Northern Ireland: Conflict and Change

We work with leading authors to develop the
strongest educational materials in politics,
bringing cutting-edge thinking and best learning
practice to a global market.

Under a range of well-known imprints, including
Longman, we craft high quality print and
electronic publications which help readers to
understand and apply their content, whether
studying or at work.

To find out more about the complete range of our
publishing, please visit us on the World Wide Web at:
www.pearsoneduc.com

Northern Ireland: Conflict and Change

Second Edition

Jonathan Tonge
University of Salford

An imprint of **Pearson Education**

Harlow, England · London · New York · Reading, Massachusetts · San Francisco · Toronto · Don Mills, Ontario · Sydney
Tokyo · Singapore · Hong Kong · Seoul · Taipei · Cape Town · Madrid · Mexico City · Amsterdam · Munich · Paris · Milan

Pearson Education Limited
Edinburgh Gate
Harlow
Essex CM20 2JE

and Associated Companies throughout the world

Visit us on the World Wide Web at:
www.pearsoneduc.com

First published by Prentice Hall Europe 1998
Second edition 2002

ISBN 0 582 42400 3

British Library Cataloguing-in-Publication Data
A catalogue record for this book is available from the British Library

Library of Congress Cataloging-in-Publication Data
A catalog record is available from the Library of Congress

10 9 8 7 6 5 4 3 2 1
06 05 04 03 02

Typeset in 11/12pt Adobe Garamond by 35
Printed in Malaysia , LSP

To my parents, Stanley and Brenda Tonge

N

Coleraine

ULSTER
Londonderry
DERRY   ANTRIM
DONEGAL

Strabane
TYRONE   Belfast
Omagh   Lough
Neagh

DONEGAL BAY
Lisburn
Armagh   DOWN
FERMANAGH
MONAGHAN   ARMAGH
Crossmaglen

SLIGO

LEITRIM   CAVAN
LOUTH
MAYO
IRISH SEA
ROSCOMMON   LONGFORD
MEATH
CONNAUGHT
WESTMEATH
GALWAY   Dublin
Galway   OFFALY   DUBLIN
KILDARE

LAOIS   WICKLOW
GALWAY BAY   LEINSTER
CLARE
CARLOW
KILKENNY
TIPPERARY   WEXFORD
LIMERICK
MUNSTER
WATERFORD
KERRY   CORK

Cork

Northern Ireland

Ancient province borders

Border between Northern Ireland
and Republic of Ireland

County boundaries

Largest cities

0   40   80 km
0   25   50 miles

Source: adapted from *Politics UK*, 4th Edition, Longman (Jones *et al.*, 2001).

Contents

List of tables

Preface

This book is aimed at students of the politics and history of Northern Ireland. It should also benefit the lay reader with an interest in the subject matter. The book combines an examination of the historical context of the conflict in Northern Ireland with an exploration of the contemporary political situation. It provides a detailed account of the attempts to create a lasting peace in Northern Ireland, assessing whether barriers to the resolution of the conflict have been removed.

The disappearance of my home office amid mountains of press cuttings over the last six years should have sufficed as a warning that the production of a second edition was tantamount to writing a new book. The extent of change in Northern Ireland over the last few years has been extraordinary. In attempting to record and assess these changes, this second edition contains a large number of rewritten chapters, a division of the party chapter into separate Unionist and Nationalist chapters (as per the Good Friday Agreement . . .) and new chapters on policing and the Good Friday Agreement.

A large number of debts have been incurred in production of this book. I wish to thank Emma Mitchell, ex-Pearson, for suggesting a second edition. Thanks are also due to the Economic and Social Research Council, for the research awards New Nationalism in Northern Ireland (R000222668); The Role of Extra Constitutional Parties in the Northern Ireland Assembly (L327253058), with Professor J McAuley; and Third Traditions in Northern Ireland (R000223414). Whilst this book is not the primary outlet for findings from the projects, the research does inform part of the chapter on political parties and some comments on responses to the Good Friday Agreement.

I am grateful to all the political figures and party administrators who have co-operated for this book and other projects. The list is too long to be exhaustively reproduced here, but special thanks must go to Mitchel McLaughlin, Alex Maskey and Dawn Doyle (Sinn Fein); Tim Attwood and Gerry Cosgrove (SDLP); Dr Stephen Farry (Alliance); Hazel Legge and David Boyd (UUP). Thanks are also due to the large range of organisations assisting in the bi-annual University of Salford study tour to Northern Ireland, encouraging discussion and debate among visiting students. The interest in the subject displayed by Salford students rarely fails to impress. Special thanks are due to Sinn Fein and the PUP for their roles as 'hosts'. To the parties already mentioned above, I wish to record thanks to the DUP, the RUC, George Patton,

Chief Executive of the Orange Order, and Professor Paul Bew, Queen's University. The staff in the Political Collection at the Linenhall Library in Belfast are always helpful and I am especially grateful to Yvonne Murphy and Allan Leonard.

On the academic side, I am heavily indebted to my colleague at the University of Salford, Dr Jocelyn Evans, for his data analysis and perceptive comments. I also wish to thank Andy Mycock and Penny Pardoe for their help. Professor Jim McAuley at the University of Huddersfield offered valuable insights into Loyalist politics. I also wish to thank participants in 'The New Northern Irish Politics' seminar series at the University of Salford in autumn 2000, all of whom provided illuminating insights. They included Professor Henry Patterson (Ulster); Professor Steve Bruce (Aberdeen) and Dr Feargal Cochrane (Lancaster).

On a personal note, I wish to thank Maria Gearing, Anita Hopkins and my son Connell, who, rightly, remains unimpressed by the amount of time his father devotes to Northern Ireland. This second edition is dedicated to my parents, Stanley and Brenda Tonge.

Finally, I wish to add the obvious disclaimer. The numerous citations above in no way constitute an attempt to scatter blame for this work. Any errors, distortions or downright dissembling are my own responsibility.

Jonathan Tonge is Professor of Politics at the University of Salford.

Publisher's Acknowledgements

We are grateful to the following for permission to reproduce copyright material:

Map (p. vi) from *Politics UK*, 4th Edition, Longman (Jones *et al.*, 2001), Pearson Education Limited.

Whilst every effort has been made to trace the owners of copyright material, in a few cases this has proved impossible and we take this opportunity to offer our apologies to any copyright holders whose rights have been unwittingly infringed.

List of abbreviations

AIA	Anglo-Irish Agreement
AOH	Ancient Order of Hibernians
APNI	Alliance Party of Northern Ireland
CEC	Campaign for Equal Citizenship
CIRA	Continuity Irish Republican Army
CSJ	Campaign for Social Justice
DSD	Downing Street Declaration
DUP	Democratic Unionist Party
EU	European Union
GAA	Gaelic Athletic Association
GFA	Good Friday Agreement
ICD	International Commission on Decommissioning
ICTU	Irish Congress of Trade Unions
INLA	Irish National Liberation Army
IRA	Irish Republican Army
IRB	Irish Republican Brotherhood
LAW	Loyalist Association of Workers
LVF	Loyalist Volunteer Force
MEP	Member of the European Parliament
MLA	Member of the Legislative Assembly
MP	Member of Parliament
NICRA	Northern Ireland Civil Rights Association
NICS	Northern Ireland Civil Service
NIHE	Northern Ireland Housing Executive
NILP	Northern Ireland Labour Party
NIO	Northern Ireland Office
NIUP	Northern Ireland Unionist Party
NIWC	Northern Ireland Women's Coalition
NORAID	Irish Northern Aid Committee
OIRA	Official Irish Republican Army
PIRA	Provisional Irish Republican Army
PSNI	Police Service of Northern Ireland
PUP	Progressive Unionist Party
RIR	Royal Irish Regiment
RIRA	Real Irish Republican Army

RSF	Republican Sinn Fein
RUC	Royal Ulster Constabulary
SAS	Special Air Service
SDLP	Social Democratic and Labour Party
SF	Sinn Fein
STV	Single Transferable Vote
TD	Teachta Dala (member of the Dail)
UDA	Ulster Defence Association
UDP	Ulster Democratic Party
UDR	Ulster Defence Regiment
UFF	Ulster Freedom Fighters
UKUP	United Kingdom Unionist Party
UPNI	Unionist Party of Northern Ireland
UUC	Ulster Unionist Council
UUP	Ulster Unionist Party
UUUC	United Ulster Unionist Council
UVF	Ulster Volunteer Force
UWC	Ulster Workers' Council

Introduction

The basis of the problem

Political conflict and change have coincided in Northern Ireland during recent decades. Between 1969 and 2000, the conflict in Northern Ireland produced a death toll exceeding 3,600. The vast majority of Northern Ireland's 1.6 million inhabitants have always desired peace, yet conflict was endemic from 1969 until the mid-1990s and sporadic thereafter. At the beginning of the twenty-first century, prospects looked the brightest for many years for the management, if not the resolution, of the political problems of Northern Ireland. The main paramilitary groups had been on ceasefire for most of the period since 1994. The 1998 Good Friday Agreement offered a historic compromise between the Unionist and Nationalist traditions in Northern Ireland.

The political problem in Northern Ireland is based upon the assertion of competing national identities. There is a majority population in Northern Ireland which sees itself as British. There is a minority of people in Northern Ireland who see their identity as Irish. From these competing identities stem the aspects of the conflict that have proved so difficult to resolve. The majority of people within Northern Ireland wish to retain governing structures in Northern Ireland based upon the political expression of their identity. This majority adopts a Unionist position, desiring the maintenance of the Union of Great Britain and Northern Ireland and the retention of Northern Ireland's place within the United Kingdom. Many of the minority population are Irish Nationalists. They see themselves as part of a wider population, the overall Irish majority on the island of Ireland. They aspire to the political assertion of this Irish identity through the creation of a united Ireland or, in the interim, a strong role for the Irish government within Northern Ireland. The Good Friday Agreement attempted to balance these competing claims by keeping Northern Ireland within the United Kingdom, whilst allowing the Irish government some say in the affairs of Northern Ireland and permitting some economic activity to be organised on an all-Ireland basis.

The division over who should ultimately govern is problematic enough. It is deepened by the religious, cultural and social divide which often coincides with the political divide. Protestants form just over half the population in Northern Ireland. An overwhelming majority see themselves as politically and culturally British. Catholics form 40 per cent of the population. Many see themselves culturally as Irish. A large number desire political expression of that Irishness, although there is less unanimity amongst Catholics over constitutional politics compared to that found amongst Protestants. The consequence of the main division of British versus Irish, allied to a religious divide, is a fracturing of society, reflected in some areas by residential segregation between communities most often identified as Protestant and Catholic. Ethnic division, based upon nationality and religion, is marked by the strongest linkage between religious affiliation and party bloc choices in western Europe. Competing political aspirations provide the basis of the modern problems of Northern Ireland.

The peace process of the 1990s, culminating in the Good Friday Agreement, emphasised that Northern Ireland's politics are undergoing change. Ethnic bloc politics may still dominate, but are not frozen. Residual paramilitarism is still evident, but at a fraction of its former scale. The title of this work, Conflict and Change, is designed to reflect that whilst a political conflict endures, the conduct of that conflict has altered. This book aims to provide the reader with an overview of the problem, whilst examining recent changes in policy and attitudes amongst the population, the Unionist and Nationalist parties, the British and Irish governments and the paramilitary organisations.

The death toll during previous decades reminds all of the seriousness of the conflict. Northern Ireland has never been a consensual society. Nonetheless the first-time visitor to Northern Ireland is sometimes surprised at its apparent normality. The political and religious divide in Northern Ireland may dominate society, but the conflict has ebbed and flowed and, even during its worst periods, was rarely in evidence in many parts.

History and politics

The aim of this book is to explore what gives the political contest its longevity, whilst also examining the subtle shifts in the politics and society of Northern Ireland during recent times. It attempts this through a systematic examination of the history and politics of Northern Ireland. The book pays considerable attention to the peace process of the 1990s as an illustration of how political transformation is difficult but attainable.

The first three chapters explore the creation and evolution of Northern Ireland as a state. Chapter 1 examines the reasons why the territorial division of Ireland emerged as a supposedly 'least evil' compromise designed to accommodate separate political and religious identities. Critics of the creation of Northern Ireland alleged that the first 50 years of its existence were built upon sectarian discrimination and political partisanship. Chapters 2 and 3 discuss the validity of such claims and explore the fragility of the Northern state in response to challenges in the 1960s.

Following this historical account, the focus is mainly upon contemporary aspects of Northern Ireland. Chapters 4 and 5 examine party ideologies, organisations and aspirations. Chapter 6 analyses the form of governance created for Northern Ireland under the Good Friday Agreement. Chapter 7 assesses the problem of policing Northern Ireland, a state which has never enjoyed the full loyalty of all its citizens. Chapter 8 attempts to define the role of religion in respect of Northern Ireland's political divide and within society. Religious labels have always been used to identify communities in Northern Ireland.

The remainder of the book is devoted primarily to an analysis of attempts at resolving the conflict. Chapter 9 provides an overview of such attempts before 1985. The following chapter discusses the lasting significance of the Anglo-Irish Agreement. It argues that the Agreement was of great importance in its own right and as a necessary forerunner of the peace process of the 1990s. Chapters 11 to 13 analyse that peace process, emphasising the importance of the development of a Nationalist coalition and changes within republicanism. The chapters detail the delicate balancing acts which led to the construction of a fragile peace process, climaxed by the production of the Good Friday Agreement after exhaustive multi-party and governmental negotiations. Chapter 14 offers an analysis of the policy learning represented within the Agreement. The final chapter discusses whether there are any alternatives to the Good Friday Agreement, and examines three aspects. First, what, if any, alternatives exist? Second, what are the main barriers to such alternatives? Third, do such alternatives carry any cross-community support?

It is worth explaining two sets of terms which are often used interchangeably in a manner which might confuse the novice reader. First, it has been claimed that a book could be written over the extent to which the terms *Catholic* and *Nationalist*, *Protestant* and *Unionist* are interchanged (Pollak, 1993). To simplify: most Catholics are Irish Nationalists, but some are not. Overwhelmingly, Protestants are British Unionists. In this book, when talking about the politics of Northern Ireland, the terms Nationalist and Unionist are employed. When talking about religion, religious labels are used. Only when examining discrimination or relying upon the survey data of others are the terms regularly interchanged.

Second, the terms *Unionist* and *Loyalist*, *Nationalist* and *Republican* are often interchanged. Again, at the risk of gross oversimplification, the terms Unionist and Loyalist both refer to supporters of the maintenance of the Union of Great Britain and Northern Ireland. The term Loyalist is normally applied to those Unionists seen as more working-class and loyal not only to the Union, but also to Ulster, or at least the six counties of Ulster which make up Northern Ireland. Irish Nationalists and Irish Republicans share many beliefs but, again, there are some differences. Both support a united Ireland, but Republicans place greater emphasis upon the political and cultural independence of that Ireland. Some might quibble with these definitions, but an entirely satisfactory outline of minor differences has yet to be achieved.

Chapter 1

A divided island

The problems of Northern Ireland are rooted in the struggle for an independent Ireland and the division of Ireland emerging from support or hostility to that struggle. This chapter examines the balance of political forces – Irish Nationalist and British Unionist – which led to the partition of Ireland earlier this century.

Until the seventeenth century, Ireland existed as a largely autonomous, but disunited country, under loose British rule. Centuries earlier, the Normans attempted to exert some form of central government, but this effort had a limited geographic and administrative remit. Political control, in so far as it existed, was exercised by Gaelic chiefs, such as the O'Donnells and O'Neills. Each had the ability to mobilise small private armies, or clans, used to preserve local dominance. In areas around Dublin, a more direct English authority was exerted, following Henry VIII's defeat of an Irish Army in 1534.

1.1 The roots of modern problems

The origins of the current political problems of Northern Ireland lie in historical conflicts between Planter and Gael. Pre-plantation, the hegemony of the clans was strongest in Ulster, the province which traditionally comprised nine counties: Antrim, Armagh, Derry, Down, Fermanagh, Tyrone, Cavan, Donegal and Monaghan. Only much later, with the partition of Ireland, was Ulster redefined to become a political-administrative unit excluding the latter three counties. Attracted by close geographical proximity and exploitative opportunities, large numbers of Scottish Protestants undertook the Plantation of Ulster in 1609.

Resentment towards the newly arrived landowners was created by two factors. Firstly, there was considerable displacement of the resident Irish from their land. By the beginning of the eighteenth century, the native Irish owned only 14 per cent of the land (Darby, 1983: 14). Secondly, there existed cultural and religious hostility to the new Protestant arrivals from the indigenous, Catholic population. This hostility translated into rebellion in 1641, an uprising crushed by Cromwell within a decade.

Catholic aspirations of retaking territory were revived by the accession to the English throne of their co-religionist James II in 1685. Deposed in the 'Glorious Revolution' of 1688 by William of Orange, James II raised an army supported by many Irish Catholics and the two protagonists clashed at the

Battle of the Boyne in Ireland in 1690. Annual celebration of King William's victory on 12 July remains important for many Ulster Protestants. Over a century later, the foundation of the Orange Order provided a forum for Protestants determined to resist the threat of 'Popery'.

Celebration of historical landmarks, such as the Battle of the Boyne, arguably risks overstating the role of religion in conflict within Ireland. Irish history has never been a straightforward tale of conflict between native Catholic Irish versus Protestant Scottish and English settlers. One irony is that William of Orange received the tacit support of the Pope in his struggle with James II. After 1690 there was considerable hostility between Protestants and Presbyterians, a tension later reduced through the establishment of an alliance in the Orange Order, a religious and cultural organisation closed to Catholics. It was a Presbyterian, Wolfe Tone, who in 1798 led the Irish rebellion against British rule. Tone's United Irishmen comprised Presbyterians and Catholics, engaged in a fruitless series of risings against colonial governance.

At the time of the formal establishment of the Union of Great Britain and Ireland, religious and national affiliations were by no means interchangeable. Many Irish Catholics supported the Union, whilst the Orange Order was in opposition (Connolly, 1990). The development of a Catholic Nationalist movement arose from the oppressive anti-Catholic laws which impinged upon civil rights. The link between religion and national identity grew as Ireland was 'governed in many respect as a crown colony because it was seen as a security problem' (Ward, 1993).

Beneficial effects of Catholic emancipation in 1829 were offset in Ireland by the impact of the famine a decade later, which helped foster an embryonic national liberation movement. Caused by a combination of the failure of the potato crop and the indifference of Ireland's authorities, the famine halved Ireland's population. Death or emigration were more common results than constitutional agitation. Nonetheless, the forerunner of the IRA, the Irish Republican Brotherhood, initially known as the Irish Revolutionary Brotherhood, was formed in 1858, with the ambition of ending British rule in Ireland.

Agrarian conflict was common during the nineteenth century. The most important organisation during this period was the Tenant League, which attempted to secure better rights for struggling tenant farmers. In its advocacy of change, the League was confronted by differing demands from farmers. Whilst all wanted increased rights, farmers in the west wanted more land to farm, to increase their returns. Elsewhere the primary concern was to lower rents. If the initial response of the British Prime Minister Gladstone, the Land Act of 1870, satisfied few, his 1881 Act was more successful in establishing fairer rents and greater freedom for farmers.

Within Ulster, the impact of the famine was much less marked. Here, the impact of the industrial revolution was evident, reinforcing perceptions of the 'separateness' of Ulster, a distinctiveness of identity that has also been portrayed in geographic terms (Bardon, 1992). It might be added that this latter notion of uniqueness has been derided elsewhere as somehow suggesting that 'the origins of the Loyalist parade are to be found in geology' (Ryan, 1994: 104).

What cannot be disputed is that a prosperous skilled working-class, over-whelmingly comprising Protestants, had emerged in Ulster by the close of the nineteenth century, based upon the shipbuilding and engineering industries. Compared to rural Ireland, Belfast, the heartland of this labour aristocracy, appeared to have much more in common with large mainland British ports.

1.2 Home Rule for Ireland

Persistent internal conflicts over land and rights emphasise that the 'ancient Irish nation is only a cherished myth' (Wilson, 1989: 20). Nonetheless, during the latter part of the nineteenth century, it appeared to the British government that there existed sufficient Irish national consciousness to demand a political response. This was based upon the granting of Home Rule to the entire island of Ireland. The rise of nationalism was not confined to Ireland. Instead its development was a feature of most European states.

According to the plans of the British government, a parliament in Dublin would be created to give the Irish limited autonomy over domestic matters, whilst the Westminster parliament would continue to legislate on defence and foreign policy, along with most economic affairs.

In introducing the first Home Rule Bill in Parliament in 1886, Gladstone could be accused of political expediency. Through such action, the Liberal Party garnered the support of the Irish Parliamentary Party, founded by Isaac Butt in 1874 and led by Charles Stewart Parnell after 1880. The capture of 85 seats by Parnell's party in the 1885 election left it holding the balance of power, a factor not unimportant in Gladstone's new advocacy of Home Rule.

Nonetheless, Liberal Party support for devolution was not merely a product of political calculation. Firstly, Gladstone possessed a genuine belief in self-government, which exonerates him from charges of self-interest. Secondary absolution is provided when one examines the consequences for the Liberal Party of Gladstone's beliefs. Divided between Gladstone Home Rule supporters and Liberal Unionists, many of whom later joined the Conservative Unionists, the party was dealt a blow which contributed significantly to its later rapid demise and exclusion from office.

A further reason for support for Home Rule was the desire to placate con-stitutional Irish Nationalists. With tension already evident between a funda-mentalist wing of Irish nationalism and its constitutional proponents, the onus was on the British government to make concessions to parliamentary supporters of partial Irish autonomy. Friction between 'respectable' and 'radical' routes to Irish independence was to become a recurring theme in Irish political history. Parnellites favoured constitutional approaches, but did not inevitably eschew more radical approaches and retained links with some Fenians who preferred a two-tier strategy (Hachey, 1984). Indeed, Parnell was briefly jailed in 1880 following opposition to land measures which appeared to offer little prospect of ownership to tenant farmers.

Schism within the Liberal Party contributed to the defeat of the 1886 Home Rule Bill. Its 1893 successor, a weaker variant proposing the transfer of fewer powers, was defeated in the House of Lords, during a period in which the Irish Parliamentary Party had temporarily split following the citation of Parnell in a divorce case. Liberal Party stances on Home Rule varied according to leader, oscillating between the hostility of Rosebery to the enthusiasm of Campbell Bannerman. Despite the latter's belief in the idea and the achievement of a large Liberal majority at the 1906 election, there had been a post-Gladstone 'policy of disengagement' from Irish self-government (Kee, 1976: 165).

The third attempt at Home Rule in 1912 was partly a product of political arithmetic. The Liberals, now led by Asquith, had enjoyed Irish parliamentary support for the passing of the 'People's Budget' of 1909 and the ending of the permanent veto of legislation held by the House of Lords in 1911. Operating with a slender majority after the two elections of 1910, Asquith, a reluctant supporter of Home Rule, reintroduced legislation. Although offering only constrained autonomy for Ireland, the Bill appeared to satisfy the Nationalist ambitions of Irish MPs.

Liberal support for Home Rule polarised the parties in the House of Commons. The Conservative Party indicated its willingness to defend the Union in its current form, fearing that the granting of autonomy to Ireland would weaken Britain's colonial governance elsewhere. Indeed, as Patrick O'Farrell declares of the Home Rule era, the 'essence of Conservative Party policy was Unionism as the nexus of imperial power and of the imperial ethos' (O'Farrell, 1975: 97). Liberal Party calculations were also centred upon the most appropriate means of preserving the British Empire, but hinged upon a more concessionary approach.

In opposing any weakening of the Union, the Conservative leader from 1902 until 1911, Arthur Balfour, preferred a policy of 'killing home rule with kindness' by addressing Irish grievances rather than revising constitutional arrangements (quoted in Wilson, 1989: 35). For more strident Conservatives, opposition to Home Rule meant advocacy of the extra-parliamentary activity undertaken by the people of Ulster. As early as the introduction of the first Home Rule Bill, Lord Randolph Churchill, in endorsing the playing of the 'Orange Card', suggested that 'Ulster will Fight and Ulster will be Right'. Churchill's polemic was partly attributable to his party-leadership aspirations. He identified that a significant body of Conservative opinion was prepared to back any measures used by Ulster Unionists to oppose Home Rule.

By the time of the Third Home Rule Bill, opposition in the House of Commons was advanced with particular vehemence by Bonar Law, a Conservative leader of Ulster Presbyterian stock. Bonar Law declared that he could 'imagine no length of resistance' to which Ulster could go which would break his support for its cause. Further endorsement of military resistance to Home Rule was again suggested by his assertion that 'there are things stronger than parliamentary majorities' (quoted in Phoenix, 1994: 112).

Not until 1912 was the partition of Ireland discussed in public, 'even as a distasteful possibility' (Laffan, 1983: 33). By the outbreak of World War I, however, it was evident that Home Rule was unlikely to embrace all of Ireland, given the strength of hostility to the measure within Ulster. The British Prime

Minister Asquith favoured an option by which individual counties in the North would be able to opt out from Home Rule for six years. Rejected by Unionists as a stay of execution, the plan was modified to allow for permanent opt-outs for the four counties with Protestant majorities. Unionists, prepared to abandon their colleagues in most Southern counties, wanted a six-county opt-out.

Although the Home Rule Bill was passed in 1914, war intervened, preventing its enactment. Special legislation was promised in respect of Ulster's constitutional position. As differing arrangements for sectors of the island were now to be devised, the eventual formal division of Ireland was inevitable.

1.3 The growth of Ulster unionism

Although Conservative support for their cause was useful, it was not the decisive factor in encouraging Ulster's Protestants to resist Home Rule. Defiance would have been the norm whatever the stances of mainland parliamentary parties. Indeed, amongst some Unionists there was suspicion over the solidity of the alliance, at least until the establishment of Bonar Law as Conservative Party leader.

Both the embryonic Irish Nationalist movement and the British government underestimated the amount of hostility proposals for Home Rule would engender in the north of Ireland. A common dismissal of the threat of self-government for Ulster if Home Rule was imposed was that of 'Orangeade'. Whilst it was true that as late as 1885, over half of Ulster's 33 parliamentary seats were won by the Home Rule Party, rioting in Belfast over the Home Rule Bill of 1886 offered an early portent of the ramification of any all-Ireland measure. Furthermore, the 1886 polling reverse served merely to end the earlier complacency of Unionists.

Opposition to Home Rule revived the Orange Order in the late 1800s. By 1905, cohesive Unionist politics developed through the creation of the Ulster Unionist Council (UUC). For the first time, the political, religious and cultural forces of unionism were fused in a single organisation, the political homogeneity of which was enhanced by the unity of defensive resistance to Home Rule. At its foundation, the UUC comprised 200 representatives, consisting of 100 from Ulster Unionist constituency associations, 50 from the Orange Order and 50 co-opted members. Doubling in size by 1918, the UUC 'fostered a partitionist mentality' as it emphasised that Ulster could not form part of any imposed all-Ireland settlement (Jackson, 1994: 42). Indeed, more militant sections of Protestant opinion, such as the Apprentice Boys of Derry, continued to swell the numbers on the Council.

Opposition to Home Rule amongst Unionists was based upon three factors. Firstly, Ulster had prospered under British rule. Sections of the Province's skilled workforce represented an advanced section of the working-class on any international comparison. This marginal superiority permitted the development of an alliance between workers and employers, the latter emphasising common cause. Economic conflicts were by no means unknown, but they did not fracture political and religious alliances. If this proved the despair of the small non-sectarian organisations of the left, it was nonetheless hardly surprising. Protestantism was not only a useful faith for securing a passage to heaven, but opened shipbuilding gates in addition to the pearly type. By 1911, 93 per cent of Belfast's shipbuilders were Protestants, compared to 76 per cent of the population (Farrell, 1980).

Secondly, there was the strong religious component to the formation of attitudes. Partial separation from Britain would lead to eventual incorporation within a 'Papist' Ireland which would offer little tolerance towards Protestant dissidents. Again, hostility towards Catholicism as a religious creed transcended social classes. The Presbyterian and Methodist Churches, along with the Church of Ireland, were active in the campaign against Home Rule. Indeed, the Presbyterian Church described resistance to Home Rule as a 'sacred duty' (Phoenix, 1994: 113).

Finally, the assertion of Ulster Protestants of their British identity was reinforced by a Gaelic revival in the south of Ireland. This merely emphasised Ulster's cultural distinctiveness, although it should be noted that Protestants have always played a part in the development of Gaelic culture. Set alongside political developments, the revival fostered the perception that Ulster was the 'antithesis of Irishness' (Jackson, 1994: 44). These three mutually reinforcing elements of an Ulster identity were hardened by the defensiveness of a siege mentality, as the Union with Britain was threatened.

Popular opposition to Home Rule was pervasive in Ulster, led by the Dublin lawyer Edward Carson and organised by the Northern businessman James Craig. Assuming leadership of the Ulster Unionists in 1910, Carson realised that opposition to Home Rule for Ireland as an entirety was not viable. Accordingly, he concentrated his efforts to ensure a veto of what he described as the 'most nefarious conspiracy that has ever been hatched against a free people' within the 'Protestant province of Ulster' (quoted in Hachey, 1984: 74–6). Rebellion against Home Rule had mass support to the extent that a Solemn League and Covenant rejecting the measure was signed by 471,000 individuals on Ulster Day in September 1912. Signatories pledged to 'use all means that may be found necessary' to defeat Home Rule.

Indications of what 'all means' actually meant became evident the following year, with the creation of the Ulster Volunteer Force (UVF). Drilled mainly in Orange Halls, the UVF attracted cross-class support throughout Ulster, with commanders often landowners (Stewart, 1967). Operating as the military wing of unionism, the UVF amounted to a 100,000 strong male force of Covenant signatories, pledged to fight for the 'mutual protection of all loyalists'.

The term 'Loyalist' is important as it is indicative of the location of allegiances of Unionists. For the UVF, it was the Liberal government that was engaged in a treasonable activity, by threatening the transfer of Ulster to the partial jurisdiction of an alien parliament. According to the Solemn Covenant of 1912, the principal aim of Ulster citizens was merely 'equal citizenship in the United Kingdom'. Ostensibly engaged in rebellion, Unionists were in effect acting as 'more royalist than the King' in maintaining allegiance to the Crown, against the political expediency of His Majesty's government. That formal British sovereignty over Ireland remained intact under the proposed Home Rule settlement was a constitutional nicety which unimpressed Loyalists. They perceived a loosening of the British link in the South as the forerunner of Irish independence.

The UVF provided the military backing by which any provisional Unionist government would be able to ignore absorption within a fledgling Irish unitary state, albeit one with a highly constrained autonomy. By its presence, the UVF indicated the inevitability of the partition of Ireland, unless the British government was prepared to either countenance civil war between the UVF and Nationalist Irish Volunteers in the South, or face down the Unionist rebellion using the British Army.

The strength of the UVF ensured that Unionists would not be obliged to accept compromise positions, such as Asquith's proposal that each county of Ulster would have an opt-out clause for six years before joining the remainder of Ireland. Unionists were adamant in their rejection of recognition of a Dublin parliament, proving impervious even to suggestions that Ulster could be over-represented within that assembly.

Remote anyway, prospects for a quelling of Ulster's threatened rebellion by the British Army disappeared entirely following the Curragh Mutiny of 1914. Ordered by the commander-in-chief of British military forces in Ireland to prepare to take action against the Ulster Volunteer Force, local commanders at Curragh Camp, led by Brigadier-General Hubert Gough, indicated that they were not prepared to take military action against Loyalists. This defiance was partly in recognition of close cultural ties and in some cases because officers were of Ulster birth or descent. Furthermore, it was recognised that any British offensive would lead to bloody conflict with scant support for the Army from the indigenous population.

It remains uncertain whether the British government would have initiated any such action. Indeed, the mutiny has been described as no more than a 'misunderstanding' (Hachey, 1984: 88). Nonetheless, the resignation of 58 officers at Curragh was indicative of the divided loyalties felt by many serving soldiers. As a symbolic gesture of solidarity and a further deterrent to an already reluctant government, the Curragh Mutiny emphasised the impossibility of any holistic Irish solution.

Indeed, by mid-1914, the ambiguous approach of the British government to the Ulster rebellion had allowed the UVF to become a powerful armed militia. On a single night in April that year, 24,000 rifles and three million rounds of ammunition were smuggled into the port of Larne. In common with other arms shipments, no arrests were made. This tacit official acceptance of activity contrasted with the later British treatment of rebels in the South.

Unionism's mandate within the traditional province of Ulster was narrow. In the 1910 election, 103,000 Unionist votes were recorded against 94,000 in favour of Home Rule. A slim majority in one province of Ireland created the formal division of Ireland into two states. Intensity of commitment rather than national extensiveness of support characterised the Unionist position. The narrow geographical parameters of majority unionism ensured a political redrawing of the geographical entity of Ulster, to enshrine a permanent Unionist majority within six counties (Antrim, Armagh, Derry, Down, Fermanagh and Tyrone), which would form the new statelet of Northern Ireland. In their defiance of the British government, Unionists were aided and abetted by the Conservative Party and sympathetic sections of the British Army. Unsurprisingly, the success of the threat of force did not go unnoticed elsewhere in Ireland.

1.4 The rise of Irish nationalism

Revolutionary Irish nationalism was subordinate to constitutional approaches until 1916. Although the Irish Revolutionary Brotherhood, soon renamed the Irish Republican Brotherhood (IRB), had been in existence since 1858, there appeared to be little agitation for armed resistance to British rule. Initially attracting participants in the 1848 Rising, the IRB's main recruits were those interested in the recreational pursuits it offered (Comerford, 1981).

Increased attention to constitutional issues followed the replacement of the outlawed Land League by the Irish National League. Remnants of agricultural unrest, some of which subsided after the 1881 Land Act, coincided with the articulation of broader political concerns by the Irish parliamentary party. Even the strident Nationalists of the IRB were prepared to support 'Home Rulers' within parliament. In part, this was due to the willingness of the latter to use obstructionist tactics. Moreover, it was a recognition of the much wider mandate and legitimacy of the elected vehicle of change, exemplified by the success of the Nationalist Party in the 1885 general election. Although never more than a 'marriage of convenience' the extent of the accord between the IRB and parliamentary Nationalists was exemplified by the election of one of the latter, Joseph Biggar, to the Supreme Council of the IRB (Hoppen, 1980).

Defeat for the Home Rule Bills of 1886 and 1893 increased pressure upon the constitutional wing of nationalism. Anxious to maintain Liberal Party support for Home Rule, the Irish Nationalists were seen as 'clinging to nurse for fear of something worse' with little immediate benefit (Hoppen, 1980: 131). Meanwhile, the establishment of an Irish identity continued to receive sporting and cultural sustenance through the development of organisations such as the Gaelic Athletic Association and the Gaelic League. Politically, the establishment of Sinn Fein (meaning Ourselves) offered a bolstering of Nationalist approaches that merged constitutionalism in an uneasy alliance with revolutionary violence.

Founded in 1905 by Arthur Griffith, an advocate of non-violence, Sinn Fein was a largely urban-based party with little support prior to World War I. It offered a manifesto of limited independence in which English and Irish citizens would retain a joint monarch. Despite the tensions surrounding the 1912 Home Rule Bill, Sinn Fein's membership remained static. Many of its members did, however, join the Irish Volunteers, the South's militia insistent upon independence for Ireland. If unable to procure arms to the extent of Carson's Unionist forces, the formation of the Irish Volunteers nonetheless indicated the likelihood of a bloody civil war if the future of Ireland could not be resolved by Asquith's government.

If the advent of World War I was seen by some Nationalists as 'England's danger, Ireland's opportunity' the perception was not overwhelming. Of 181,000 Irish Volunteers, only 11,000 persisted with the national liberation struggle, the remainder preferring to join Britain's fight with Germany. Here marked the point of departure between constitutional and physical force approaches to nationalism. The primary advocate of the former was John Redmond, the leader of the Irish parliamentary party. Redmond boasted of the allegiance of Irishmen to the British Crown, whilst a rump of Irish volunteers were plotting the Easter Rising designed to overthrow British rule.

Greeted with incredulity by the British government and Irish populace alike, the 1916 Easter Rising was a revolt by 1,600 Irish volunteers, mainly from the IRB core, who had assumed control of the organisation. Capturing landmarks in Dublin, the rebels were quelled after a week of conflict in which 450 people were killed. The proclamation of independence read by Padraic Pearse outside the General Post Office in Dublin attracted indifference from a public more concerned with the damage caused to the city.

A transformation in popular attitudes towards the rebellion was effected by the reaction of the British government. Concerned not to legitimise armed struggle by granting prisoner-of-war status to those arrested, the government executed a number of rebels for treason. The benefit of the new martyr status of Ireland's attempted liberators was Sinn Fein. Although not involved in an official capacity in the Rising, the party offered a political outlet to supporters of an independent, united Ireland.

Such was the backlash over the execution of the rebels that Sinn Fein won a decisive victory at the 1918 General Election. Standing on an abstentionist pledge, the party captured 73 of the 105 seats. Had all seats been contested, Sinn Fein would undoubtedly have won an overall majority of votes cast. These elections remain of importance to many Irish Nationalists. Firstly, they amounted to the most widely franchised elections held in the country, as women over 30 were granted the vote for the first time. Secondly, they were to be the last time that all citizens of the island of Ireland could vote as a unit. Thirdly, and most crucially, they offered a democratic mandate for the establishment of a thirty-two-county independent Ireland. For Sinn Fein, this contest assumed almost talismanic significance as the last elections to have ever 'counted'. The subsequent division of Ireland is thus seen as undemocratic and unlawful. This refusal to accept the validity of partition is why the terms 'six counties' and 'twenty-six counties' are used by Republicans instead of 'Northern Ireland' and 'Southern Ireland'.

It is a moot point whether the 1918 elections should be interpreted as a decisive mandate for a unitary independent state. The Sinn Fein share of the vote was exaggerated in terms of seats. Almost one-quarter of the seats gained were uncontested (O'Leary and McGarry, 1996). Furthermore, the success of the party was partly due to residual hostility towards Britain over its handling of participants in the 1916 Rising. It is difficult to perceive the vote as an endorsement of Sinn Fein's agenda for a new Ireland as this had scarcely been formulated. Additionally, the electorate could not vote to accept or reject partition in a referendum-type contest. Nonetheless, for Irish Nationalists and Republicans today, the elections are indicative of the illegitimacy of the separate Northern state, with Union with Britain endorsed by a minority of the island's population. The creation of Northern Ireland was perceived as a triumph of the threat of Unionist force over democratic procedures and thus served only to legitimise the use of subsequent Nationalist violence.

Following its election victory, Sinn Fein established the Irish parliament, Dail Eireann, in 1919, an institution which remained unattended by Unionists and Home Rule parliamentarians. The Irish Volunteers became the Irish Republican Army, defenders of the embryonic Irish Republic proclaimed in the 1916 Rising. They were determined to end British rule in Ireland and rejected plans for the division of the country. Led by Michael Collins, the IRA fought an effective and brutal guerilla war against the special auxiliary forces of the British government, known colloquially as the 'Black and Tans'. As both sides traded atrocities and fought each other to a standstill, there was growing unease in Britain over the conduct of Crown forces. A Labour Party commission established by Arthur Henderson condemned aspects of British military policing.

1.5 The partition of Ireland

The formal division of Ireland was enacted through the Government of Ireland Act 1920, which superseded the Home Rule provisions of 1914. The 1920 Act established two parliaments under British jurisdiction, one based in Dublin, the other located in Belfast. The former was to control certain affairs of the 26 counties of what became known as Southern Ireland. The latter parliament was to exercise limited authority over six counties in north-eastern Ulster. Each parliament was to be bi-cameral, comprising a lower chamber directly elected by proportional representation and an indirectly elected upper chamber.

The division of the island was based upon politics rather than geography. At the tip of the Southern state, County Donegal lay further north than any part of Northern Ireland. The exclusion of three counties of Ulster – Donegal, Cavan and Monaghan – from the Northern state appeared to diminish claims of the distinctiveness of the ancient province of Ulster. Instead, Ulster's boundaries were redrawn to ensure the creation of a Northern state with a decisive, in-built Protestant and Unionist majority, immune from the threat posed by higher Catholic birth rates. Incorporation of all nine counties of Ulster within Northern Ireland would have produced a vulnerable 56 per cent to 44 per cent Protestant to Catholic ratio (Buckland, 1981). Within the six counties selected, Protestants comprised two-thirds of the population.

Initially, the 1920 Act pleased neither Nationalists nor Unionists. Objections from the latter were overcome by recognition that partition was the least unfavourable option, given Westminster's unwillingness to continue to rule Ireland directly and the fear of Unionists of absorption within a unitary Irish state. Thus, Home Rule was granted to the opponents of Home Rule. Nonetheless,

Unionists accepted the deal, which gave them a parliament with limited jurisdiction within their preferred size of state. The previous three Bills had been a product of combined Liberal and Nationalist political forces. This final effort bore the hallmarks of Conservative and Unionist dominance (Laffan, 1983).

For Nationalists, the weak parliament offered under the Act was an unacceptable substitute for independence. In common with its Northern counterpart, the Southern parliament would have control of domestic matters, but the Westminster parliament would determine defence and foreign policy, in addition to taxation.

Opposition to the modest scale of autonomy provided the primary motivation for the War of Independence continued by the IRA until 1921. Hostility to partition was but one dimension of the conflict. The 1920 Act had offered Nationalists a modicum of an all-Ireland settlement. It proposed the creation of a Council of Ireland to facilitate matters of mutual co-operation between the two new parliaments, but the measure never came to fruition.

Forced to reconsider its approach in respect of the Dublin parliament, the British government negotiated the Anglo-Irish Treaty in 1921, which amounted to a 'compromise between the ideal of Irish unity and the reality of Northern Ireland's position' (Buckland, 1981: 38). The treaty created the Irish Free State, which granted greater autonomy to the South, affording it dominion status. This meant that Southern Ireland would remain part of the British Empire. The Anglo-Irish Treaty compared the status of the new state with that granted to Canada, similar in that the political leaders of both countries pledged allegiance to the Crown, who appointed a Governor General to oversee constitutional and political arrangements. Both states also formed part of the British Commonwealth.

Under the 1920 Government of Ireland Act, the division between north and south had been seen as ultimately reconcilable. By allowing the South greater autonomy from Britain under the 1921 treaty, between Northern and Southern Ireland 'partition was confirmed' (Follis, 1995: 186). Northern Ireland soon acquired its own political and social system distinct from that of the rest of the island. Even common features, such as proportional representation in elections North and South, were soon at variance, with Unionists in the North abandoning the method in favour of a first-past-the-post system, diminishing Nationalist representation.

Republicans were divided over whether dominion status could be viewed as a sufficient step towards full independence. The Anglo-Irish Treaty did offer a more substantial parliament than that proposed in the Government of Ireland Act one year earlier. Sinn Fein won 124 of the 128 seats in that parliament, but did not take up its places, occupying only its own Dail (parliament) as the 'true' legislative body of Ireland. Accordingly, the 1920 parliament in reality failed to exist.

The debate over internal constitutional arrangements deflected some attention from partition for a short time. Eventually, the Dail's narrow acceptance of the treaty, by 64 votes to 57, led to the resignation of de Valera as Ireland's first president and the polarisation of forces around the issue of partition.

In attempting to resolve the problem of the division of Ireland, the Anglo-Irish Treaty was obliged to balance the competing claims of Nationalists and Unionists. Its solution was to establish the Irish Free State as the holder of nominal authority over the island of Ireland, but concede Northern Ireland the right to opt out in favour of its own state, an option that, to the surprise of no one, was immediately and permanently exercised.

Superficially at least, the Anglo-Irish Treaty appeared to bolster the prospect of a united Ireland by establishing a Boundary Commission to assess the validity of the borders of Northern Ireland, redrawing them when necessary. For Nationalists, this offered the prospect of the disestablishment of the Northern state, as it could be reduced below viable size by future Commissions. Furthermore, the Free State would be able to nominate one of the three Commissioners.

For Unionists, the prospect of rapid dismemberment of their embryonic state was real, but potential change to the boundaries of Northern Ireland was rapidly sidelined. Firstly, the terms of reference of the Commission were highly ambiguous. It was to determine boundaries in 'accordance with the wishes of the inhabitants', but no guidance was provided as to the unit of expression of these wishes, be it the Northern state, Southern state, local county or electoral ward (Wall, 1966). Secondly, the Northern Ireland representative for the Commission declined to co-operate. Thirdly, the recommendations of the Commission offered no succour to Nationalists, offering a net population gain to the Free State of only 23,500.

The Boundary Commission proved such a failure for Nationalists because it argued that the onus of proof fell upon those desirous of change. Substantial majorities were needed for alteration. Furthermore, the Commission believed its task was based upon assessment of the settlement of the Government of Ireland Act 1920, not the Anglo-Irish Treaty of 1921 (Laffan, 1983: 101). Ultimately, its modest proposals for boundary change were ignored and Nationalists also lost the Council of Ireland created via the 1920 Act.

Uncertainty surrounding the impact of the 1921 treaty had earlier increased violence in all parts of the island. An IRA campaign developed in the North to complement the earlier guerilla war of independence in the South. Sectarian tensions led to riots. Co-operation between the Northern and Southern political administrations would be difficult to achieve, even though regular meetings were a declared ambition of the treaty. An initial meeting between de Valera and James Craig, the first Prime Minister of Northern Ireland, ended in discord and there ended dialogue for many decades. A boycott of Belfast goods by the Southern state in the early days of Northern Ireland did little to assist the cordiality of relationships.

1.6 Civil war in Ireland

It was in the South that the worst violence erupted, as the previous unity of Republicans concerning the national question disintegrated into a civil war between pro- and anti-treaty forces. Previous alliances disintegrated into deadly conflict as politics became a 'kaleidoscope of shifting emotions and ambivalences' (Keogh, 1994: 3). Sinn Fein's domination of the Dail Eireann between 1919 and 1921 produced 'simplistic one-dimensional politics which ill-fitted its participants for the experience of treaty negotiations' (Fanning, 1983: 2). Now Nationalists were divided over whether to accept the compromise of a semi-autonomous, twenty-six-county Irish Free State.

A pro-treaty provisional government of the Irish Free State quickly superseded the authority of the Dail. The military arm of this government was the Free State Army, pitted against some former colleagues such as de Valera, operating in the anti-treaty IRA. Compromises between pro- and anti-treaty forces were attempted by the pro-treaty leader of the provisional government, Michael Collins. In the election of June 1922, only 36 anti-treaty Sinn Fein candidates were elected to the 128-seat Dail, despite an electoral pact between pro- and anti-treaty Sinn Fein candidates which allowed over half of the treaty opponents to be returned uncontested.

With the IRA reviving the Easter Rising tactic of occupying buildings, pro-treaty forces engaged in military action against the organisation. In these operations the Free State Army was aided by loans of weapons from the British government. Superior equipment, greater numbers, wider support and the backing of the Roman Catholic Church were all factors which made victory inevitable for the Free State forces. This success was achieved at a considerable price: 11,000 suspected IRA activists and supporters were interned by the close of the conflict, whilst 77 had been executed purely as reprisal measures for the killing of pro-treaty supporters. Michael Collins was executed by the IRA in his native Cork. His successor, William Cosgrave, merely increased the military offensive, declaring that Free State forces might be obliged to eliminate 10,000 Republicans to establish self-government in Ireland according to the terms of the Anglo-Irish Treaty (Lawlor, 1983).

Again, military force was seen as the most useful tool of resolution of political issues. Not until 1927 were constitutional politics fully restored in the South, as de Valera led the newly formed Fianna Fail party into the Dail, to oppose Cumann na Gaedheal, renamed Fine Gael in 1933. The politics of the civil war were to dominate the South for several decades.

1.7 Was partition inevitable?

Political historians are allowed the luxury of hindsight in assessing whether partition was the most appropriate attempt to resolve the Irish problem. Despite the advantage of being able to analyse consequences, there remains division over whether the splitting of Ireland into two states was the only realistic approach. What then were the options open to the British government?

1.7.1 Partition as undertaken

An orthodox approach is that the division of Ireland was indeed the least worst option to be undertaken. The immoveable object of Unionists' demands for retention of their British connection was ranged against the irresistible force of Irish nationalism. Given the coexistence of conflicting identities within a single land mass, it was, as Tom Wilson puts it, 'indeed the case that there had to be some losers' (Wilson, 1989: 40).

In this case, the obvious loser was the Nationalist minority trapped in an alien Northern state and a much smaller Unionist minority in a similar position in an Ireland heading for full independence. Partition was designed to satisfy partially, or least offend, the aspirations of as many people as possible. The onus was now placed upon Nationalists to accept that there was a democratic basis for the Northern state. The British government could not be expected to foresee the inequitable treatment of this minority that lay ahead.

1.7.2 The creation of a single Irish parliament controlling all of Ireland

The establishment of a semi-independent, united Irish state might be justified on a utilitarian basis, in that it would have created the greatest happiness for the greatest number within Ireland. However, this is to ignore the qualitative element attached to such a solution. The strength of hostility of Unionists to incorporation within a united Ireland was stronger than the desire of most Irish citizens for their inclusion. Furthermore, the Unionist perception that the Southern state would eventually shed its British connections was vindicated. The strongest argument against the imposition of self-government for all of Ireland was nonetheless the threat of force. Undoubtedly there would have been considerable conflict if the British government had attempted this settlement. Given the possible reluctance of the British Army to engage with conflict with Unionists, it would have been difficult to impose Home Rule.

1.7.3 The creation of a unified Irish state, but with devolution for the North

Exercise of this option would, like the 1920 Government of Ireland Act, have also created two parliaments, but with the Irish parliament as the overseer. Most of the problems attached to the creation of a single Dublin parliament remained with this option. Although Lloyd George raised the possibility of a devolved Belfast parliament for the North within an all-Ireland settlement, it was rejected by Unionists as undermining their right to remain full British citizens. Any such solution made a Dublin parliament superior to its Belfast counterpart. Significant opt-outs for the latter would undermine Republican aspirations of a unified state. In other words, this solution would have pleased few, but was entirely unacceptable to Unionists.

1.7.4 The continuation of the Union between Britain and Ireland

Political pressure for change in the relationship between Britain and Ireland had been growing for some time. Although two Home Rule Bills had been defeated, the demand for a weakening of British control was irrepressible by the time of the third Bill and the final, post-World War I version. Successive Irish elections had confirmed the need for the creation of self-government. The Government of Ireland Act was a minimal recognition of the aspirations most clearly expressed by Sinn Fein's 1918 election victory.

1.7.5 The creation of a deliberately vulnerable Northern Ireland

If Northern Ireland had been created on geographic logic, a nine-county state would have emerged, embracing all of Ulster. It is just possible that such a state might have been 'sold' to Unionists. Within a few decades, the growing Nationalist population might have voted the state out of existence. Any such settlement would have accentuated political tensions to such an extent that the state would probably have been ungovernable.

1.8 Conclusion

Even the Conservative leader of Britain's governing coalition, Austen Chamberlain, doubted the logic and legitimacy of partition. Whilst to many it was an indefensible flawed compromise, it was to others understandable, borne primarily of the fear of Ulster Unionist reaction to the imposition of Home Rule. The division of Ireland enshrined the threat of violence as the ultimate arbiter of Irish politics. One of the signatories to the treaty which divided Ireland, Michael Collins, asked: 'Will anyone be satisfied at the bargain?' (Lyons, 1973: 439). Whilst many in the South did accept the treaty, the bigger challenge would be found in Northern Ireland. For partition to have at least some chance of succeeding, tolerance of minority identities was now required. Here was a new state where the aspirations of the Nationalist minority could not be wholly fulfilled, but needed to be sated.

Chapter 2

An 'Orange state'? Northern Ireland 1921–68

The big test for Protestants within the new state of Northern Ireland concerned their ability to treat fairly a dissident minority Catholic population. An in-built Protestant and Unionist majority had been created. This could have led to displays of either magnanimity or triumphalism towards the sector of the population dissatisfied with the new settlement. In the event, the latter option was exercised, resulting in considerable discrimination against the Catholic Nationalist population.

2.1 An insecure state

From the outset, Northern Ireland was an insecure state, persistently under threat, even if such threats were more rhetorical than real. The obvious threat came from a Catholic and mainly Nationalist minority population that resented the creation of what it saw as an artificial state devoid of geographical, historical or political logic. Suppression of symbols of the Irish identity of the Nationalist minority was commonplace. Commemorations of the 1916 Easter Rising were banned. Prohibition of displays of the tricolour, the Irish national flag, was also introduced.

Northern Ireland's viability as a separate entity faced potential challenges as both Unionist and Nationalist populations regarded themselves as sub-sets of other national groupings. Unionists pledged allegiance to the British state. The creation of Northern Ireland was the least worst option in terms of reflecting this loyalty. Nationalists saw themselves as trapped in an illegitimate, British-held part of an Irish state temporarily partitioned.

An abject lack of consensus was immediately reflected in internal security arrangements. With over 400 people killed and 2,000 injured in conflict in the first two years of the state's existence, the Special Powers Act was introduced in 1922, which suspended normal legal processes. The Act provided sweeping powers of search, arrest and detention. Designed to last one year, it endured until 1972, its longevity reflecting the absence of consensus within the state.

Primary operators of the Special Powers Act were the Royal Ulster Constabulary and the reserve police force, the Ulster Special Constabulary, or 'B' Specials. Both armed, their creation fuelled the perception that Northern Ireland, an immature sub-state, had 'institutionalized violence' (Townshend, 1983: 384). The RUC failed to attract a proportionate one-third Catholic membership. The actual figure peaked at 17 per cent and such recruitment averaged 10 per cent. The 'B' Specials were a part-time force seen by many Catholics as a sectarian militia, being exclusively Protestant, often ill-trained and partisan. Its recruitment was based upon Ulster Volunteer Force (UVF) structures so closely that entire UVF units transferred into the reserve police force (Farrell, 1980). Orange lodges provided an alternative source of recruitment.

Few Catholics were willing volunteers to what was often perceived as an illegitimate police force. Some potential recruits were also subject to discouragement from their own community. Aside from self-exclusion, Catholics were unwanted within the 'B' Specials. Policing within Northern Ireland was not perceived as neutral, but instead was viewed by Nationalists as based upon the reduction of their political threat. For many Protestants, Catholic absence from the security forces was confirmation of the disloyalty of the Nationalist population.

Catholic alienation from the legal apparatus of Northern Ireland was compounded by the exclusion of Nationalists from many senior posts in the judiciary. Even the jury system disproportionately excluded Catholics as juries comprised ratepayers.

In the early years, much police activity was directed against the Nationalist population, despite the most common source of disturbance arising from Loyalist attacks upon Catholic areas, forcing thousands to flee their homes. Of the 457 people killed between July 1920 and July 1922, the majority were Catholics (Farrell, 1980). Civil war in the South ensured that much IRA activity was diverted elsewhere. Despite this, 16 battalions of British troops were stationed in the Province to consolidate Unionist rule, along with a regular police force, 19,000 'B' Specials and other auxiliary policing groups, including over 5,000 full-time reservists. Internment (detention without trial) was introduced in 1922, ceasing in 1924 after over 500 people had been held, mainly Catholics.

In other aspects of the Northern Irish polity, the exclusion of Catholics appeared to confirm the notion of an 'Orange state' run for the self-preservation of the Unionist population. Discrimination was abetted by two features of Northern Ireland. First, the Province enjoyed considerable political autonomy, due to the disinterest in the Province displayed by the British government. Second, however, there was little financial room for manoeuvre. Almost 80 per cent of Northern Ireland's income was determined by Westminster, to which revenue from income tax and customs and excise accrued. As the economy of Northern Ireland declined, so competition for economic dividends became more fervent. Obvious losers in such a contest were to be the Catholic minority. Discrimination was alleged in three particular areas: elections, employment and housing.

2.2 Electoral discrimination

Perhaps the most overt forms of discrimination were found in the arena of electoral practices. For many Nationalists, discrimination was in-built, as a Protestant Unionist majority had been contrived and could not be challenged.

Table 2.1   Electors and elected in Derry 1967

Ward	Voters		Elected
	Catholic	Non-Catholic	
Derry North	2,530	3,946	8 Unionists
Waterside	1,852	3,697	4 Unionists
Derry South	10,047	8,781	12 Unionists
			8 Nationalists

Source: adapted from Darby (1976).

Under the conditions of the 1920 Government of Ireland Act, elections in Northern Ireland were to be conducted using a system of proportional representation, designed to achieve representation for the Nationalist minority. Yet by 1922, this had been abolished by the Unionist government in favour of a 'first-past-the-post' system in local elections, a measure repeated in 1929 in respect of contests for the Northern Ireland parliament. Perpetuation of single-party government was guaranteed.

Voting qualifications were also based upon finance, disproportionately disenfranchising Catholics. For elections to local councils, only homeowning ratepayers could vote. Poorer Protestants were also affected, but greater proportionate reliance amongst Catholics upon public housing meant that many forfeited their right to elect local representatives. Property requirements made a significant impact upon the size of the local electorate. For Westminster and Stormont elections, the number of voters approached 900,000. Local electoral contests were determined by an electorate of only 600,000.

Catholics were also disadvantaged by the existence of business franchises, by which companies could hold up to six extra votes, exercised through nominees. As businesses were more frequently owned by Protestants, this device tended to favour Unionist candidates. One other anomaly was the award of four seats in Stormont to Queen's University, at the time largely Protestant, with the consequence that Unionist candidates were easily the most successful contestants, winning 75 per cent of the seats.

Most blatant of all electoral devices was gerrymandering, a term which refers to the manipulation of electoral boundaries. Within Northern Ireland, it was used to considerable effect to reinforce Unionist electoral dominance. Local electoral ward boundaries were devised to ensure Unionist council majorities, even in predominantly Nationalist areas. Most notorious was the example of Derry, where, as Table 2.1 indicates, a substantial Catholic majority was not reflected in terms of returned councillors.

In Derry, Unionist votes were in effect worth almost double those cast for Nationalists. Even allowing for a small Catholic Unionist vote, the Council should have been dominated by a substantial Nationalist majority. Instead, Catholics were crammed into a large ward yielding a number of Nationalist councillors. Much smaller areas were used to create similar numbers of

Unionist councillors, permanently in control of the Council. It was apparent, therefore, that Unionist control was 'too consistent for too long to be anything other than deliberately contrived' (Lyons, 1973: 756).

Gerrymandering was repeated elsewhere. Towns such as Dungannon and Omagh saw Nationalist population majorities turned into representational minorities. Newry and Strabane were rare examples of significant councils controlled by Nationalists. Overall, Unionists controlled 85 per cent of councils, even though they amounted to only 66 per cent of the population (Buckland, 1981).

2.3 Discrimination in employment

There are three main strands to the allegation that Roman Catholics were victims of employment discrimination.

2.3.1 Discrimination in industrial location decisions

The contention was that Catholics were disproportionately adversely affected by the location of most industries in the east of the Province. This part of Northern Ireland was more Protestant and Unionist than the West. Even those who dispute that systematic discrimination occurred accept that Catholic areas of the Province were often losers from locational decisions. Areas with Catholic majorities received only three-quarters of the amount of employment location awards enjoyed by Protestant areas between 1949–63 (Wilson, 1989). A consequence was a growing disparity in employment typology between the industrialised East of Northern Ireland and the more rural West.

2.3.2 Discrimination in employment prospects

At the time of the suspension of the Northern Ireland parliament in 1972, almost one-third of Catholic males were unskilled. Overall, Catholic males were twice as likely to be unskilled as Protestants (Quinn, 1993). Unemployment was much more acute amongst Catholics than Protestants. Indeed, even after reforms of employment laws in the 1970s and 1980s, substantial differences remained. Amongst Catholic and Protestant groups in Northern Ireland sharing the same set of circumstances, being skilled, but without formal qualifications, aged 25–44 with two children, Catholic rates of unemployment were twice as high (Smith and Chambers, 1991).

2.3.3 Discrimination in public-sector appointments

The exclusion of Catholics from the public and private sectors appeared to receive official sanction. Basil Brooke, Prime Minister of Northern Ireland from 1943–63, had declared that 'we would appeal to Loyalists . . . to employ Protestant lads and lassies'. Given such polemic, it was scarcely surprising if what resulted was a 'consistent and irrefutable pattern of deliberate discrimination against Catholics' (Darby, 1976: 78).

Exclusion was particularly marked in three areas of public activity. First, the avowedly sectarian nature of the security services discouraged Catholics. Second, the civil service contained few Catholics in the highest positions. Only one Catholic permanent secretary could be found within the service by the late 1950s. Third, local councils, when Unionist-controlled, frequently excluded Catholics from jobs. In 1928, only 5 per cent of the workforce of Belfast Corporation was Catholic, although Catholics amounted to one-quarter of the population of the city (Johnson, 1985: 215). In the mid-1960s, Derry Council employed 177 workers, of whom only 32 were Catholic (Coogan, 1995: 32). The Cameron Report found that Unionist councils used their power of appointments in a way which benefited Protestants (Cameron, 1969).

2.4 Discrimination in housing

Both Catholic and Protestant communities endured poor housing, partly as a result of the antipathy towards housebuilding held by many councils in the Province. Only 50,000 houses were built between the wars. A reluctance to build houses need not in itself have led to poor housing, as Northern Ireland's pre-war population remained static, a consequence of high Catholic emigration rates (Johnson, 1985).

After World War II, discrimination increased as competition developed for quality new housing. Three dimensions to discrimination existed. Firstly, there was a tendency to allow Catholics to continue to reside in slum dwellings. Despite amounting to the poorer sector of the population, they were less likely to be rehoused. Secondly, Catholics perceived themselves as victims of the arbitrary allocation decisions of councils. Unlike mainland Britain, housing was determined by *ad hoc* arrangements within individual councils. Thirdly, the primary aims of councils often appeared to be the preservation of residential segregation or the absorption of rehoused Nationalists within overwhelmingly Unionist areas.

Numerous examples of apparent favouring of Protestants occurred. For example, of the 1,048 houses built in Fermanagh between 1945 and 1967, 82 per cent were allocated to Protestants, even though Catholics amounted to the majority population (Farrell, 1980: 87). In Dungannon in 1965, 194 new houses were all used to rehouse Protestants. A particular grievance was the rehousing of single Protestants, ostensibly at the expense of Catholic families. Slum conditions affected both communities. Discrimination was a device which affected the chance held by an individual of removal from such squalor.

Even amongst those hostile to the Republican agenda of a united Ireland, there was sympathy for the plight of Northern Nationalists. Thus, Conor Cruise O'Brien wrote that what occurred in Northern Ireland was the formation of an 'institutionalized caste system' with Protestants in control (O'Brien, 1972: 129). The hierarchy of the Catholic Church regularly lamented discrimination against its followers.

2.5 The extent of discrimination

There remains disagreement over whether discrimination occurred and controversy over its extent. Nearly 50 years after the creation of an alleged 'Orange state', there was scant accord over whether Catholics were being victimised within Northern Ireland, as Table 2.2 indicates, based upon the views of respondents in 1968.

This lack of public consensus over whether discrimination was a reality was replicated in political and academic circles and did not augur well for problem resolution. A Unionist rejection of the premise that Catholics were being treated unfairly was perhaps unsurprising. Protestant superiority was seen as the natural order, justified by the need for eternal vigilance against suspect Catholics. Electoral hegemony for Unionists was not seen as unjust, but rather as a justifiable product of the creation of Northern Ireland, with its attendant demographic and religious balance.

Without doubt, some Catholics have exaggerated the pervasiveness and degree of discrimination against the Nationalist population. This approach is seen most clearly in those accounts of the state which compare the plight of Catholics in Northern Ireland to that endured by blacks in the United States (*see* for example, O'Dochartaigh, 1994).

Amongst Protestants, there are those who claim that discrimination was largely 'religion-blind' as the working-class as an entirety was disadvantaged. Systematic discrimination did not occur. Differences between the Protestant and Catholic communities were 'not deliberate injustices perpetrated by a Unionist administration' (Campbell, 1996). Accordingly, much subsequent 'anti-discrimination' legislation has been ill-judged, erroneously attempting to redress a problem that did not exist. The result has been that Protestants are the modern victims of discrimination (Campbell, 1987; 1995).

Orthodox views lie somewhere between these two poles, with the debate over the extent of discrimination centred upon three themes:

(a) the 'politics of denial' in respect of discrimination which has emerged from some Unionist quarters (McGarry and O'Leary, 1995: 106);
(b) the degree of self-exclusion by the Catholic population;
(c) the perception of 'disloyal' Catholics.

Table 2.2 Views on discrimination in Northern Ireland in 1968
Proposition: '. . . in parts of Northern Ireland Catholics are treated unfairly. Do you think this is true or not?'

	Religion (%)	
	Protestant	**Catholic**
Yes	18	74
No	74	13
Don't know	8	13

Source: adapted from Rose (1971).

2.5.1 The politics of denial

The refutation by some Unionists that discrimination occurred on a widespread scale might be dismissed as predictable. Nonetheless, it is worth noting that in a formal, legalistic sense, it should have been impossible for Northern Ireland to operate as a sectarian state. Stewart (1977) claims that Stormont did not itself pass discriminatory laws, being forbidden to do so by the Government of Ireland Act 1920. Discrimination, if it occurred, must have occurred as consequence of local actions, whether committed by councils, employers or individuals. Indeed, the Unionist regime was not as homogeneous as might be assumed. There were debates within the Unionist Party concerning the appropriate means of treating Catholics (Bew, Gibbon and Patterson, 1996). Nonetheless, sectarian urges sometimes held sway.

Whatever the constitutional obligations of Unionists, it was apparent that Catholics were disadvantaged within Northern Ireland. Stormont did not act positively to eradicate discrimination. Instead, Catholic deficiencies were sometimes blamed. In 1955, one academic asserted that Catholics 'often *were* inferior, if *only* in those personal qualities that make for success in competitive economic life' (Wilson, 1955: 208–9).

Such an argument suggested a greater economic competence amongst the Unionist population, based upon a combination of the Protestant work ethic and superior schooling. More subtle supply-side explanations also influence modern Unionist accounts of differences in status between the two communities. Perceptions of the inferiority of Catholics have been displaced by stress upon the accidental nature of disparities between the two communities. Catholics question why the gap in skills training was not rectified.

More subtle than inferiority arguments was the denial of discrimination in some of the aspects of the state about which Catholics complained. Electoral discrimination has been denied, in that the Unionist majority produced at each election to the Northern Ireland parliament merely reflected the political balance of forces within Northern Ireland (Barritt and Carter, 1962). In local elections, the Protestant working-class also suffered disenfranchisement through property qualifications. Accordingly, it is claimed that this was not a device of deliberate religious discrimination.

In housing, it has been pointed out that the proportion of Catholics living in council housing was higher than that found within the Protestant sector (Calvert, 1972). Catholics did not, therefore, suffer from an unwillingness of the state to deal with their housing difficulties. Furthermore, both Protestants and Catholics acquiesced in the residential segregation perpetuated by councils.

Equally, claims of locational discrimination have been questioned. For example, Wilson (1989: 105) argues that 'the widely held belief that Londonderry was the victim of sectarian discrimination in industrial promotion cannot be sustained'. This argument dismisses the idea that the East of the Province was systematically favoured over the predominantly Catholic West. Although Catholics comprised a higher proportion of the population in the West, three-fifths nonetheless lived in the three eastern counties of Northern Ireland. Any deliberate favouring of this eastern area would, therefore, have helped the majority of the Catholic population.

Differences in wealth and status between Protestants and Catholics were acknowledged. Indeed, the terms 'lower class', 'labourers' and 'poor' were used as synonyms for Catholics by Protestants (Harris, 1986: 153). If use of these terms was partly stereotypical and derogatory, there was sufficient empirical evidence to indicate the existence of a residual Catholic underclass of casualised, unskilled labour.

2.5.2 Catholic self-exclusion

It has been suggested that whilst Catholics were the victims of discrimination, 'exclusion was often self-imposed' (Buckland, 1981: 66). Catholics were seen as having withdrawn from Northern Ireland. Self-exclusion possessed several features. Firstly, the Nationalist Party engaged in long periods of abstention from Stormont, with a sole overriding policy of anti-partitionism. Only by 1965 did the Nationalist Party agree to become the official opposition. Secondly, there was an unwillingness to apply for certain public-sector appointments, notably in administration and the police. Thirdly, Catholics were alleged to have withdrawn from the state by their insistence upon their own system of education.

Critics of the final argument suggest that agreement to educate a community as it desires is the baseline of a liberal, pluralist society. In no sense does it represent withdrawal from the state, nor is such a departure seen in negative terms elsewhere in the United Kingdom. The two previous arguments are also problematic. A political system based upon majoritarianism rendered the Nationalist party politically impotent, leading to prolonged abstentionism. There appeared to be no attempt to recognise the validity of the political aspirations of the Nationalist population. This inhibited some Catholics from applying to join the institutions of state, as they might become participants within an alien political system. Prospects for advancement within such institutions were in any case highly constrained.

The two communities were also divided on cultural grounds. Social meetings were rare, partly because so many events were centred upon the respective churches. Some Catholics attempted to preserve Gaelic culture and language. Sport acted as one community marker. Catholics generally favoured Gaelic games, whilst Protestants played sports such as soccer and rugby. Many Catholics also enjoyed the latter and the extent of the wider cultural divide can be overstated. The idea that Catholics engaged in cultural self-exclusion by maintaining traditions is highly problematic.

2.5.3 Perceptions of disloyal Catholics

For many Unionists, Catholics were essentially disloyal citizens within the state. Overwhelmingly Nationalist, perhaps more so than nowadays, the Catholic population was seen as holding an external allegiance. This loyalty, to an Irish state claiming sovereignty over Northern Ireland, was for many Protestants incompatible with full acceptance of Catholics as citizens of Northern Ireland, with the attendant economic benefits which accrued, relative to the South of Ireland.

According to Unionists, Nationalist disloyalty led to self-exclusion, as Catholics refused to co-operate with what they regarded as an illegitimate state. Additionally, it has been suggested that councils held by Nationalists pursued allocative discrimination with even greater vigour than their Unionist rivals (Rose, 1971).

Against these arguments, it should be noted that Nationalist control of councils was rare. Furthermore, Catholics saw themselves as unwelcome within the Northern state and were immediately excluded from influence. For Nationalists, partition legitimised sectarianism by creating a majoritarian political system designed to favour those holding a particular religious creed and ethnic identity.

Although perceived as disloyal, Nationalists were essentially non-rebellious subjects between 1921 and 1968. This weakens the argument that Catholics were necessarily excluded because they were engaged in some form of permanent revolution designed to bring about the collapse of Northern Ireland. Despite the discrimination to which they were subject, the Nationalist response was one of sullen, tacit acquiescence, not determined state overthrow.

2.6 Explanations of discrimination

Explanations of why discrimination occurred differ over three main issues:

1. the value of Protestant privileges;
2. the extent of Protestant unity across social classes;
3. the role, if any, of the British government, in promoting sectarianism.

Nationalists believed that discrimination was an endemic feature of the sectarian state of Northern Ireland. An artificial state based upon Protestant triumphalism was certain to exercise discrimination against Catholics. For Protestants, union with Britain was now justified on democratic grounds by the creation of a two-to-one Unionist majority. All that seemed to be needed was regular reassurance from London that this majority would guarantee Northern Ireland's place within the United Kingdom.

The British government appeared, if not anxious, at least willing enough to confirm the constitutional status of Northern Ireland. For example, it responded to the withdrawal of Ireland from the Commonwealth and the creation of an Irish Republic in 1949 by asserting that there could be no change in the constitutional status of Northern Ireland without the consent of Stormont. Given constitutional guarantees, a large in-built majority and relative peace in Northern Ireland, in what sense was discrimination functional?

One explanation of discrimination was that it centred upon *economic* factors. Unionist hegemony was reinforced by uniting the Protestant middle and working-classes in an organic relationship. Protestants enjoyed economic superiority over their Catholic counterparts. Until the 1960s, there was only a small Catholic middle-class. Marginal superiority characterised the position of the Protestant working-class, which, although poor, enjoyed a slightly better standard of living than the Catholic working-class. The latter suffered greater unemployment and casualisation of labour.

Although advantages were slight, economic superiority was useful in maintaining the loyalty of working-class Protestants to the Unionist regime. Internal dissent was neutered by the token privileges offered by the perpetually governing Unionist Party to its supporters.

These arguments are necessary but insufficient, as working-class unionism also possessed a non-material basis. It *is* possible to assert that marginal economic superiority produced a largely unquestioning brand of unionism, in which loyalty to Ulster, its leaders and the British Crown overrode potential class antagonisms.

Enjoyment of superior economic fortune derived partly from the nature of Northern Ireland's economy, which remained internalised, as the activities of multinational companies were not in evidence. Instead there were three pillars of Northern Ireland's economy: agriculture, linen and shipbuilding, which combined accounted for almost half the workforce in the Province up to World War II (Johnson, 1985: 191). Many of these concerns were locally owned, with employers displaying a tendency to employ co-religionists. Such Orange clientelism was difficult to challenge in an era which predated detailed fair employment legislation.

Largely a product of Marxist or Republican analyses, *imperial or colonial* explanations of discrimination emphasise the usefulness of sectarian discrimination in the perpetuation of British rule. These approaches often perceive Northern Ireland as one of Britain's last colonies. Discrimination in favour of a sector of the indigenous population was designed to bolster and legitimise colonial rule, by boosting local support for colonial dominance.

Republican approaches tend to imply that the Protestant working-class was the victim of false consciousness. Duped into supporting unionism through the benefits of marginal superiority, Protestants would have been better served by making common cause with working-class Catholics in challenging British economic domination. According to Irish Republicans, Britain was held as ultimately responsible for the preservation of a sectarian state, in which a contrived majority was allowed certain privileges, as reward for the preservation of British interests.

Marxist Republicans, such as James Connolly, had argued that the partition of Ireland would inevitably create a sectarian state based upon sectional interest. British policy was seen as based upon divide and rule, as the fracturing of working-class interests was seen as functional for capital by reducing the impact of labour organisations. Competition for scarce resources amongst groups divided by religious affiliation prevented the development of class antagonisms.

Criticisms of such arguments centre upon the extent to which sectarianism was of use to British interests and the value of the economy of Northern Ireland. Sectarianism might instead be viewed as a consequence of the failure of the Unionist leadership to 'rise to the challenge of political maturity' (Quinn, 1993: 14). British capital had minimal use for sectarianism, whilst British political élites had little interest in religious bigotry beyond mild disdain. Northern Ireland was run at one remove from the rest of the United Kingdom, with its internal affairs a minimal concern of a section of the Home Office. Indeed, as Follis (1995: 123) notes, the relationship between the 'imperial government' and local Loyalists was rarely convivial, insisting that: 'Far from being close allies of the British Government, the Ulster Unionists heartily reciprocated London's resentment and suspicion'.

Equally, the latter criticism concerning the economic value of the 'Orange state' suggests that sectarianism was largely internally devised. Britain had little interest in the perpetually declining economy of Northern Ireland. Against this, it should be noted that Northern Ireland possessed a strong economy when the decision to partition Ireland was undertaken. After 1921, however, the economy declined sharply, with unemployment averaging 27 per cent during the 1930s. Accordingly, the economic exploitation of Northern Ireland produced diminishing returns.

Others, who might be described as left-wing Unionists, fuse economic and political explanations and produce an analysis based upon *social class* (Bew, Gibbon and Patterson, 1996). They reject the view of Republicans or many other Marxists that the Protestant working-class had its identity 'bought' by favours. National loyalty was important, but the Protestant working-class was less deferential to its leaders than has been claimed. In 1932, Protestant workers from the Shankill district of Belfast rioted in support of impoverished Catholics in the Falls area. Sectarianism was useful for the state as it prevented this solidarity becoming permanent. Capitalists could threaten Protestant workers with the loss of national identity and the removal of privileges.

Although British loyalty to Northern Ireland was not wholehearted, the national loyalties of the citizens in the Province outweighed class affiliations. The Unionist middle-class ascendancy remained unthreatened by serious challenge from below by poorer co-religionists. Protestants prepared to engage in such agitation were seen as damaging the state. Ironically, the Catholic Church provided an ally to Protestant hegemony, in denouncing agitation on social issues as inspired by Communists.

Non-economic explanations of why discrimination was prevalent within Northern Ireland between 1921 and 1968 lie in the perception of political threat to the state. Of all explanations, this relies the most exclusively upon an internal rationale, based upon the siege mentality of unionism. Each aspect of Unionist discrimination was designed to allay concerns over the threat of absorption of the six-county Northern state within a united Ireland.

The abolition of proportional representation and gerrymandering of local electoral boundaries can be explained within this framework. Local elections had offered the greatest potential Nationalist resistance. Indeed, immediately after the creation of Northern Ireland, rebel councils declared allegiance to the Southern state. Abolition of proportional representation reduced the numbers of rebel bodies. Gerrymandering consolidated the switch to Unionist control.

Protestants were fearful of the entry of Catholics into the security apparatus of the state or the upper echelons of society, due to their doubtful loyalty. Catholic adherence to the symbols of the Irish Republic, such as the flying of the illegal tricolour and the commemoration of the Easter Rising, served to emphasise Unionist fears.

Thus, Protestants were unsure how to treat the Catholic population. The police force was torn between a desire to attract Catholics and integrate them into the state and the desire to act decisively against 'traitors'. One result was that there were, in effect, two police forces. One, the 'B' Specials, was nakedly sectarian. The main police force, the RUC, spent its time 'teetering uncertainly between impartiality and partisanship' (Whyte, 1983: 29).

Finally, the political fears of Protestants were reinforced by hostility to the doctrines of Roman Catholicism and the perception of a 'Popish conspiracy' (Elliott and Hickie, 1971: 40). Discrimination was necessary against followers of an expansionist religion, in order to defend a Protestant state.

Yet, purely religious discrimination was rare. What occurred was political and social discrimination against an Irish nationalist population who were Catholics. The rights of Catholics to practise their religion and educate their children in the faith were scrupulously defended by the Protestant Unionist regime.

A cynic might suggest that this zeal owed something to the usefulness of the perpetuation of sectarian division. Nonetheless, it should be stressed that whilst sections of the Protestant population were contemptuous of the religion held by their fellow citizens, systematic discrimination that occurred was an attempt to secure the state from the challenges of Irish *nationalism*. Unsystematic discrimination, extending even to the sectarian murder of Catholics purely because of their religious label in the early years of the state, also occurred.

2.7 Political stagnation

Perhaps the most remarkable feature of Northern Ireland during this period of endemic discrimination was the lack of challenge to the state. From 1922 to 1955, there were 97 political murders. The Border Campaign of the IRA between 1956 and 1962 killed six RUC personnel. That particular phase of violence ended with a statement from the IRA lamenting the lack of support from Nationalists in Northern Ireland. Periodic campaigns saw the reintroduction of stringent security measures. Internment was reintroduced on both sides of the border during the 1950s campaign.

By the late 1950s, some prosperous Catholics were prepared to accept the permanency of Northern Ireland. Indeed, many enjoyed the benefits of a much more comprehensive system of welfare than that available in the Republic, introduced by the 1945–51 Labour government against initial Unionist opposition. Whilst condemning partition, Catholic bishops were unyielding in their hostility to armed republicanism, denouncing as a mortal sin membership of organisations committed to such activities.

Despite the passivity of Nationalist responses to their subordinate position, there remained little attempt to integrate Catholics within political structures. Unionists were reluctant to make even slight concessions to Nationalist demands as they feared that such moves would be seen as a sign of Unionist weakness and that further demands would follow. Nationalists, therefore, found it impossible to make political progress.

An Anti-Partition League created in 1945 attempted to unite different shades of Nationalist opinion. For some time, sections of the League did not pursue an abstentionist stance, but little was achieved. The League had particular support in rural areas and was influenced by the clergy. Radical urban Catholics might have supported the Northern Ireland Labour Party (NILP) which held progressive social stances. However, constitutional politics dominated and the NILP suffered a decline in Nationalist support when it developed a Unionist position on the border question.

As a gesture of frustration with the lack of political progress, the Nationalist population occasionally supported more militant Republican candidates. A member of the fringe Republican party, Saor Uladh, was successful in Tyrone in a Stormont General Election in 1953. Two Sinn Fein candidates were elected in the 1955 General Election. If Unionists interpreted such results as evidence of the continuing disloyalty of Catholics, the success of Sinn Fein owed more to the absence of rival Nationalist candidates on that occasion.

2.8 The threat from the South?

Within Unionist demonology, the twenty-six-county state in the South of Ireland posed a direct threat to the security of Northern Ireland for two reasons. Firstly, the Southern state was overtly hostile to the division of Ireland. Secondly, the hegemonic role of the Catholic Church within that state inhibited Protestant securities. For Unionists, events in the South following partition vindicated their belief that Home Rule would indeed have ensured Rome rule. Accordingly, it was necessary for Unionists to maintain eternal vigilance against the perceived threat of territorial encroachment from the South.

Indeed, as Northern Ireland consolidated its Protestant British identity, Southern Ireland attempted to enshrine a Catholic, Gaelic lifestyle amongst its populace. The conclusion of the Irish Civil War in 1923 facilitated the development of an immature democracy within the 26 counties of the Irish Free State. Three problems confronted the new state. Firstly, there was a need to assert Irish nationality despite continuing British ties and partition. Secondly, there lay the difficulty of maintaining the claim to jurisdiction over the north-eastern corner of Ireland. Finally, economic strength needed to be developed. Attempts at resolving these dilemmas succeeded only in strengthening Unionist hostility towards the South and fostering the 'No Surrender' mentality within Northern Ireland.

By 1927, the creation of a new opposition party, Fianna Fail ('warriors'), by Eamon de Valera allowed a recognisable system of government and opposition to emerge. Fianna Fail represented the anti-partition wing of republicanism defeated in the Irish Civil War. It rose to power in 1932 on rhetorical pledges to end partition and emphasise Ireland's status as a sovereign nation. This attempt to free Ireland from imperial ties was confirmation for unionists that limited autonomy for the south would result eventually in full independence.

An explicit assertion of Irish identity was established in the 1937 constitution, which confirmed the links between the Irish state and the Roman Catholic Church. The 1937 constitution:

1. created a new state: Eire, or Ireland;
2. laid the foundations for the establishment of an Irish Republic in 1949;
3. rejected the permanency of partition;
4. enshrined the position of the Catholic Church.

Separatism, unity and theocracy were the core themes of the new settlement in Southern Ireland. The first theme concerned the establishment of Ireland as a genuine nation in its own right, beyond the status of 'West Britain'. From the outset, de Valera attempted to steer the Free State towards the status of a republic. This was achieved by 1949, as Ireland withdrew from the Commonwealth. As the South weakened its British links, the British government sought to reassure Unionists in the North by declaring that there could be no change in the status of Northern Ireland without the consent of Stormont.

Commitments to Irish unity expressed within the Irish Republic were largely rhetorical, as there was little that the Irish government could do to achieve this goal. Fianna Fail's strong pledges to the aspiration of a united Ireland nonetheless had some electoral value, whilst helping to ensure that the South of Ireland would remain entombed in civil war politics for several generations. Furthermore, under the 1937 constitution, it became a constitutional imperative of all Irish governments, irrespective of political persuasion, to seek means of creating Irish unity. Article 2 declared that the national territory consists of 'the whole island of Ireland, its islands and the territorial seas'. Article 3 recognised the *de facto* reality, declaring that 'pending the reintegration of the national territory . . . the laws of the state would only apply to the Free State area'.

Territorial claims to the North were obviously anathema to Unionists, who were also alienated by the extent of influence held by the Catholic Church in the South. In developing a Catholic state and aspiring to Irish unity, Unionist sensitivities were not of primary concern to the Dublin government. The motivations of de Valera stemmed from his belief in the need to establish Ireland as an independent and secure state, based upon the moral certainties which arose from his personal piety.

As Murphy argues, Ulster was viewed merely as Ireland's fourth green field, held under alien capture (Murphy, 1995). There was no attempt to forge any kind of understanding or accommodation with Northern Unionists. As both governments on the island developed political arrangements which reflected their insecurities, any lingering hopes for dialogue between the two evaporated. De Valera did take strong action against the IRA during its periodic revivals. However, even internment without trial and executions did little to assuage

Unionists who believed such measures were enacted for the internal security of the Republic.

A theocracy can be defined as government by God directly or through a priestly class. The 1937 constitution attempted both as it empowered the Catholic Church whilst its introduction invoked 'the name of the Holy Trinity from whom is all authority'. From the liberal and secular 1922 model, the Irish constitution moved towards a theocratic 1937 model which indirectly provided the Catholic Church with significant input within the polity (Whyte, 1980). The shift was preceded by ecclesiastical censorship and prohibition in various aspects of life. Even certain forms of dancing or dress were seen as morally incorrect (Hoppen, 1980).

Most explicit was Article 44 which recognised the 'special position' of Roman Catholicism as the 'religion of the great majority of the citizens'. Article 41 insisted that 'no law shall be enacted providing for the dissolution of marriage'. The same Article confirmed the patriarchal nature of society, by insisting that 'mothers shall not be obliged by economic necessity to engage in labour to the neglect of their duties in the home'.

The moral dimensions of the Irish constitution need not have offended Protestants in Northern Ireland, many of whom shared the conservative social stances of the Catholic Church. Theological differences and an outright hostility to the Catholic Church were of greater importance. Catholic moralism was based upon absolutist beliefs which impinged upon the political arena. This was seen in social policy in 1951, when the Catholic Church opposed the creation of limited forms of state welfare, arguing that they were the responsibility of families. It was the viewpoint of the Catholic Church which triumphed over the proposals of Dr Noel Browne, the government minister.

In both North and South, theological underpinnings to society were abetted by the absence of a significant party of the left. In the Irish Republic, also lacking an urban proletariat, this helped to prevent the development of anti-clerical sentiment. Political independence permitted the development of legislation designed to consolidate symbols of national identity. The relative weakness of the Irish language allowed the Catholic Church a central role as the symbol of that identity.

It remains doubtful whether the nature of Northern Ireland was influential upon the manner in which Southern Ireland developed, although polarisation was increased. An 'Orange state' may have existed in the North even if the Republic had been a beacon of liberal pluralism. Nonetheless, perceptions remained important. The special position of the Catholic Church in the South deepened Unionist hostility. In 1983, a survey found that 74.5 per cent of Protestants cited 'fear of the power of the Roman Catholic Church' as a reason for being Unionist (Moxon-Browne, 1983: 38).

If the influence of the Church was an irritant to Unionists, so was the constitutional claim of the Irish Republic to Northern Ireland. This provided an excuse for a siege mentality. The Republic had no possibility of exercising its claim, as the North was well aware. As Wichert (1991: 151) asserts, the belief in a united Ireland 'grew into mere ideology and became part of the national identity, much used in political speeches and manifestos, but not something that was thought in practice attainable or politically desirable'.

Protestants in the South were actually disproportionately wealthy, represented in significant numbers within the professions. There was, however, a decline in the South's Protestant population, from 10 per cent in 1911 to 4 per cent by 1971, partly arising from the demand of the Catholic Church that children raised in mixed marriages be brought up as Catholics.

Overall, the Republic provided scant economic incentives for acceptance of Irish unity, offering a backward, agrarian economy. In order to protect Irish agriculture, de Valera engaged in protectionism, imposing tariffs upon imports. Always unsuccessful, the measure reinforced an image of a garrison state Ireland, attempting to insulate itself from the external world.

During the Second World War, the Irish Free State remained neutral. The geographic value of the Southern state to Britain rendered Northern Ireland's position within the United Kingdom expendable. Britain offered de Valera a declaration of support for a United Ireland in principle, which would become an 'accomplished fact' after the war (Fisk, 1983: 178). In return, Britain required that Eire either join Britain in the war against Germany, or as a minimum become non-belligerent rather than neutral, a move which would, for example, allow British use of the Irish naval ports it relinquished in 1938.

In rejecting the proposal, de Valera pointed out that an attachment indicated that the consent of the Unionist government at Stormont would be required for its implementation, agreement unlikely to be forthcoming. Of equal concern was the desire to protect Irish neutrality. Finally, de Valera believed at the time of the offer that Britain was likely to lose the war. Infamously, a telegram of condolence was sent to the German embassy upon the death of Hitler. Unsurprisingly, the gesture served only to strengthen the bond between Northern Ireland and the remainder of the United Kingdom, even though the British government had scarcely confirmed the link in its proposals to the Free State.

2.9 Conclusion

By the 1960s, many of the old certainties of the 'Orange state' remained intact. Unionist hegemony was seemingly assured. However, this picture of relative tranquillity was illusory. Weaknesses within the economy were evident, making it more difficult to retain the privileges of Orangeism. Divisions within unionism between modernisers and fundamentalists were emerging. Above all, preservation of the old order depended upon a lack of challenge from below. A common aspect of rebellion is that it stems from challenge to relative deprivation (Gurr, 1970). As Nationalists switched from sullen acquiescence to protest against their condition, the old order collapsed, never to return.

Chapter 3

From civil rights protests to insurrection

During the 1960s, debate was growing within the Unionist and Nationalist communities. Unionists pondered the best means of advancing their cause, particularly after the rise to the leadership of the relative moderate, Terence O'Neill, in 1963. The new Unionist leader believed that the best way to secure political dominance was to treat the Catholic minority on a more equitable basis. Nationalists meanwhile pondered the most appropriate means of rectifying their inequitable treatment in a polity in which they exerted scant influence. The political stagnation of the 1950s was about to be displaced by challenge and confrontation.

3.1 The modernisation of unionism

O'Neill was only the fourth Prime Minister of Northern Ireland. He wished to modernise the Province and the party in perpetual government. Along with other enlightened Unionists, O'Neill recognised that there was scope for the introduction of a more liberal form of governance in the 1960s.

A member of the Orange Order, in common with others in the Unionist hierarchy, O'Neill did not envisage more pluralistic forms of decision-making in Northern Ireland. Power-sharing with Nationalists was not envisaged. What was seen as useful on the basis of Unionist rational self-interest was the development of a more tolerant, co-operative regime. This strategy amounted to the granting of limited concessions to Catholics in order to achieve greater consensus within society.

The reformism of O'Neill was a broad agenda, designed to secure the economic and political futures of Northern Ireland. Economically, Northern Ireland was neither prosperous nor ailing. The gross domestic product, for example, rose at a faster rate than elsewhere in the United Kingdom in the 1950s and 1960s, although this amounted to only a moderate international performance (Wilson, 1989).

In an era characterised by centralised planning, the Wilson Plan attempted to find ways to modernise the economy and generate sufficient jobs to curb the persistently high unemployment endured in the Province (Wilson Report, 1965). O'Neill (1972: 67) was to lament: 'We had all the benefits of belonging to a large economy . . . but we threw it all away in trying to maintain an impossible position of Protestant ascendancy at any price'.

A moderate patrician, O'Neill believed that Catholics could be 'civilised' through economic concessions. By refusing to support the Border Campaign of the IRA from 1956–62, Catholics had indicated their willingness to accept the constitutional status quo, at least for the foreseeable future. This acceptance might be strengthened if they were now treated with tolerance and fairness.

For O'Neill, intolerance was not a symbol of the political virility of loyalism. Stressing the pragmatic basis of the link with Britain, the Prime Minister of Northern Ireland eschewed Protestant triumphalism, whilst nonetheless reaffirming stereotypes of the superiority of the creed. Thus, he declared that 'if you treat Roman Catholics with due consideration and kindness, they will live like Protestants' (*Belfast Telegraph*, 10 May 1969).

What was proposed was a modest package of reforms. They amounted to the politics of minimalism and concession, not the politics of equality or assimilation. The main reform proposals were:

1. the suspension of Derry City Corporation;
2. a review of local government;
3. reform of the franchise for local elections;
4. appointment of an ombudsman to investigate complaints against local maladministration.

It was believed that such reforms would be sufficient to appease the Catholic minority. Concentration upon discrimination in local government did target one of the most obvious arenas of discrimination. There were no proposals for reform of employment law nor for changes in policing.

3.2 The birth of the civil rights campaign

As Unionists examined their future strategy, Nationalists began to do likewise. Abstentionism and non-co-operation with the state, whilst often enforced by exclusion from power, amounted to the politics of futility. Middle-class Catholics, in particular, began to wonder aloud whether there might be more appropriate political strategies, hinting that anti-partitionism might be subordinated to more immediate agendas. Some Catholics argued that there was a duty to co-operate with the civil authority. Reformism displaced rebellion as the primary vehicle of change.

Two factors underpinned the shift in Catholic attitudes. First, the minority community enjoyed a growing self-confidence. Catholics assumed prominent positions of authority elsewhere, not least in the United States, where Kennedy had been elected as president in 1963. Catholics again looked to the United States as an example of how to conduct a civil rights campaign. Although there were numerous differences in their standards of treatment, parallels were drawn between the blacks' struggle in the USA and the possibilities for the 'liberation' of Catholics in Northern Ireland. Relatively liberal papal declarations in Vatican II had seen the removal of some of the mystique and suspicion attached to Catholicism. Tentative ecumenism even developed in Northern Ireland as relationships thawed slightly between the major churches.

Second, despite discrimination, there emerged a growing Catholic middle-class. This should not be overstated. At the end of the 1960s, it was still dwarfed by the Protestant middle-class (Aunger, 1983). Nonetheless it was influential. Prominent members of the civil rights campaign, such as John Hume, emerged from the growing Catholic section of the population who were articulate products of grammar schools, unwilling to acquiesce in the relative deprivation of their co-religionists.

In 1964, an embryonic civil rights campaign began with the establishment of the Campaign for Social Justice (CSJ). Formed by a Dungannon doctor, the organisation attempted to attract interest in the plight of the minority in Northern Ireland. Two features of the campaign are worthy of note. Firstly, it primarily engaged in the standard pressure-group activities of lobbying and the raising of issues, rather than civil disobedience. Secondly, the main appeal of the group was to British Labour MPs at Westminster. Appeals to British MPs for internal reforms within Northern Ireland indicate that, at its outset at least, the civil rights campaign was not welded to the Irish Republican ideal. The CSJ was unconcerned with traditional Nationalist border politics of anti-partitionism.

If the raising of consciousness was a primary goal, the CSJ was a success. Within a year, the Campaign for Democracy in Ulster was formed, comprising Labour MPs anxious to end discrimination in the Province. Some, such as the Manchester MP, Paul Rose, were extremely active in highlighting the inequitable treatment of Catholics. Traditional nationalism was far from dead, as the fiftieth anniversary of the Easter Rising was celebrated with as much vigour as the state permitted in 1966, a year also marked by the sectarian assassination of two Catholics by a reborn Ulster Volunteer Force. However, the desire for internal change was now at the forefront of Catholic politics.

Middle-class Catholic resentment had been increased by the decision in 1965 to locate Ulster's second university in (Protestant) Coleraine rather than (Catholic) Derry. By 1967, civil rights activity was growing to the extent that the Northern Ireland Civil Rights Association (NICRA) was formed, operating as an umbrella group for the different forms of activity. Although an essentially moderate organisation, NICRA was prepared to extend earlier pressure-group activity into civil disobedience. A difficulty with the pressure-group approach is that it operates in a pluralist political framework which assumes a basic degree of consensus in society. As the activities of NICRA were to highlight, no such consensus existed.

3.3 The demands of the civil rights movement

NICRA sought specific redress of grievances, via the following demands (Connolly, 1990: 50):

1. one man, one vote to be extended to local elections;
2. cessation of gerrymandering;
3. equitable housing allocations, via a points system;

4. abolition of the Special Powers Act;
5. disbandment of the 'B' Specials;
6. introduction of complaints mechanisms in local government.

Equally significant was what was *not* included. There were no demands for an end to partition, nor calls for a review of the border. Also absent was an insistence upon power-sharing. Toleration and fair treatment were desired as a precursor to participation in the Ulster polity. Moderation characterised the movement and its set of demands, which amounted to an extension of O'Neill's modernisation programme (Probert, 1978).

Furthermore, the very title of the Civil Rights Association implied a tacit recognition of the state. Use of the term 'Northern Ireland' was a departure for those Nationalist elements who previously referred to the country as the 'Six Counties'. Nor was the movement inspired by Communists, as claimed by some opponents. According to one radical member of the civil rights movement: 'NICRA was a reformist organisation, out for limited change within the North, not an end to the northern state, much less a transformation of Irish society north and south' (McCann, 1992: 179).

3.4 Unionist responses

Despite the moderation of the civil rights agenda, Unionists were divided between 'reformers and resisters' (Quinn, 1993: 24). Neither wished to see Unionist domination undermined, but differed on the pragmatic means of consolidation. Reformers held sympathy with several of the aims of NICRA. Resisters viewed all challenges to aspects of the state either as unnecessary, as discrimination did not exist, or as the conduct of war by other means by the republican movement. A tough response was, therefore, required.

Catholic resentment was fuelled in January 1968 by a widely publicised case in Dungannon involving the allocation of a council house to a single Protestant woman in seeming preference to a homeless Catholic family. A defence of the actions of the local council was based upon the fact that the Catholic family were squatters from another area, whereas the Protestant was local. The case, although extreme, was not unique, but received particular attention due to the involvement on behalf of the family by the local Nationalist MP, Austin Currie.

NICRA staged a large march in August 1968. Two months later, a second proposed demonstration was rerouted by the Home Affairs Minister, William Craig. Invoking the Special Powers Act, Craig used legislation from which Orange marches had appeared exempt. Using physical force, the RUC prevented the marchers from entering the city centre. Although a programme of reforms was announced in November 1968, the situation continued to deteriorate. In January 1969, Peoples Democracy, a radical, mainly student, element of the civil rights movement, which enjoyed some support from non-Catholics, staged a march from Belfast to Derry. Loyalists attacked the march at Burntollet, aided and abetted, it was claimed, by off-duty 'B' Specials (Farrell, 1980).

It was evident that the summer 'marching season' in Ulster, in which hundreds of mainly Loyalist parades take place, might lead to further escalation of conflict. In August, Catholics attacked the police following the Protestant Apprentice Boys' march in Derry. Two nights of rioting ensued as the police attempted to force entry into the Catholic Bogside. Sectarian violence spread to Belfast, with hundreds forced to flee their homes. Four-fifths of those made homeless were Catholics (Wichert, 1991: 111). Eight Catholics and two Protestants were killed in the violence. Bogside became part of 'Free Derry', a self-policed, 'no-go' area for the security forces until the entry of the British Army in Operation Motorman in 1972.

The Cameron and Scarman Reports into police conduct praised the police, but acknowledged that there had been serious breaches of discipline (Cameron, 1969; Scarman, 1972). Nationalists were less sanguine concerning the capabilities of the police, particularly the 'B' Specials. Instead, they had welcomed the arrival of British troops as peacekeepers who would prevent attacks by Protestant mobs. Sympathy, but little else, was granted to Northern Nationalists by the Irish Prime Minister, Jack Lynch, who declared that his government 'could not stand by' whilst sectarian pogroms continued. Field hospitals were set up near the border.

3.5 The arrival of the British Army

Understandably, most interpretations perceived the conflict in Northern Ireland in 1969 as one of intercommunal strife. Underlying tensions had manifested themselves in sectarian conflict. In response, the British government sent in British troops to restore order. A long-term objective was to stabilise British rule in Ulster.

Other than a handful of diehard Republicans, few in Nationalist areas of Belfast and Derry were overly concerned with long-term strategies in 1969. Rather, the arrival of British troops was welcome after the collapse of any lingering trust in the internal policing arrangements in the Province. Although remarkable in view of subsequent events, scenes of unbridled hospitality for arriving troops were common in Catholic ghettos. Cordiality was fostered by a Home Secretary, James Callaghan, not unsympathetic to the demands of the civil rights movement, backed by a British Labour Prime Minister, Harold Wilson, who had little love for the Unionist regime.

After the surprise election of a Conservative government in June 1970, Nationalists found themselves dealing with a somewhat less sympathetic Home Secretary, Reginald Maudling. An early indication of Maudling's approach to the nuances of Irish politics may have been provided by his alleged comment as he boarded the return flight after an initial visit: 'Bloody awful country; give me a whisky'.

Sage elements within the British Army realised, with some prescience, that their honeymoon period could not be sustained. Few doubted that without political progress, the Army would be placed in a conflictual position. For some Nationalists, the response of sections of the state to the civil rights campaigns illustrated that reforms would have to be imposed upon Unionists. If the intervention of the Army was seen as a device to reinforce the status quo, it was likely that confrontation would ensue. Similarly, the Army would need to deal gingerly with local residents. A permanent presence might create perceptions of the Army as a surrogate RUC.

According to some critics, a 'succession of mistakes in security policy made a major contribution to the escalation of the conflict' (Boyle and Hadden, 1994: 83). This interpretation lays great stress upon the reactive nature of developments. Armed conflict developed partly as a response to the errors of the Army. Untrained as peacekeepers, the Army alienated the Nationalist working-class by using powers of search and detention. In April 1970, the Army fired baton rounds against Catholics in Ballymurphy. Two months later, the growing estrangement of the Army from Nationalists was virtually complete, following the imposition of a thirty-six-hour curfew upon the Lower Falls in Belfast, as part of an arms search.

The introduction of detention without trial during the following year merely reinforced hostility. Internment appeared an inept military tactic, largely based upon uncertain information. Two reasons explain the hardline approach. Internal conflicts within unionism made it necessary for the Unionist Party leadership to be seen to be taking a tough stance against Nationalist disquiet (Guelke, 1988). Second, the close relationship between the Conservative and Unionist parties ensured that Westminster sanctioned a firm approach.

Most disastrous of all were the events of Bloody Sunday in January 1972, in which 13 unarmed Catholics were shot dead by the British Army, an event which even stirred passions in the Irish Republic to the extent that the British Embassy in Dublin was incinerated. Nationalists of different hues rejected the subsequent Widgery Report which alleged that the British Army had come under sniper fire from the IRA (Widgery, 1972). Nearly three decades later, events were reinvestigated by the Saville Inquiry.

Two developments occurred as relationships between Nationalists and the Army grew poisonous. Firstly, Unionism fragmented. Secondly, the IRA, derided in ghetto graffiti as the organisation that 'ran away' in 1969, splintered but gained in strength.

3.6 Unionist fragmentation

Despite the robustness of the initial response to civil rights agitation displayed by the security forces, the Unionist leadership was criticised internally for its weakness. Increasingly, O'Neill became caught in a political pincer, trapped on his left by the demands of the civil rights movement and scorned on his right by those who equated moderation with treason and opposed all concessions. Fear of change and loss of position provided two motivations for resistance to reform. As Probert (1978: 79) suggests, 'O'Neill inevitably came into conflict with those elements of the Unionist alliance who sought to preserve the traditional privileges ... the local bourgeoisie and the Protestant labour aristocracy'.

Devoid of the clear support of local business owners and confronted by increasing Protestant working-class hostility to the patrician approach of Orange grandees, O'Neillism was clearly in trouble as a reformist political project. As O'Neill attempted to defend his agenda, he dismissed William Craig as Minister for Home Affairs, after the latter had begun to make sympathetic gestures towards the idea of an independent Ulster. Hardliners such as Craig believed that sections of the Unionist Party were too conciliatory towards both the Westminster government and the civil rights movement. The establishment of the Cameron Commission of Inquiry into the disturbances in the Province had angered hardline Unionists. Two cabinet ministers resigned in protest, whilst several Unionist MPs now demanded a change of Party leadership.

An election to Stormont was called in February 1969, which confirmed the emergence of fault lines within unionism. At the forefront of calls for the replacement of O'Neill was the Reverend Ian Paisley, who challenged the Prime Minister in his own Bannside constituency and polled only 5 per cent fewer votes. The Protestant Unionist Party, which had existed on the margins of Ulster politics since the late 1950s, now emerged as a credible challenger to the official Unionist Party.

Indeed, the election was marked by the disintegration of the political homogeneity of Unionism. Once a solid, united force, Unionists divided along bizarre lines. Official Unionist candidates were either pro- or anti-O'Neill, depending upon the affiliation of their constituency party. Against Official anti-O'Neill Unionist candidates stood Independent pro-O'Neill Unionists. Similarly, Independent Unionists stood against pro-O'Neill Official Unionists.

Although moderates emerged from the elections with credible results, the position of the Unionist leadership had been fatally weakened. During the following month, O'Neill received a very lukewarm vote of confidence, by 338 votes to 263, from the Ulster Unionist Council. Whilst Paisley and Major Ronald Bunting, the two principals in the organisation of anti-civil rights protests, began short gaol sentences, O'Neill resigned. He was replaced by his cousin James Chichester-Clark, proof that Orange family dynasties had not totally expired, but an inadequate response to a deteriorating situation.

3.7 The formation of the Provisional IRA

The crisis in unionism over responses to the civil rights campaign deepened with the re-emergence of the IRA. Moribund and marginalised since the abject failure of the Border Campaign, Unionist responses to the civil rights campaign had provided the tiny organisation with a new lease of life, whilst simultaneously highlighting internal frictions which led to a split.

Although the core aim of the establishment of an independent, thirty-two-county socialist Irish republic remained, differences in strategy were apparent within the IRA during the late 1960s. Republicans were divided over the extent to which economic, electoral and military agendas should be prioritised.

Between 1962 and 1969, the IRA was very weak. Demoralised by failure, its recruitment was minimal and it was devoid of a military strategy. Social and economic agitation was seen as the most viable future strategy. This involved the creation of a broad liberation front, embracing trade unionists and disaffected groups in coalitional strategies. Under the leadership of Cathal Goulding, the organisation became increasingly Marxist and political, to the chagrin of vaguely socialist militarists within its ranks (MacStiofain, 1975). Concurrently, the IRA became almost as much concerned with the nature of the Southern state and its alleged cultural domination by Britain, as it was with partition. This departure enraged traditionalists concerned with the primacy of 'Brits Out'.

Above all, the IRA leadership misread the situation in Northern Ireland. Involved in the civil rights campaign from the outset, but as marginal actors, the IRA nonetheless issued a document, *Ireland Today*, as late as 1969, arguing that 'the 26 counties is the area in which the greatest anti-imperialist unity is possible' (Republican Education Department 1969: 5, quoted in Patterson, 1989: 105).

Given that the citizens of the Irish Republic were showing minimal interest in 'anti-imperialism', it was a curious interpretation, particularly at a time of considerable unrest in Northern Ireland. Despite the backlash amongst many Unionists, the IRA argued that political reform created by the civil rights movement would change the attitudes of the Protestant working-class, allowing it to make common cause with its Catholic counterpart. The fracturing of unionism was optimistically seen as supportive evidence (Patterson, 1989).

Marxist theorising carried little clout amongst several of the small number of remaining IRA personnel in the North. They formed part of communities bearing the brunt of sectarian attack from Loyalists. Whilst they might agree with the position of the leadership that orangeism formed part of a wider British imperial strategy, they were more concerned with the immediate need of resisting Loyalist attacks. Such individuals did respond to these attacks with what tiny firepower they could muster, one example being when they opened fire on a Loyalist mob attacking a Catholic Church in Belfast in August 1969.

Men of personal piety such as Sean McStiofain and Ruairi O'Bradaigh formed part of the new group of leadership critics. Denounced as bigots by Goulding, the Northern remnants of the IRA were tiring of the social approach and downgrading of military action by the IRA leadership. A final decision to split came when the leadership decided to end abstentionism. In the (unlikely) event of Sinn Fein candidates winning sufficient support, they would be allowed to take their seats in the Dail. It was hoped that this would boost urban working-class support for Sinn Fein in the Republic.

This downgrading of the military in favour of the political was too much for the traditionalist militarists in the movement. In January 1970 at the Sinn Fein *ard fheis* (conference) they formed the Provisional IRA as a breakaway organisation from what now became known as the 'Official' IRA.

A limited amount of support for the Provisionals came from nationalistic elements within the Fianna Fail ruling party in the Irish Republic. Such elements desired a return to green republicanism rather than the red Marxist republicanism and Communist agitation of the Official IRA. Indeed, the

Provisionals lay within the tradition of armed sacrifice for 'Mother Ireland' from which Fianna Fail had emerged. Sections of the party were relieved that the Provisionals were much more interested in military action in the North than pursuing social agendas in the South.

The extent to which aid from Southern Nationalists was significant in the formation of the Provisional IRA is disputed. Patterson (1989) argues the role of Fianna Fail had some significance, an argument rejected by Bishop and Mallie (1987). Coogan (1995) leans to the latter view. Although 'relief money' headed northwards from sympathetic Nationalists, he claims that the one consignment of arms smuggled to the North through Fianna Fail went to the Officials. Two cabinet ministers in the Republic, Charles Haughey and Neil Blaney, were charged with gun-running, but later acquitted. Fianna Fail helped to set up the strongly Nationalist *Voice of the North* newspaper. Members of the Official IRA, the recipients of much less funding from the South, were critical of the basis of support for the Provisionals.

The differences between the two IRAs could be exaggerated. Despite the magnitude of the split, 'there was little to choose in tactics or intentions' (Bowyer-Bell, 1989: 374). Indeed, some of the most brutal killings were carried out during this period by the Official IRA, including the bombing of the Parachute Regiment barracks at Aldershot, as a reprisal for Bloody Sunday. The bomb killed cleaners and a chaplain. The Officials called a ceasefire in 1972, having alienated sympathisers in Derry by killing a local soldier on leave from the British Army. At the risk of caricature, the differences of emphasis between the two IRA organisations can be seen in Table 3.1.

Devoid of assistance from politicians, the British Army's peacekeeping procedures undermined its initial welcome. Nationalist hostility grew rapidly, a process accelerated by increasing IRA activity which in turn led to greater repression. The Provisional IRA recruited at speed. Some areas of Belfast, such as the Lower Falls and Markets, remained loyal to the old IRA leadership, as did parts of Derry. In many other places, the uncomplicated approach of the Provisionals appealed.

As the campaign of the Provisionals switched to an offensive in February 1971, with the killing of the first British soldier, there was a belief in the potential of a short, sharp war approach in speedily obtaining a united Ireland. Certainly IRA activity increased enormously after the introduction of

Table 3.1 Differences between Republican paramilitary organisations 1970–72

Official IRA	Provisional IRA
Marxist	Socialist
Atheist	Catholic
Belief in need for Protestant working-class support	Defence of Nationalist area an initial priority
Social and political agenda	Military agenda; abstentionism

internment and following the upsurge in anti-British sentiment after Bloody Sunday. Detention without trial had been opposed by the British Army on the basis that it possessed insufficient knowledge. Political posturing overrode subject knowledge and a largely useless haul of terrorist suspects was conducted in Nationalist areas. Allegations of ill-treatment of detainees fuelled hostility. The Compton Committee of Inquiry conceded that prisoners had been ill-treated whilst rejecting claims that systematic brutality had occurred (Compton Report, 1971).

In 1972, there were over 10,000 shootings in Northern Ireland. Much of the city centre of Belfast was bombed, sometimes in a concerted series of explosions, as occurred on 'Bloody Friday' that year. Fifteen devices were detonated separately in a seventy-five minute period, killing nine people, mostly civilians. Such was the ferocity with which armed insurrection displaced civil rights protests that the Provisional IRA appeared to have bombed its way to the negotiating table when invited to secret talks by the Home Secretary, William Whitelaw, in July 1972. A delegation, which included Martin McGuinness and Gerry Adams, engaged in fruitless 'negotiations'. The IRA's belief that it might win through a quick campaign would slowly begin to change to a strategy of 'long war'.

3.8 The civil rights movement and the IRA

In the eyes of some Unionists, the transition from civil rights demands to an IRA offensive appeared relatively seamless, vindicating suspicions over the true nature of the original campaign. The following two very broad categories of explanation have been forwarded to explain how demands for civil rights eventually translated into armed insurrection.

3.8.1 The 'trojan horse' thesis

This alleges that the civil rights movement was a forerunner of a new IRA campaign, directly linked to the organisation, which at the time had opted for an unarmed strategy. In effect, the thesis defines the civil rights movement by outcomes. An IRA campaign emerged at a later date. As such, the civil rights movement must have been instrumental in fermenting that campaign.

Exponents of this idea do not deny the presence of non-violent idealists within the civil rights movement, but suggest that it was used as a flag of convenience by those with wider political agendas. This assessment can still be found. According to David Trimble, the leader of the Ulster Unionist Party, 'the behaviour and tactics, of civil rights, the civil rights movement, soon clarified the matter . . . this was really just the Republican movement in another guise' (quoted in Coogan, 1995: 63). Estimates of the IRA's strength varied greatly. The British government believed it had 3,000 members by 1966, whilst the Irish government offered a more realistic estimate of 1,000 (*Irish Post*, 11 January 1997). The Irish government believed that recruitment was increasing, but that this was not indicative of an imminent armed campaign.

Undoubtedly, the civil rights movement amounted to an uneasy coalition. Moderates, such as John Hume and Ivan Cooper, within the Derry Citizens' Action Committee mingled with radicals, such as Michael Farrell and Eamon McCann, in Peoples Democracy and the Derry Housing Action Committee. The movement was united in its hostility to discrimination and its contempt for the 'green Toryism' of the Nationalist Party upon which the community had long relied. Radicals were particularly critical of Orange and Green (Protestant versus Catholic) politics and contemptuous of the sectarian state. They regarded the Nationalist Party as a confessional party, influenced by the clergy and sectarian in outlook (Farrell, 1980).

Civil rights demands did undermine the state and attacks upon the civil rights movement were partly responsible for the formation of the Provisional IRA. However, these two statements combined do not prove that the civil rights movement was a trojan horse for armed republicanism. Certainly there were those within the Republican movement who saw the possibilities that might arise from a civil rights campaign (MacStiofain, 1975). Indeed, the leader of the IRA, Cathal Goulding, claimed to have been directly involved in the creation of NICRA. Purdie (1988; 1990) points to the presence of longstanding Republican agitators, including IRA personnel, within the civil rights movement. Although purporting to demand civil rights for all, demonstrations featured the singing of Irish rebel songs and Nationalist ballads.

Finally, those who claim a direct link point to the fact that most of the demands of the civil rights movement were met between 1968 and 1972, yet violence increased dramatically, proof that Nationalists were disinterested in internal reforms.

3.8.2 The 'separate entities' thesis

This refutes the claim of a direct lineage between the civil rights movement and the rebirth of the IRA. Despite the assertion of Goulding, the IRA appears to have played little active role within a movement centred upon internal reform. Some IRA members did become involved in citizens' defence committees, but otherwise played little part (McCann, 1980).

Broadly, the separate entities thesis is based upon the following contentions. Firstly, the creation of the Provisional IRA occurred partly *because* the civil rights movement had no wider agenda. Secondly, the IRA revived partly because the Unionist response to the civil rights movement was so hostile, forcing the IRA into attempting a defensive role within Nationalist areas against the police and *ad hoc* Loyalist mobs. Later, the IRA enlarged in response to the actions of the British Army. Thirdly, to speak of the civil rights movement as an 'IRA front' is fallacious given the state of the latter organisation at the time of civil rights protests. Coogan (1995: 55) argues: 'there was no IRA activity. And for a very good reason: there was no IRA'. Fourthly, the political culmination of the civil rights movement was not the formation of the IRA but the creation of the Social Democratic and Labour Party, established in 1970 as a moderate Nationalist party with a commitment to progressive social policies.

Quinn (1993: 24) bridges differing perspectives arguing:'"Provoism" was a response to the fear of a loyalist backlash against reform of civil rights. In effect the IRA hijacked the civil rights movement and redirected it towards old-fashioned physical force'. This argument rejects the idea that the civil rights movement was a Republican vehicle. It nonetheless sees a link between the two forms of political activity that occurred, if only because the IRA 'captured' hitherto peaceful protest. Unionist fears were justified in the sense that they believed the civil rights movement would result in a challenge to the state. It was incorrect, however, to assert that it was simply the Republican movement adopting new tactics. NICRA contained a large middle-class element characterised by moderation.

3.9 The growth of Loyalist paramilitary groups

As both wings of the IRA began to recruit, a concurrent development was the rise of Loyalist paramilitaries within working-class areas, particularly in Belfast. A forerunner of such activity was the establishment of the Ulster Protestant Volunteers in 1966, linked to Ian Paisley. The most prominent group to emerge was the Ulster Defence Association (UDA). It was formed in 1971 as an amalgamation of large local defence forces, such as those already functioning in the Shankill and Woodvale districts of Belfast. In mounting roadblocks and attempting limited forms of self-policing, the UDA acted as a reactive force, attempting to imitate the 'no-go' Nationalist areas of Derry.

Pledged to defend Ulster by all means necessary, the UDA saw itself as a defensive, non-sectarian organisation designed to resist Republican aggression. Loyalty was stronger to Ulster than to Britain. Few olive branches were to be offered to the Nationalist community, according to an early UDA newsletter:

> ... the Roman Catholic population do not regard themselves as part of Ulster. They regard themselves as part of the Republic of Ireland. They are on the side of murder, terrorism, intimidation, and the total destruction of loyalists. The exceptions are so very, very few that we simply cannot trust any of them ... (UDA 1971, quoted in Guelke, 1988: 64).

Attractive as a defensive mechanism within an increasingly beleaguered Protestant population, the UDA attracted considerable support, claiming 35,000 members in 1972. Its size was one reason why it was difficult to ban. Another was that its sectarian assassinations of Catholics were carried out under the title of the Ulster Freedom Fighters, unlike the Ulster Volunteer Force (UVF) which claimed responsibility for its killings. Having murdered two people in 1970, Protestant paramilitaries killed 20 more in 1971. Besides fundraising, there were three main dimensions to UDA activity: 'respectable' community development, paramilitary parades and sectarian assassination (Bruce, 1994).

As the IRA launched its offensive in February 1971, other large Protestant organisations were to emerge. One was the West Ulster Unionist Council, led by Harry West, operating on behalf of conservative elements within the Unionist Party. Another was the Loyalist Association of Workers, led by Billy Hull, with strong roots within the trade-union movement.

More significant than either was the Ulster Vanguard, created by William Craig. Despite his disenchantment with the Ulster Unionist leadership, Craig had remained a party member. Desirous of a broader, more resolute form of unionism, Craig established the Vanguard movement as a coalition of Unionist forces determined to resist threats to Ulster. A populist movement was indeed created, incorporating prominent Unionists such as Martin Smyth, a leading figure within the Orange Order.

Veering between constitutional and extra-constitutional approaches, the Vanguard movement tapped into the fears of Protestants to the extent that it proved capable of mobilising up to 60,000 people at rallies. Vanguard had links with paramilitary organisations and with trade unions, the latter providing the useful weapon of industrial action in protest at unpopular Westminster actions (Crawford, 1987).

From the plethora of Loyalist associations, it was the mainly constitutional loyalism of Ian Paisley's Democratic Unionist Party, formed in 1971, that was to emerge as the main challenger to the Unionist Party. This development has been ascribed to four factors. First, the party, in its earlier guise as the Protestant Unionist Party, had been the first to challenge O'Neill. Second, the party had relative clarity in policy, helped perhaps by the near-absence of internal democracy. Vanguard mooted the notion of an independent Ulster without clarifying the idea. Later, Vanguard lost support by appearing to favour power-sharing with Nationalists. Third, it was difficult for coalition movements such as Vanguard to convert into political parties. The establishment of the Vanguard Unionist Progressive Party in 1973 split the movement. Finally, paramilitary associations had different aims from constitutional parties and had difficulty in attracting support outside working-class districts.

3.10 The abolition of Stormont

As Republican and Loyalist paramilitary groups gathered in strength, Northern Ireland became increasingly ungovernable. The IRA waged a virulent campaign of violence, initially against economic targets, but increasingly against security personnel. Although both sides officially eschewed sectarian violence, no-warning bombs in pubs frequented by members of the 'other' community undermined such denials.

Internal reforms continued, but did not satisfy Catholics and angered hardline Protestants. The abolition of the 'B' Specials in late 1969 was a particular source of disquiet, only partly assuaged by the establishment of a replacement, the Ulster Defence Regiment (UDR). As part of the British Army, it had been hoped that the UDR would project a more neutral image than its predecessor. Disenchantment with the British Army amongst Nationalists rendered that hope forlorn. Some Catholic recruitment was attained in its formative years, but this declined sharply as it was targeted by Republicans. Another reform was the creation of the Northern Ireland Housing Executive in 1972, which removed the ability of local authorities to operate discretionary, sometimes discriminatory, housing policies.

Unable to procure further substantial security commitments from the British government, Chichester-Clark resigned in March 1971, to be replaced by Brian Faulkner. Instrumental in the introduction of internment, Faulkner demanded tougher security measures, suggesting to the British government that failure to act would lead to his resignation and the risk of the demagogic Ian Paisley as Prime Minister.

Faulkner appeared to misread historical lessons in his faith in internment, which originated from its apparent success against the IRA in the 1950s. A lack of political support amongst Nationalists defeated the IRA in that campaign, not internment.

Until the introduction of detention without trial in August 1971, 34 people had been killed during the previous seven months. The death toll in the remaining five months was 140. Hundreds of Protestants were forced to flee the Ardoyne area of Belfast following rioting, whilst Catholics evacuated other areas.

As geographic and political polarisation increased, Faulkner engaged in one conciliatory gesture by appointing a Catholic, G.B. Newe, to his Cabinet. Newe, who had instigated a debate on the appropriateness of Catholic participation in the state back in 1958, was the first Catholic to hold such office in a Northern Ireland government.

Tougher security measures under Faulkner failed to reduce levels of violence and the British government decided it should assume direct responsibility for security in Northern Ireland. Undermined by this action, the Unionist government resigned, replaced by direct rule by the Westminster government. In effect, the Secretary of State for Northern Ireland assumed the powers of the former Prime Minister of the Province, assisted by a small team of ministers. A Northern Ireland Office was created, based in London and Belfast, to oversee administration.

Unsurprisingly, the abolition of Stormont upset Unionists. After all, it was their parliament, which had presided over a statelet of comparative tranquillity until recent years. A huge strike was called to coincide with the final days of the parliament. For many Nationalists, the imposition of direct rule might have been welcome in earlier years as a means of alleviation of sectarian discrimination. Now, however, it was the 'old' enemy of the British government which had resurfaced as the target of wrath.

Imposing direct rule held advantages and disadvantages for the Westminster government. A positive feature from a Westminster viewpoint was that it allowed direct control of all security issues. Clinging to the notion of neutrality, the British government also hoped that a non-discriminatory form of direct rule might be more acceptable to Catholics than the sectarian excesses of devolved Unionist government. There was also some optimism that it might be easier to develop political initiatives through bypassing a Unionist administration.

On the debit side, the abandonment of the 'arm's-length' distance provided by devolved approaches meant that unrest could no longer be presented simply as one between two warring communities. Rather, the British government was now engaged in direct conflict with Irish Republicans, a conflict that it believed it had eliminated through partition 50 years earlier. Furthermore, the suspension of Stormont amounted to a tacit acceptance that Unionist government had not worked. How, therefore, was its restoration ever to be justified?

3.11 Conclusion

By 1972, the terms 'ungovernability' and 'Northern Ireland' had become synonymous. Limited options existed in the early 1970s for the prevention of conflict, but these rested upon a rapid pace of reform and trust amongst Nationalists concerning the role of the British Army. These options disappeared by 1972. Designed as a temporary measure, direct rule proved enduring. Its imposition represented the death of traditional unionism, which had proved unable to deal with challenges to its ascendancy. Demands for internal reform had been construed from the outset by Unionists as rebellion and had translated into such within the Nationalist community. Republicans believed that removal of the Stormont regime represented a triumph en route to the establishment of a united Ireland. However, the removal of a government was not tantamount to the seizure of power.

Chapter 4

Unionist and Loyalist politics

The first three chapters of this book examined the historical basis for political difficulties in Northern Ireland. The focus now switches to the current politics and governance of the state, before assessing attempts to manage political problems. This chapter and Chapter 5 analyse the ideology and organisation of the main political parties, on which there remains surprisingly little information, despite the voluminous literature on the politics of Northern Ireland.

4.1 The party system in Northern Ireland

Ethnic bloc politics characterise Northern Ireland. The major parties in Northern Ireland are divided into two main groupings, Unionist and Nationalist, drawing the overwhelming majority of their support and members from, respectively, British Protestants and Irish Catholics. The link between religious denomination and choice of political party has led to the labelling of political parties in Northern Ireland as confessional parties. The divide between unionism and nationalism does not exist because of the stances of political parties on religious questions. Such stances do not exist. All parties claim to welcome support from Catholic, Protestant and dissenter. The link between denomination and political grouping derives from the different positions held by Unionists and Nationalists on the constitutional future of Northern Ireland.

Despite the ethnic bloc polarity of Northern Ireland's politics, intra-ethnic rivalries are also very important. Competition between and within parties inside the Unionist and Nationalist 'family' represents a vital dynamic to Northern Ireland's politics, highlighted by the ongoing divisions within unionism over the 1998 Good Friday Agreement.

An optimistic interpretation of the Good Friday Agreement was that it might contribute to a thawing of ethnic bloc politics, as Catholics and Protestants voted outside their ethnic party bloc. The single transferable vote (STV) system of proportional representation is used for non-Westminster elections in Northern Ireland. This might allow voters to at least transfer their lower preference votes to candidates from the rival ethnic bloc. Thus, a pro-Agreement Unionist might wish to vote for as many pro-Agreement candidates as possible, even if this means lower preference voting for the SDLP. This could lead to a realignment of politics, with a new cross-community centrist bloc emerging, embracing moderate pro-Agreement parties. A pessimistic interpretation of the Agreement was that the ethnic bloc divide would increase through the reinforcement of 'Green' (Nationalist) and 'Orange' (Unionist) politics, as parties attempt to persuade their 'own' electorate that they can get the best deal for unionism over nationalism and vice versa.

4.2 The nature of unionism

At the core of unionism lies a determination that Northern Ireland will remain as part of the United Kingdom. Arising from this are demands placed upon the British government that it secures the constitutional position of Northern Ireland. Equally, unionism rejects the claims of Irish nationalism that the geographic unity of Ireland must necessarily translate into political unity. Unionists view Northern Ireland as a legitimate entity, historically, culturally and politically part of the United Kingdom.

Unionists see themselves historically, politically and culturally as British. They, therefore, support continued union with Great Britain and vote for Unionist parties, in a similar manner to the way that Nationalists see themselves as Irish and so support Nationalist parties which promote the political advancement of that Irish identity. Some Unionists also see Protestantism as an integral part of a British identity.

Whilst support for parties stems from a political logic, politics in Northern Ireland are nonetheless often perceived as sectarian. There are three main charges comprising this allegation. First, the main Unionist parties have formal or informal links to Protestant organisations or churches. Second, Nationalist parties remain rooted in 'green' politics and make little attempt to attract support from the Protestant community. Thirdly, the unwillingness of 'mainland' British political parties to organise in Northern Ireland creates a political vacuum in which sectarian politics flourish. Although there is evidence to support all these charges, the basic political divide would exist even in a secular (non-religious) Northern Ireland. Seventy-one per cent of Protestants 'think of themselves' as Unionists, and seventy per cent of Catholics 'think of themselves' as Nationalists (Murphy and Totten, 2000: 295). The polarity in respect of Protestants voting for Unionist parties and Catholics voting for Nationalist parties is even starker.

Unionism has been identified with a conditional loyalty towards Britain (Miller, 1978). Whilst support for the Crown has endured, loyalty to other British political institutions has been provided partly on the basis of Unionist self-interest. When decisions have been taken against the perceived interests of Unionists, disobedience has followed. Historical examples are provided by the refusal to accept Home Rule and the workers' strike which ended the power-sharing executive of the Sunningdale Agreement in 1974.

Critics of the conditional-loyalty thesis point out that the loyalty of citizens is always conditional upon effective, consensual governance (Coulter, 1994). Conditional loyalty is, therefore, not exclusive to unionism. Also, it is argued that it is loyalty to Unionists which has been conditional, due to the British government's refusal to secure an unequivocal, permanent place for Northern

Table 4.1   Protestant identity in Northern Ireland 1968–89 (%)

	1968	1989
British	39	68
Ulster	32	10
Irish	20	3
Northern Irish	n/a	16

Note: the category of Northern Irish did not appear in the 1968 survey.
Source: adapted from Moxon-Browne (1991).

Ireland within the United Kingdom. Northern Ireland's place is subject to the agreement of the majority within Northern Ireland, a condition not applied to other parts of the Kingdom. Only 5 per cent of the Ulster Unionist Council, the ruling body of unionism's largest party, believe that the Westminster government can be trusted on the future of Northern Ireland (Tonge and Evans, 2001a).

Unionism is also sometimes seen as a form of British nationalism. Unionists are sometimes perceived by outsiders as 'more British than the British'. Few other British citizens engage in vivid displays of the symbols of Britishness found in many Loyalist areas of Northern Ireland. This symbolism is associated with the siege mentality of Unionists, dwelling in a contested part of British territory.

Critics see the repositories of loyalty, such as the Crown and Protestantism, as part of a bygone era. Others see symbolic displays merely as patriotism. What can be asserted is that unionism asserts a particular type of Britishness, with variations such as Orangeism rarely found elsewhere. Until Unionists lost their own parliament in 1972, most saw their primary identity as Ulster citizens. British identity was important, but faced less of a challenge and was thus not as salient. After the challenge to Northern Ireland's position arose in the early 1970s, identity shifted, as Table 4.1 demonstrates.

4.3 Devolution and unionism

Unionism has been an ideology constructed upon resistance, whereas nationalism has been an 'active ideological force' (Aughey, 1994: 54). This is because Ulster unionism is an ideology upon the defence of the status quo. Maintenance of the Union with Britain has demanded greater thought under sustained challenge. Prior to the civil rights challenges of the late 1960s, unionism was largely stagnant. The mantras of 'A Protestant parliament for a Protestant people' and 'What we have we hold' sufficed for political philosophy (Quinn, 1993: 61).

Not everyone agrees that unionism was devoid of dynamism during that era. Evidence has been supplied of a continually evolving unionism, in which there was considerable friction between the Orange leadership and the Protestant working-class, whatever the veneer of Unionist unity (Bew, Gibbon and Patterson, 1996).

What is not disputed is that internal debates within unionism increased after the loss of Stormont and imposition of direct rule from Westminster in 1972. Following the loss of their own parliament, Unionists were obliged to rethink the optimum means of governing Northern Ireland. Debates within unionism have increased in volume since the 1998 Good Friday Agreement, with a clear division evident between Unionist supporters and opposers. Until 1998, a key debate within unionism was between those who wanted full integration into the United Kingdom and those who wished for devolved government to be returned to Northern Ireland. Some Unionists believed that full integration was the most appropriate method of guaranteeing the status of Northern Ireland within the United Kingdom. The integrationist wing is still alive within the Ulster Unionist Party, with nearly half its ruling council supporting the idea, despite the wider restructuring of the United Kingdom. Integration might end continuing uncertainty over the future of Northern Ireland by allowing it to be treated like any other part of the United Kingdom. Integrationists have been sub-divided, between electoral and administrative integrationists.

Electoral integrationists wish to see the Conservative and Labour parties contest elections in Northern Ireland. Forty per cent of the Ulster Unionist Council support this idea. Supporters of electoral integration believe that it will be beneficial for two main reasons. Firstly, allowing mainland parties to stand will enfranchise the people of Northern Ireland who are at present debarred from voting for the party which forms the British government. Secondly, permitting non-sectarian parties to stand will lessen the polarisation of politics.

Both the Conservative and Labour parties have been reluctant to organise in Northern Ireland. Local Conservatives have contested elections since 1989, but have not attracted large support. Neither party sees much gain through involvement, which would represent a further drain upon resources. Until the 1980s, the Conservative Party was formally attached to the Ulster Unionist Party, whilst the Labour Party is linked to the Social Democratic and Labour Party. The latter link has been criticised by some Unionists within the Labour Party who denounce the SDLP as the 'ugly sister'.

Devolutionists achieved their goal with the creation of devolved assembly under the Good Friday Agreement. British government policy since direct rule aimed to return some powers to local politicians in Northern Ireland through a devolved, power-sharing adminstration. Devolutionists believe that many of the internal affairs of Northern Ireland will be dealt with more effectively this way, whilst the status of Northern Ireland within the United Kingdom will not be weakened. Autonomy is limited, as major issues of foreign, defence and economic policies, plus security issues, continue to be determined by the Westminster parliament as reserved powers.

Unionists have long rejected any Nationalist fears that a devolved assembly could return to the discriminatory pre-1972 Stormont regime. Most, although not all, Unionists accept the concept of enforced power-sharing with Nationalists. Unionists have differed over the best method of protecting the rights of the Nationalist minority. Some devolutionists have argued for a bill of rights as the appropriate mechanism. Those less keen on enforced power-sharing believe that proportionality throughout government will suffice through the responsible exercise of power.

4.4 Forms of unionism

Porter (1996) has argued the existence of three types of unionism – cultural, liberal and civic – each with its own distinctive characteristics. The Good Friday Agreement is designed to move unionism towards a civic form, embracing Nationalists and nationalism to an unprecedented extent. Cultural Unionism offers an exaggerated sense of Protestant Britishness. According to Steve Bruce, unionism and Protestantism are inextricably linked. This is because 'beyond evangelical Protestantism, no secure identity is available' (Bruce, 1986: 258). This argument suggests that Protestants in Northern Ireland form a distinctive ethnic group, whereas Catholics are an integral part of the Irish nation.

For Unionists such as Ian Paisley of the Democratic Unionist Party, this association of religion and politics is indeed acknowledged and desired. It is the duty of Unionists to oppose a united Ireland. This opposition 'takes on a political character because of the influence of the Roman Catholic Church in the Republic of Ireland and the attempts to reunify the North with the South' (MacIver, 1987: 361). Others argue that unionism is not reducible to a core Protestantism. Severance of unionism from its connections with Protestant sectarianism would allow unionism to develop as a political creed centred upon the principles of liberty and justice.

Liberal unionism argues a rational, contractarian case for the Union, condemnatory of the sectarian excesses of previous generations. The rational case for the Union is based upon the principle of majority consent for the status quo in Northern Ireland, but also suggests that the United Kingdom offers an appropriately liberal and enlightened environment for all the citizens of Northern Ireland. Unionism offers progressive values, freedom and equality. Critics of such arguments question the assumed superiority of the British state and citizenship. These assumptions may remain even though the Irish Republic has moved from a Catholic theocracy to a liberal, secular democracy.

Civic unionism is the most ambitious Unionist project, attempting to reconcile a stout defence of the Union with an acknowledgement, even embrace, of the rival claims of nationalism. Civic unionism endorses a plurality of identities and political ambitions in Northern Ireland. It accepts the Irishness of the majority and the need for political recognition of this through the Irish dimension of limited cross-border institutions. The consent principle keeps Northern Ireland within the Union, but the pursuit of a (peaceful) Nationalist political project should not be a bar to a stake in Northern Ireland's political institutions.

4.5 Unionist parties

4.5.1 The Ulster Unionist Party (UUP)

Sometimes known as the Official Unionist Party, the UUP is the largest political organisation in Northern Ireland. It holds more seats than its rivals at

Table 4.2   Election results in Northern Ireland 1982–2001

Election	Percentages				
	UUP	DUP	SDLP	SF	Other
1982 Assembly	29.7	23.0	18.8	10.1	18.4
1983 General	34.0	20.0	17.9	13.4	14.7
1984 European	21.5	33.6	22.1	13.3	9.5
1985 Local	29.5	24.3	21.1	11.4	13.7
1987 General	37.9	11.7	21.1	11.4	17.9
1989 Local	30.4	18.7	21.0	11.2	18.7
1992 General	34.5	13.1	23.5	10.0	19.9
1993 Local	29.4	17.3	22.0	12.4	18.9
1994 European	23.8	29.2	28.9	9.0	19.1
1996 Forum	24.2	18.8	21.4	15.5	20.1
1997 General	32.7	13.1	24.1	16.1	14.0
1997 Local	27.8	15.6	20.7	16.9	19.0
1998 Assembly	21.3	18.1	22.0	17.6	21.0
1999 European	17.7	28.5	28.2	17.4	8.2
2001 General	26.8	22.5	21.0	21.7	8.0
2001 Local	23.0	21.5	19.4	20.7	15.4

Sources: adapted from Connolly (1990); Aughey and Morrow (1996); Arthur and Jeffery (1996); *Irish News*, 24 May 1997; *Belfast Telegraph*, 13 May 2001.

Westminster and Stormont. Table 4.2 confirms how the UUP regularly attracts the most votes in elections, exceptions being European contests and the 1998 Assembly election.

The dominance of the UUP, until 2001 at least, was most apparent at Westminster elections, when the first-past-the-post system is used. The use of STV for other contests encourages smaller parties to contest local elections and has perhaps accelerated the fragmentation of unionism.

Until the late 1960s, the leadership of the Ulster Unionist Party contained wealthy patricians, although it was supported by Protestants across different social classes. The UUP's attachment to the Conservative Party was such that it enjoyed full voting rights at Conservative Party conferences (Flackes, 1983). This relationship declined sharply following the introduction of direct rule in 1972, as Ulster Unionists opposed many of the political initiatives introduced by the Westminster government. Subsequent relationships between the UUP and the parties at Westminster have varied in cordiality. These variations have been ascribed to the fickleness of British political parties in their attitudes to Northern Ireland (Dixon, 1994).

In 1973, the Ulster Unionists rejected the Sunningdale Agreement on power-sharing with a Council of Ireland, leading to the resignation of the party leader, Brian Faulkner. During the mid-1970s, the UUP formed part of the United Ulster Unionist Coalition. This again opposed power-sharing with Nationalists in the 1975 Northern Ireland Constitutional Convention.

In 1982, the party did participate in the Northern Ireland Assembly, but only on the basis that it enhanced scrutiny of aspects of direct rule. The UUP strongly opposed the Anglo-Irish Agreement of 1985, which gave the Republic a definite but limited say on certain political matters in Northern Ireland. The 1995 Framework Documents also provoked a hostile reaction from the UUP, for similar reasons, but, by 1998, the limited cross-border and intergovernmental arrangements of the Good Friday Agreement were deemed acceptable by a majority within the party.

Elected party leader in 1995, David Trimble wished to reappraise relations with the Dublin government. He met the Irish Taoiseach for talks shortly after becoming leader, the first such meeting for 30 years. This event was designed to emphasise the view of the UUP that friendly relations with the South were possible. In return, the party states that 'these relationships must preserve the political independence and territorial integrity of states which are fundamental principles of international law' (Ulster Unionist Information Institute, 1995).

The UUP's mid-1990s policy document, *The Democratic Imperative*, tacitly accepted that an *entirely* internal settlement in Northern Ireland would be impractical. Nonetheless, the role of the Irish government would be highly circumscribed (Ulster Unionist Party, 1996). The UUP made clear its wish to place any settlement with an Irish dimension within a confederal context. The establishment of a Council of the British Isles, comprising elected representatives and designed to examine matters of common interest between Great Britain and the Republic of Ireland, became an important plank of the UUP's demands in the negotiations leading to the Good Friday Agreement.

Although traditionally more integrationist than its main rival, the Democratic Unionist Party, the UUP broadly welcomed the return of devolved government to Northern Ireland in 1999. The UUP's integrationist phase occurred under the leadership of James Molyneaux from 1979 to 1995, although, even during this period, some devolution of political authority to Northern Ireland was supported. The UUP was less keen than Nationalist parties on government through a Northern Ireland Executive, knowing that Sinn Fein would form part of that body. The UUP was, however, obliged to shift ground from its belief that governance should take place through a committee system, based upon the electoral strengths of parties and reflecting existing departments of government in Northern Ireland.

Structurally, the most striking feature of the UUP is its decentralisation. It is, in effect, 18 constituency parties within a party. There is a central executive and a party standing committee, but they exert little authority over these local parties, which guard their autonomy. The lack of central writ has been exacerbated by the divisions within the ruling 858-member Ulster Unionist Council over whether to support the Good Friday Agreement. The Council contains a wide range of representatives, although three-quarters come from constituency parties. The Protestant Orange Order has 122 representatives on the UUC which determined the new party leader and 18 representatives on the party's standing committee of 300. A further 12 members of the Council are from the Association of Loyal Orange Women. Orange delegates must also be

Table 4.3 Voting in the Ulster Unionist Party leadership contest 2000 by the Ulster Unionist Council members, according to Orange Order membership (%)

	Orange Order members	Non-Orange Order members
Trimble voters	48.7	51.3
Smyth voters	67.9	32.1

N = 295
Chi square = 11.02, 1df, p < .001.

Source: author's survey, 2000. *See* Tonge and Evans (2001a).

individual members of the UUP. Over half (51 per cent) of the members of the UUC are members of the Orange Order; fewer than 1 per cent are Roman Catholics. Eighty-six per cent of UUC members claim to be practising members of their religion. The party Council elects the executive of the party. The annual party conference debates policy. The 'broad church' that makes up the UUP, united by defence of the Union rather than bound by rigid structures or ideas, has led to the labelling of the organisation as more of a movement than a party (Hume, 1996).

Initially, David Trimble was seen as a hardline UUP leader. He courted the Orange vote, being proactive in supporting the right of the Orange Order to march unfettered at Drumcree in 1995. He was the founder of the Ulster Society, to which 500 Orange lodges are affiliated. Subsequently, however, Trimble spoke of the need to redefine the UUP's link with the Orange Order, aimed at reducing its influence. The link was already in decline, although all leaders of the UUP have been members of the Order. Some members of the party have questioned whether the UUP should be closely linked with an exclusively Protestant organisation (McDowell, 1995). The UUC is divided almost equally over whether to end the link, with Orange Order membership a significant attitudinal variable (Tonge and Evans, 2001a). Trimble's attempt to move unionism from its ethnic to a civic form has structural and political problems. The decentralised basis of his party means that it difficult to act against sources of dissent. In playing out its divisions, the Ulster Unionist Council met on a large number of occasions after the Good Friday Agreement in an attempt to tie the party to a tougher stance on IRA decommissioning. In 2000, Trimble was challenged for the party leadership by the Rev. Martin Smyth. The leader resisted the challenge by the uncomfortably narrow majority of 57 per cent to 43 per cent. As a former Grand Master, Smyth picked up many Orange votes among the UUC, but many fewer from outside the Order (*see* Table 4.3).

Trimble's modernisation project is also confronted by the difficulty that his support base is found among older members of the UUC. Younger members of the Council are much more inclined towards 'No' unionism, apparent from a breakdown by age of UUC voting in the Good Friday Agreement referendum (*see* Table 4.4).

Table 4.4 Voting in the Good Friday Agreement referendum by the Ulster Unionist Council, according to age

Age	Vote	
	Yes	No
15–24	0.0	100.0
25–34	45.5	54.5
35–44	66.7	33.3
45–54	68.7	31.3
55–64	79.3	20.7
65–74	76.1	23.9
75+	81.6	18.4

N = 293
Chi square = 35.01, 6df, p < .001.

Source: author's survey, 2000. *See* Tonge and Evans (2001a).

The difficulty for Trimble lies, according to one assessment, in resisting 'stupid unionism, locked in the mental world of the 1950s' (Bew, 1998). From the (limited) evidence of UUC voting, it appears, however, that older Unionists are readier to embrace change than their younger counterparts. Trimble's insistence, in September 1998, that the Northern Ireland Assembly would be a 'pluralist parliament for a pluralist people' was a direct repudiation of unionism's past conduct of a Protestant parliament for a Protestant people. Apparently the confirmation of Northern Ireland's place in the United Kingdom, the return of devolved government, the sight of former militant Republicans at Stormont and unparalleled economic prosperity are insufficient to convince sceptics within the UUC. Only 27 per cent believed that the UUP had achieved most of its objectives in the Good Friday Agreement. Nearly 70 per cent voted 'yes' in the Good Friday Agreement referendum, but, within two years, only 44 per cent were prepared to say that they would do likewise. Aside from preservation of the Union and rejection of joint British–Irish sovereignty, the UUC is divided on what constitutes the best solution for Northern Ireland, as Table 4.5 indicates.

The modernisation of the UUP is a long-term project dependent upon substantial internal reform and a consolidation of devolved government. Part of the uncertainty derives from short-term issues such as decommissioning and policing, but there remains considerable debate over the most appropriate form of devolved power-sharing.

4.5.2 The Democratic Unionist Party (DUP)

Founded in 1971, the DUP attracted many initial recruits from the Protestant Unionist Party which existed for a brief period during 1969–71. Sharing the core beliefs of the UUP, the DUP is regarded as the advocate of a more

Table 4.5 Ulster Unionist Council solutions for Northern Ireland

Solution	Agree/Strongly agree	Disagree/Strongly disagree	Neither agree nor disagree
Power-sharing WITH cross-border bodies	35.7	60.7	3.6
Power-sharing WITHOUT cross-border bodies	44.2	42.4	13.4
Full integration into the UK	55.6	29.9	14.5
Direct British rule	18.3	66.1	15.6
Joint sovereignty	3.1	95.5	1.4
United Ireland	3.7	95.5	0.8

Source: author's survey, 2000. *See* Tonge and Evans (2001a).

hardline unionism. This includes persistent demands for vigorous security policies and a refusal to deal with Sinn Fein, except where unavoidable, within local councils and in the Assembly. At its formation, the DUP claimed that it would be right-wing on constitutional issues but left-wing on social policies, an appeal designed especially for working-class Loyalists.

Opposed to power-sharing in the Sunningdale Agreement and the Constitutional Convention of the mid-1970s, the party benefited from the proposal of its rival for working-class votes, the Vanguard Party, to form a temporary partnership with the Nationalist-oriented Social Democratic and Labour Party. This idea led to the destruction of the Vanguard Party and the consolidation of the DUP as the UUP's main rival.

After participating in the Northern Ireland Assembly in 1982, the DUP strongly opposed the Anglo-Irish Agreement of 1985. It has been a persistent critic of the peace process, arguing that it was a flawed attempt to pacify insatiable Republican demands. As such, the party took no part in the negotiations leading to the Good Friday Agreement in 1998, even though it is desirous of devolved government for Northern Ireland. The party highlighted political and moral objections to the Agreement, with concerns over prisoner releases, policing changes and the presence of Sinn Fein in government all prominent. The party rotated its ministers within the Northern Ireland Executive, adding to the sense of impermanence sometimes associated with the new political institutions. Having outlined its objections from the outset, the DUP believed it could capitalise on increasing Unionist disillusionment with the Good Friday Agreement and reassert its role as the stoutest defender of the interests of the Unionist bloc.

The DUP is insistent upon the need for the British government to end ambiguity over the future of Northern Ireland within the United Kingdom. It is also vocal in its denunciation of the Irish Republic's involvement in Northern Ireland. Accordingly, the party treats Anglo-Irish political manoeuvres with suspicion. According to the DUP, the internal political workings of Northern Ireland need to be routinised before even limited co-operation with the Republic can be developed. The DUP has moved away from its old belief in a system of majoritarianism (majority rule) within devolved government, in favour of power-sharing and participation for the Nationalist minority (but not Sinn Fein). This would be achieved through a guaranteed role for constitutional Nationalists on legislative committees proportionate to their electoral strength. There was a certain irony in the absence of the DUP from the negotiations leading to devolved government for Northern Ireland, as no party is more desirous of a strong Assembly with a full range of functions (Hazleton, 2001).

Led by the Rev. Ian Paisley from the outset, the DUP has relied heavily upon his enduring appeal. Regarded as a demagogue by detractors, Paisley emerges as the most popular political figure in European elections where Northern Ireland is treated a single constituency. Paisley's mix of politics and fundamental religion provides a populist agenda. He is seen as the most fervent defender of his people from the spectre of a united, Catholic Ireland. Paisley tends to combine matters political and spiritual for the benefit of domestic audiences. For example, although he opposes the alleged threat of a European Catholic super-state, he rarely mentions God or religion in the European Parliament (Moloney and Pollok, 1986).

Paisley's hold over the DUP is unchallenged. Indeed, in the early days of the DUP, it was admitted even by Paisley's colleagues that the DUP was 'Paisley's fan club . . . there was no Party' (Bruce, 1986: 107). Paisley was viewed by some supporters as a leader 'chosen by God to protect Ulster' (Connolly, 1990: 104). The leader insists that his politics stem from his religion. He argues that the law should be obeyed unless it contravenes the laws of the gospel. Thus, although Paisley is a constitutional politician who condemns the actions of Loyalist paramilitaries, he has occasionally been prepared to defy the British government should it attempt to deliver Ulster's Protestants into a united Ireland. In 1981, 500 of Paisley's supporters gathered on a hillside in Antrim to wave firearms certificates. This form of activity was labelled the Carson Trail, in which normal respecters of the law indicate their willingness to defend Ulster by various means, in the manner that Edward Carson threatened to oppose Home Rule earlier this century.

Many within the DUP also fuse politics and religion. The party comprises a disproportionately high number of Free Presbyterians amongst its activists. In the 1970s and 1980s, 64 per cent of party activists were members of the Free Presbyterian Church (Bruce, 1987: 644). Less than 1 per cent of the population of Northern Ireland are members of the Free Presbyterian Church, founded by Paisley in 1951. For some Free Presbyterian members of the DUP, the problems of Northern Ireland can be attributed to the expansionism of the Roman Catholic Church.

Despite the informal links between Church and party, support for the DUP is much more broadly based. Non-religious loyalists lend the party considerable electoral support. In East Belfast, for example, Peter Robinson is regularly returned as a DUP MP, although the area contains a relatively high number of citizens who are, at most, only nominally Protestant. The DUP is successful in eliciting support from a combination of rural, often fundamentalist, Protestants and much less religiously committed working-class Loyalists, impressed by the stout defence of Ulster offered by the party.

4.5.3 Other Unionist parties

Whilst the UUP and DUP capture the vast majority of Unionist votes, other Unionist parties attract limited support. The UK Unionist Party (UKUP), led by Robert McCartney, adopts the most integrationist stance of all Unionist parties. Its primary aspiration is for Northern Ireland to be treated in the same manner as any other part of the United Kingdom. The party wishes unionism to shed its association with religious sectarianism. The UKUP was highly critical of the Good Friday Agreement, arguing that it weakened Northern Ireland's place in the United Kingdom. Having achieved a respectable five seats in the Northern Ireland Assembly, on a 4.5 per cent vote share, the party promptly split, with the majority of its Assembly members forming the Northern Ireland Unionist Party, led by Cedric Wilson. The split appeared to owe more to personality than politics, which remained rigidly anti-Agreement. Also found among the anti-Agreement forces are the three elected members of the United Unionist Assembly Party, which polled a combined 23,000 votes (2.9 per cent) in the 1998 Assembly elections.

4.6 'New Loyalist' parties

Two parties linked to Loyalist paramilitaries have gained a small amount of electoral support. Both parties were instrumental in establishing a Loyalist ceasefire in 1994 and in delivering the support of a section of the Loyalist working-class (especially in Belfast) for the Good Friday Agreement in the 1998 referendum. The willingness of these parties to break with the old 'no surrender' shibboleths of unionism and the propensity of either to criticise established Unionist political forces, in particular the DUP, has led to their labelling as 'new Loyalist' parties.

Close to the Ulster Volunteer Force, the Progressive Unionist Party (PUP) is the more electorally significant of the two Loyalist parties. It possesses a radical socialist agenda, whilst supporting the constitutional status quo. Critical of the previous treatment of Catholics by Unionist regimes, the PUP rejects the notion of a Protestant ascendancy, arguing that the working-class of both communities was mistreated by the Unionist leadership (McAuley, 1997). One of the PUP's leaders, David Ervine, declared that the 'ruling élite of Unionism practised discrimination and we stood by and let it happen. We didn't treat our minority properly and were comfortable to receive a few crumbs from the table' (*Irish World*, 5 April 1996).

Aside from a belief in community-based socialism, the PUP is radical in three other respects. Firstly, it endorses dialogue with Republicans inside and outside the Northern Ireland Assembly. The party argues for a new realism, recognising the need for an accommodation with nationalism (Moore and

Patterson, 1995). Change can only occur, however, with the consent of Unionists. Secondly, the party accepts an Irish dimension to the identity of Unionists, using the expression 'Irish but peculiarly British' (Price, 1995: 67). Thirdly, the PUP is critical of the sectarian connotations of unionism. It prefers a secular approach. The party even campaigns on issues not normally associated with Northern Ireland's politics, such as abortion and gay rights (McAuley, 2001).

Linked to the paramilitary Ulster Defence Association, an organisation outlawed in 1991, the Ulster Democratic Party combines a progressive social agenda with the promotion of the idea of an Ulster identity. The idea of an independent Northern Ireland once formed part of UDA thinking, articulated in the policy document, *Beyond the Religious Divide* (New Ulster Political Research Group, 1979).

By the 1980s, the idea of independence had been abandoned. The political representatives of the UDA now advocated that Northern Ireland should remain British. The policy document *Common Sense* provided a weaker variant of the idea of a common Ulster nationality (Ulster Defence Association, 1987). Politically, it suggested this could be fostered by proportionality in government. Unionists and Nationalists would fill positions in government according to their level of electoral support.

Mainstream unionists are hostile to fringe Loyalists. This is especially true of the DUP whose urban electoral base the PUP and UDP have attempted to erode. This antipathy is reciprocated. Fringe Loyalists regard Paisleyism as tribalism, with Paisley the 'Grand Old Duke of York' marching Loyalists up the hill only to retreat again (Bruce, 1994: 34). Scepticism over whether the concept of new loyalism really existed increased in 2000 when a Loyalist feud led to seven deaths. The dispute between the UDA and UVF highlighted longstanding tensions over territory and activity. The failure of the UDP to win seats in the Northern Ireland Assembly diminished the enthusiasm of that wing of 'new loyalism' for the Good Friday Agreement, to the point where by summer 2001 the UDA was no longer supportive.

4.7 The political centre

The political centre in Northern Ireland is included in the chapter on unionism as its main electoral representative, the Alliance Party (APNI), is latently Unionist, in that it supports the constitutional status quo of Northern Ireland remaining in the United Kingdom, based upon majority consent. The political centre in Northern Ireland occupies narrow, diminishing ground. Although it may create a new cross-community centre forged from several moderate parties, the Good Friday Agreement has not helped the existing centre party, by reducing it to the label of 'other' party within a Unionist–Nationalist political framework.

Formed in 1970, the Alliance Party's electoral support has ebbed gently from its high-water mark of 14.4 per cent in 1977. The party has a tendency to perform better in opinion polls than in elections (Whyte, 1991). Nowadays, the party averages around 7 per cent of the vote and its support is mainly confined to the East of Northern Ireland. Led by Sean Neeson, Alliance holds six seats in the Northern Ireland Assembly, but does not hold a seat within the Executive. It has operated as a bi-confessional party amid a confessional party system (McAllister and Wilson, 1978; Leonard, 1999). Alliance attracts support among Protestants and Catholics, although Protestant support tends to be higher. Approximately 10–12 per cent of Protestants voted Alliance in the mid-1990s (McGarry and O'Leary, 1995: 200). However, this figure has fallen slightly. Of the party's 1,000 members, 66 per cent are Protestants, 18 per cent Catholics and 13 per cent do not claim any religion (Tonge and Evans, 2000b). Alliance's aim is to create a distinctive third tradition, designed to overcome the Unionist versus Nationalist zero-sum politics which it believes infests Northern Ireland. Having long argued for devolved power-sharing government, the party strongly supports the Good Friday Agreement, even though it has reservations about some aspects which legitimise competitive politics between Unionists and Nationalists. In the words of one senior party figure, 'compromise is an honourable necessity' (Ford, 1996). In addition to support for power-sharing, the central themes of the party are participation, accountability and transparency (Alliance Party, 1995).

Although Alliance's innate unionism has deterred some Catholic support, the party believes that the variety of identities in Northern Ireland need not be a barrier to the overcoming of crude Unionist and Nationalist politics. Indeed, Alliance members possess a variety of primary identities. Thirty-one per cent see themselves as British, 29 per cent as British-Irish, 19 per cent as Northern Irish and 17 per cent as Irish. Although Alliance is a non-sectarian party, there are differences according to religion in respect of lower preference vote transfers among members. Protestants are less likely to vote transfer to Nationalist parties.

The other centre party represented in the Assembly has a shorter history. Founded in 1996, the Northern Ireland Women's Coalition (NIWC) won two Assembly seats in 1998, on a 1.6 per cent vote share. The NIWC was formed to 'highlight the dearth of women in politics and, specifically, around the negotiating table' (Fearon, 2000: 155). The party has attempted to raise the profile of women in a polity in which gender issues have often appeared subordinate to constitutional questions (Ward, 1997). Fully supportive of the Good Friday Agreement, the NIWC's key negotiating roles were to consolidate women's rights and to draft review procedures for the Agreement. The NIWC also added to the inclusiveness of the Agreement dealing with reconciliation and victims of violence.

4.8 Conclusion

Politics in Northern Ireland remain polarised between Unionists and Nationalists, although the internal divisions between pro- and anti-Good Friday Agreement Unionists are arguably of equal importance. The Good Friday Agreement recognises and legitimises the stark Unionist–Nationalist divide. Its initial concern is to ensure that neither bloc has the upper hand. The withering of blocs through cross-community voting may eventually happen, but only in the long term. Whilst there are instances of Protestants voting for Nationalist parties and Catholics voting for Unionist parties, they are exceptional, not prolonged.

Class and issue politics are still downplayed in favour of traditional ethnic bloc politics of the constitution, despite the insistence of the British government that the status of Northern Ireland cannot change without the consent of the majority. Class politics are evident and deserve greater consideration (Coulter, 1999). However, this type of politics tends to develop separately within Loyalist and Republican communities with little connection. Much of the dynamic of politics arises from the ongoing debates *within* Unionist parties rather than between the political groups. Meanwhile, the non-sectarian centre ploughs infertile ground. It is difficult to dissent strongly from the assertion that in Northern Ireland, the middle ground 'has continued to remain mythical' (Arthur and Jeffery, 1996: 51). It remains questionable whether a new, cross-community, centrist bloc of pro-Good Friday Agreement forces, probably comprising moderate UUP and SDLP elements, can ever be forged.

Chapter 5

Nationalist and Republican politics

5.1 Nationalist themes

Nationalist interpretations of Northern Ireland have many nuances. Nonetheless, four core themes can be identified. These are:

1. the partition of Ireland was unjust;
2. politics in Ireland should, therefore, concentrate upon the rectification of this injustice;
3. a purely internal settlement is impossible in Northern Ireland;
4. self-determination for the Irish people is necessary.

Nationalists believe that the settlement produced by the Government of Ireland Act 1920 was illogical, impractical and unfair. They also note that partition was designed as a temporary measure. The state of Northern Ireland had minimal historical rationale and was scarcely viable as an economic entity. Built upon Protestant triumphalism, its most enduring feature was religious sectarianism, with discrimination against Catholics endemic. This sectarianism was inevitable in a state founded upon a contrived Protestant, pro-British majority. In response, Irish nationalism attempts a political, moral and practical agenda. Attempting to redress a perceived wrong, nationalism rejected the partition of Ireland as divisive and unnecessary.

Politics in the Irish Republic were characterised by anti-partitionist rhetoric from the outset. In the 1980s, Charles Haughey, the leader of Fianna Fail, the main Republican party in the South, described Northern Ireland as a 'failed political entity'. Nationalist parties in the North have periodically been less interested in making Northern Ireland work than with boycotting the state or seeking its dismantling.

Nationalists advocate the ultimate creation of a unitary Irish state. In the interim measure, they insist that attempts at purely internal solutions are futile. Instead, there must be guarantees that the Irishness of nationalists in Northern Ireland must be recognised using the Irish Republic as a guarantor. Nationalism rejects the idea that a conversion to Britishness is attainable amongst the minority Northern population. Whilst full unity remains the optimum Nationalist solution, a Nationalist compromise was evident in the overwhelming support given by that community to the Good Friday Agreement, which gave an Irish dimension to political arrangements in Northern Ireland, but fell short of joint authority or Irish unity.

Linked to the rejection of a settlement confined to Northern Ireland is the insistence of Nationalists upon self-determination for the Irish people. This means that all people within the island of Ireland need to resolve the Irish question without outside interference. In the New Ireland Forum 1984, Nationalist parties on both sides of the border agreed that a solution had to be 'freely agreed to by the people of the north and by the people of the south' (New Ireland Forum Report, 1984: 27, para 5.2(3)). The Good Friday Agreement was a partial move towards self-determination, being ratified by the populations in Northern Ireland and the Irish Republic.

5.2 Republicanism's core ideas

The core aim of Irish republicanism has remained unchanged throughout the existence of the organisation. The establishment of a thirty-two-county, united, democratic, socialist Irish republic has been a permanent goal. Drawing upon the ideas of the French Revolution of liberty, equality and fraternity, Republicans wish to establish a united Ireland of equal treatment for Catholic, Protestant and dissenter. Such an aspiration involves the eventual withdrawal of Britain from Northern Ireland and an end to partition. During most periods, these aims were to be achieved by force if necessary. During the Troubles, the use of force was designed to render Northern Ireland ungovernable, sapping the British will to remain. Recruits to the IRA were given the *Green Book* which declared that 'war is morally justified and that the Army is the direct representative of the 1918 Dail Eireann parliament, and that as such they are the legal and lawful government of the Irish Republic' (*see* Coogan, 1987). Most modern Republicans have abandoned the idea of the IRA representing a government-in-waiting as entirely outdated and irrelevant to the vast majority of Irish citizens, although a few 'purists' within Republican Sinn Fein still cling to this view.

Seven core ideological undercurrents underpinned the political and military thinking of the IRA (Coogan, 1987): republicanism, nationalism, militarism, romanticism, socialism, anti-imperialism and anti-colonialism.

5.2.1 Republicanism

The British presence in Northern Ireland prevents the development of a true Irish Republic. Such a state, embracing all Irish people, can only develop after the end of partition. Traditionally, the role of the Southern authorities and constitutional Nationalists in Northern Ireland in 'collaborating' with British rule was seen as 'treasonable'.

5.2.2 Nationalism

According to the *Green Book* given to IRA volunteers, the nationhood of all Ireland has been a recognised fact for more than 1,500 years. There is a belief in a distinctive Irish nation state.

5.2.3 Militarism

The right to engage in 'armed struggle' to overthrow British rule in Ireland has been central to the IRA's approach. It is justified on an historical basis. The organisation claims that this war has evolved over 800 years and thus has strong justifying antecedents.

5.2.4 Romanticism

In addition to the belief in an identifiable and definable Irish nation state, the Republican movement has emphasised the need for the cultural assertion of Irishness. The promotion of Gaelic culture has been stressed as a means of overcoming 'West Britishness'. Furthermore, the IRA has also fostered the notion of the necessity of 'blood sacrifice' to achieve its goals. Martyrdom and commemoration of the dead are recurring themes.

5.2.5 Socialism

Although it has fluctuated between differing strands of the ideology, the IRA has always claimed to be a socialist organisation, arguing for common ownership and equality within a united Ireland.

5.2.6 Anti-imperialism

Opposition to the perceived economic exploitation of a colonial, imperialist aggressor has been an important dimension of the attitudes of the IRA. The economic value of Northern Ireland was seen as a contributory factor in the division of the island.

5.2.7 Anti-colonialism

The IRA's *Green Book* described the six counties of Northern Ireland as a 'directly-controlled old-style colony'. It was seen as a remnant of Britain's colonial Empire. The Southern state was seen as subject to the continuing social, economic and cultural domination of London, according to the *Green Book*. As such, it was viewed as a neo-colonial state.

Tactically, these ideological undercurrents were translated during the Troubles into a belief in the necessity of a 'long war', the fusion of economic and military campaigns, propaganda offensives and the exercise of 'discipline' upon the Nationalist community.

5.3 Nationalism and republicanism compared

There are different strains of nationalism. Many Nationalists see themselves as Republicans and vice versa. Generally, Republicans are more critical of the British role in Ireland and their variety of Nationalist politics reflects this critique. The main differences of emphasis amongst Nationalists rest upon the following issues.

5.3.1 The extent to which the Irish people are a single nation

Traditionally, Irish Nationalists and Republicans saw Ireland as a single geographical and political unit, populated by one identity. As Quinn (1993: 65–6) puts it: 'anti-partitionists relied on simple ethno-geographical determinism: the people of Ireland were one, the island of Ireland was one, therefore the governance of Ireland should be one'.

Influenced by revisionist historians, some Nationalists began to question this assumption. Modern Nationalist dialogue speaks of the need to reconcile the two traditions in Ireland. There was a need to recognise the British identity of Protestants in the North of Ireland. Nationalism needed to switch focus from a territorial claim towards a rethinking of Irish identity. This had to be 'pluralist and inclusive' in order to embrace Northern Unionists (Fitzgerald, 1996: 6). The Irish Republican tradition within nationalism has a somewhat different approach. Republicans believe that all the peoples within the island are essentially Irish, whilst acknowledging differing cultural expressions of that Irishness. They argue that partition prevents the full development of Irish nationhood.

5.3.2 The degree to which the British government is responsible for the problem of Northern Ireland

Nationalists blame the British government for the partition of Ireland. They point out that it was imposed against the wishes of the majority of the people of Ireland. Socialist Irish Republicans, in particular, stress the value of partition in protecting Britain's economic interests in the North-East of the island (Bambery, 1990). In gratitude for the maintenance of her colony, Britain then rewarded that section of the indigenous population that favoured her continued rule – the Northern Unionists – with a series of economic favours.

Many Republicans continue to support this view of Britain as an imperial power. Constitutional Nationalists are less convinced. They suggest that Britain has become increasingly neutral on the future of the Union, a position acknowledged in recent political initiatives such as the 1993 Downing Street Declaration and the Good Friday Agreement. This neutrality was perhaps borne of the huge cost to the British government of its presence in Northern Ireland.

An underlying theme of republicanism is that Britain will eventually withdraw. The belief in the inevitability of victory has sustained the 'armed struggle'. Thus, according to Smith (1995: 227), 'Republican ideology is teleological – it sees an end to history. Republicans see history as one of continued advance to a pre-destined goal'.

5.3.3 The necessity of Unionist consent for constitutional change

At the heart of the problem of Northern Ireland lies the issue of whether the consent of Unionists should be a prerequisite for constitutional change. Should Unionists be obliged to accept a united Ireland against their will? Traditionally,

Irish Republicans believed that once realigned in a united Ireland, former Unionists would realise that their true interests lay in acceptance and co-operation. Protestants 'would need to have their understandable but mis-guided fears about civil and religious liberties answered' (Adams, 1985: 9). Present arrangements allow Unionists an undemocratic veto over progress, according to Republicans.

Constitutional Nationalists believe that Unionists must be persuaded rather than coerced into a united Ireland. This has led to attempts to address the fears of Unionists, mainly through cultural, social and economic reforms in the Irish Republic.

5.3.4 The use of force to establish a united Ireland

For much of the twentieth century, Nationalists opposed partition with vigor-ous rhetoric, but offered few practical ideas as to how it was to be ended (O'Halloran, 1987). During the final third of the century, the physical-force tradition of republicanism was used as a device alongside political strategies. Constitutional Nationalists always argued that the use of terrorism was morally wrong and tactically counter-productive. They argued that violence was a barrier to Irish unity as it further alienated Unionists. Militant Republicans argued that the use of violence, whilst incapable in isolation of achieving a united Ireland, maintained the issue on the political agenda.

5.4 The Social Democratic and Labour Party (SDLP)

Established in 1970 following the civil rights campaign, the SDLP was, until the 2001 elections, the largest Nationalist party in Northern Ireland. In 2001, it had three Westminster MPs and 24 MLAs. The party was founded in an attempt to bring a new dynamism to Nationalist politics, which had fre-quently been stagnant under the abstentionism of the old Nationalist Party. From the outset, the SDLP has favoured a united Ireland, to be achieved through peaceful means. Its 1972 policy document, *Towards a New Ireland*, desired a declaration of British withdrawal, preceded by the establishment of joint British–Irish sovereignty over Northern Ireland as an interim measure (Social Democratic and Labour Party, 1972).

In its early years, the party fused nationalism with left-of-centre politics. It had aspirations for cross-class unity and readily countenanced power-sharing within Northern Ireland, provided that this was accompanied by a significant all-Ireland dimension. The presence of a Council of Ireland encouraged the SDLP to participate in the power-sharing executive in 1974, which lasted a mere five months following the Sunningdale Agreement.

By the 1980s, the SDLP favoured joint Anglo-Irish government initiatives as a means of advancing constitutional change in Northern Ireland. Under electoral pressure from Sinn Fein, the party was an architect of the New Ireland Forum in 1983–4. Constitutional Nationalist parties throughout Ireland combined to propose solutions to the problem of Northern Ireland. Although each was rejected, the role given to the Irish government in Northern Ireland through the Anglo-Irish Agreement in 1985 bolstered the fortunes of the SDLP.

Emphasising the need for an agreed Ireland, the SDLP accepts that Unionists cannot be coerced into a united Ireland. Instead, a new Ireland needs to be forged on the basis of a consensus between North and South. The party recognises that all responsibility for the Irish problem cannot be placed upon the British government. As the party leader argued, 'it was the people who were divided, not the territory' (quoted in *Irish Times*, 6 November 1998). Rather than self-determination, what is required is co-determination (Farren, 1996). The people of Ireland, North and South, would together determine the future of Ireland. Neither the population of the North, nor that in the South, would be able to impose its will alone.

In establishing co-determination as the basis for future settlements, the SDLP attempts to set up institutional arrangements which straddle the border. North–South co-operative bodies are seen as one mechanism to do this. These organisations would exist in economic, political and cultural arenas. The party insists that these bodies would not be a 'trojan horse' for a united Ireland (Farren, 1996: 45). The other co-operative mechanism is a formal East–West relationship between the London and Dublin governments.

Virtually all of this thinking was evident in the Good Friday Agreement. Indeed, it is no exaggeration to claim that the Agreement is an SDLP document (Murray, 1998). Unsurprisingly, therefore, a substantial majority (82 per cent) of the SDLP's claimed 3,000 members believed that the party obtained most of its objectives in the Good Friday Agreement. Seventy per cent believed that the Good Friday Agreement made a united Ireland more likely, but, irrespective of the ultimate direction of the Agreement, two-thirds of members accepted the proposition that power-sharing was more important to the SDLP than Irish unity (author's survey, 2000).

Critics have suggested that the SDLP has betrayed its original ambition of operating as a 'red' socialist party, in favour of the adoption of a 'green' Nationalist stance. Before accepting a place in the House of Lords, the party leader, Gerry Fitt, resigned in 1979 over this policy shift, as the party became less enamoured with the prospect of an internal settlement in Northern Ireland. The shift towards nationalism appeared to gather pace under the leadership of John Hume. A greening of the SDLP took place after the collapse of consociational, power-sharing arrangements in 1974. A new type of member, more Nationalist than hitherto, was attracted to the party. Indeed, there exists a 'Catholic' wing to the party disinterested in the party's original socialist leanings which is closer to the party mainstream than those members identifying themselves as socialist (Evans, Tonge and Murray, 2000). The SDLP membership strongly supported early paramilitary prisoner releases and radical policing changes, while strongly opposing Orange Order parades in National-ist areas. Half of the party membership favours electoral pacts with Sinn Fein (Evans, Tonge and Murray, 2000). Two-thirds of SDLP vote transfers are to Sinn Fein (O'Kelly and Doyle, 2000).

Theoretically, determination of policy rests with the party conference, which also elects the senior leadership and executive. A majority of party members feel they have little influence within the party. Major party initiatives have often been launched by the party leader. Regarded as instrumental in the establishment of the peace process in the 1990s, John Hume began an intermittent dialogue with the leader of Sinn Fein, Gerry Adams, in 1988. In addition to promoting the need for an IRA ceasefire, the talks were designed to shift Sinn Fein's position towards acceptance of the need for Unionist consent if a united Ireland were to be created. The subsequent Downing Street Declaration, Framework Documents and Good Friday Agreement all bore the hallmarks of the SDLP's unity by consent approach.

Despite the achievement of party objectives, the SDLP faces problems. As the percentage of Catholics in Northern Ireland's population has increased, the party's vote has held firm. Indeed, the party became the largest in terms of votes cast in the 1998 Assembly elections. Nonetheless, Sinn Fein overtook the SDLP in the 2001 Westminster and local elections and has occupied much of the SDLP's political ground. If Nationalist voters are impressed by 'green' ethnic bloc politics, the gap may increase. The average age of an SDLP member is 57.

5.5 Sinn Fein

Once regarded as merely the political wing of the IRA, Sinn Fein has long emerged as a significant electoral and political force in its own right. It is the only significant all-Ireland party, holding 2,600 members in its 246 branches in the Irish Republic (Lyons, 1999). Sinn Fein now polls a majority of the Nationalist vote in Northern Ireland. Its electoral rise began after the Republican hunger strikes in the 1980s, when it developed an organisation to provide a political outlet for the military campaign of the IRA. Sinn Fein's electoral support in Northern Ireland increased to record levels in the second half of the 1990s, allowing the party to capture four seats in the 2001 General Election.

During the 1970s, Sinn Fein operated as little more than a welfare adjunct to the IRA's military campaign. The IRA believed it could force a British withdrawal through a military campaign. As Ryan (1994) demonstrates, this belief permeated the Republican movement and was relayed optimistically in propaganda. As the limitations of a military campaign became apparent, more astute Republicans sought complementary strategies. Sinn Fein moved leftwards in the late 1970s, attempting to fuse republicanism and socialism (Patterson, 1997). Its leaders were dismissive of Loyalists who claimed to be arguing for socialism within the unit of Northern Ireland. According to Adams, such 'socialists' were guilty of 'parochialism of the municipal gasworks and waterworks' variety (Adams, 1995: 128). The struggles for national independence and socialism were seen as interdependent.

The link between the paramilitary role of the IRA and the political campaigns of Sinn Fein was amplified by the latter's director of publicity, Danny Morrison. Speaking at the party's *ard fheis* (annual conference) in 1981, Morrison outlined the dual strategy, asking *ard fheis*: 'will anyone here object if with a ballot paper in this hand and an armalite in this hand we take power in Ireland?'. Sinn Fein supported 'armed struggle' to remove the British presence from Ireland.

Assisted by a considerable residue of sympathy arising from the deaths of ten Republican hunger strikers during the same year, the new electoral approach made inroads into the Nationalist vote held by the SDLP. In the 1983 General Election, the party captured the seat of West Belfast. The victor, Gerry Adams, became president of Sinn Fein later that year. Adams refused to take his seat in the Westminster parliament, continuing the tradition of abstentionism held by the party. Sinn Fein refused to participate in the Northern Ireland Assembly during 1982–6, arguing that it attempted to inspire an internal settlement in Northern Ireland and, therefore, legitimise partition.

Until the mid-1980s, the principle of abstentionism was applied also to the Dail, the Dublin parliament. Sinn Fein believed the last 'true' Irish parliament was that established in 1919, following the all-Ireland elections of 1918 when the party won a majority of seats. The parliament created in the South after partition was derided by Sinn Fein:

> The only thing Irish about the Irish Parliament in Leinster House is its name – the Dail, otherwise it is a British parliamentary system handed down by ex-colonial rulers (Adams, 1985: 8).

The decision to end abstentionism was a symbolic shift of huge importance. The extent of subsequent change in republican politics is detailed in Chapter 10. What follows here is a brief outline. Following the bolstering of constitutional nationalism in the 1985 Anglo-Irish Agreement, the electoral fortunes of Provisional Sinn Fein ebbed for several years, despite a considerable amount of effort put into community politics. With stalemate also evident in the IRA's campaign, fresh political approaches were sought. These involved, in 1986, the abandonment of abstentionism in the event of Sinn Fein winning a seat in the Southern parliament and tentative moves towards pan-nationalist dialogue in Northern Ireland by 1988. As talks between the leaders of the main Nationalist parties took place, Sinn Fein hinted that seemingly fundamental demands might be the subject of compromise. *Towards a Lasting Peace in Ireland* suggested that indications of a British withdrawal might provide sufficient basis for negotiation (Sinn Fein, 1992). At Sinn Fein's *ard fheis* in 1992, it was agreed that 'the combined forces of Irish nationalism' would 'be the main vehicle for national liberation' (O'Brien, 1999: 225). Armed struggle was being downplayed. *Towards a Lasting Peace* indicated revised thinking on unionism. The party declared that the consent of Unionists was essential for a lasting peace, but it remained doubtful whether this consent was required in advance of fundamental constitutional change. Sinn Fein's new strategy centred upon urging the British government to act as a persuader to Unionists for a united Ireland. It argued for national self-determination, defined as all the people of Ireland determining their political arrangements as a single unit.

Sinn Fein remained linked to the Provisional IRA. The two organisations have separate organisational structures, but are historically and politically linked with some overlap of personnel. During the peace process in the mid-1990s, prior to the collapse of the first IRA ceasefire, Gerry Adams insisted that the IRA 'haven't gone away'. Concurrently, he put distance between the two organisations by insisting that 'Sinn Fein is not the IRA. Sinn Fein is not involved in armed struggle. Sinn Fein does not advocate armed struggle' (*Irish Times*, 20 June 1996). Unionist critics have argued that the two organisations are inseparable, whilst to other critics, Sinn Fein/IRA links provide a 'good cop, bad cop' approach to politics. Nonetheless, to the Nationalist electorate PIRA increasingly meant Peaceful IRA, and Sinn Fein became increasingly constitutional in its approach to politics.

After the IRA renewed its ceasefire in 1997, Sinn Fein was admitted to multi-party negotiations leading to the Good Friday Agreement in April 1998. The Republican movement had helped destroy Unionist party rule at Stormont in 1972 and believed it was halfway to an independent Irish Republic. With the forging of the Good Friday Agreement, the party leadership decided to end abstentionism in respect of Stormont, a move overwhelmingly supported by party members at the party's *ard fheis* in 1998. A new, pragmatic and constitutional republicanism had emerged from a former revolutionary movement, committed to the Good Friday Agreement. It sought accommodation with Unionists and offered a much more participatory version of republicanism than hitherto. New republicanism moved beyond its old war against British rule and its 'no concessions to Loyalists' approach of the 1980s. Instead, Adams insisted by 2001 that:

> I think it's a mistake for people to look at it (the political problem) in terms of unionism and nationalism. I think the [Good Friday] agreement carved out a new majority, not unionist or nationalist. Without reneging on republicanism, we have to find accommodation with our opponents (*Guardian*, 30 April 2001).

5.6 Republican ultras

Given the extent and speed of change, perhaps the most remarkable achievement of Adams was to avoid a major split. A small number of Republican 'dissidents', 'ultras' or 'purists' nonetheless emerged, divisible into three categories. A few ideological purists, led by the deposed president, Ruairi O'Bradaigh, formed a small breakaway group – Republican Sinn Fein – after the decision to end abstentionism from the Dail in 1986. Republican Sinn Fein adopts the policy positions held by Provisional Sinn Fein in the 1970s. This includes a demand for British withdrawal from Northern Ireland within the lifetime of a parliament and support for the Eire Nua programme of a federal Ireland comprising parliaments in each of its four historic provinces. Each parliament, including that in Ulster, would be granted considerable autonomy. Republican Sinn Fein is linked to the Continuity IRA.

The Real IRA was formed in the autumn of 1997. It comprised defectors from the Provisional IRA. These dissidents were unhappy at the resumption of an IRA ceasefire, given the British government's public insistence that any political agreement would be based upon consent within Northern Ireland.

Any hopes held by the Real IRA of attracting large numbers of defectors disappeared with its killing of 29 people at Omagh in August 1998, the worst atrocity of the Troubles in Northern Ireland. Sinn Fein condemned the bombing unequivocally and the action appeared to confirm the futility of 'armed struggle' to the Provisional IRA and many other Republicans. Nonetheless, the Real IRA, which called a ceasefire in the immediate aftermath, appeared to have revived somewhat by late 2000. Its political outlet is the 32 County Sovereignty Committee, withering in its criticism of the Provisionals' 'sell-out' and promotion of the equality agenda within Northern Ireland. Its vice-chairwoman, Bernadette Sands-McKevitt, sister of Bobby Sands, insisted that her brother 'did not die for cross-border bodies with Executive powers. He did not die for nationalists to be equal within the Northern Ireland state' (quoted in Hennessy, 2000: 112). Unlike Sinn Fein, however, the 32 County Sovereignty Committee lacked an urban base and the killing of a rare Real IRA figure in Belfast in 2000 by the Provisionals further discouraged its spread (Breen, 2000b). Parallels with the 1956–62 IRA low-level Border Campaign, lacking in public support, might be drawn with Real IRA activity. Its weaponry and militarism suggest that a limited form of Republican armed campaign may endure.

The final category of Republican dissidents offers a peaceful rejection of Sinn Fein's strategy. Comprised mainly, but not exclusively, of former Provisional IRA members, the Irish Republican Writers' Group uses its publication, *Fourthwrite*, to criticise Sinn Fein's entry to Stormont, whilst rejecting a return to an armed campaign.

5.7 Conclusion

Nationalist parties have made considerable electoral gains in recent years, as the vote shares of the SDLP and Sinn Fein have risen. The SDLP has also achieved many of its political objectives, having contributed substantially to the three Strands of the Good Friday Agreement, achieved an Irish dimension and had the future of Northern Ireland co-determined by the people of Ireland, North and South. Sinn Fein has been obliged to compromise its Republican principles to maintain its electoral rise and has moved from being a supporter of armed struggle to a constitutional political party. The party insists such a change is merely tactical, designed to further the overall objective of Irish unity. Pan-nationalism, a constructor of the peace process, has been displaced by even greater electoral competition within the Nationalist bloc.

Chapter 6

Governing Northern Ireland

The 1998 Good Friday Agreement fundamentally altered the mode of governance for Northern Ireland. From the suspension of Stormont in 1972 until 1998 (apart from the first five months of 1974) Northern Ireland was governed directly from Westminster, by the Secretary of State for Northern Ireland. Direct rule imposed neo-colonial governance upon Northern Ireland. Legislative proposals were either approved or rejected by the Westminster parliament. When approved, policy was administered through the Northern Ireland Office and a number of public agencies. Administration of policy was undertaken by the 30,000 members of the Northern Ireland Civil Service (Carmichael, 2001). Local government, being particularly weak in Northern Ireland, did not offer democratic compensation. The Good Friday Agreement reintroduced devolved government for Northern Ireland. It was introduced as part of the Labour government's overall strategy of 'democratising' the United Kingdom through a programme of devolution embracing Northern Ireland, Scotland and Wales, although there were important differences within each country. The consociational principles underpinning the Agreement are designed to ensure that Unionists and Nationalists are obliged to share power. These principles prevent the domination of one community by the other.

6.1 'Old Stormont': Northern Ireland's parliament 1921–72

Prior to the abolition of Stormont in 1972, Northern Ireland was run as an adjunct of the Home Office, administered by a section also responsible for the licensing of London taxi cabs. Disinterest characterised the attitude of the British government to Northern Ireland. This lack of concern did not extend to the award of financial autonomy. Instead, Northern Ireland had few fund-raising powers in its own right.

Devolution of powers to Northern Ireland was an arrangement that suited Unionists and the British government. The latter did not have to involve itself in a region about which it had minimal concern. Unionists enjoyed the relative autonomy of their own parliament, buttressed by the Ireland Act 1949 which guaranteed the permanence of Northern Ireland's place in the United Kingdom, subject to the will of that unionist bastion.

Northern Ireland thus possessed its own parliament, cabinet, civil service and police force. These were seen by the minority population as sectarian institutions from which they were excluded. Yet, although most powers out-side the spheres of foreign, defence and economic policy were accredited to Stormont, the broad thrust of domestic policy mirrored that arising from Westminster. For example, the principles of the welfare state developed in Northern Ireland at a broadly similar pace to that elsewhere in the United Kingdom, although separate Acts were required. The Northern Ireland economy had to bear much of the strain of generating social security payments, most of which were locally financed. What frequently differed in Northern Ireland was the application of policy. It was this diversity of approach that was often seen by the minority community as arbitrary and discriminatory.

6.2 Direct rule 1972–98

Supposedly a transient measure, the introduction of direct rule in 1972 endured beyond expectation. In ending 50 years of Unionist rule, the British government assumed full responsibility for future events, pending the develop-ment of a constitutional settlement. That direct rule was envisaged as a holding operation is indicated by the title of its accompanying legislation, the Northern Ireland (Temporary Provisions) Act. Power resided with a succession of Secretaries of State for Northern Ireland, shown in Table 6.1.

Direct rule was described as a 'semi-colonial' form of administration (Wichert, 1991: 179). Acting as a Governor-General, the Secretary of State presided over Northern Ireland and did not necessarily require the consent of local political parties for decisions. Powers invested in the post were much greater than those afforded to the Secretaries of State for Scotland or Wales. All political and security matters were under the control of the Secretary of State, although operational matters were determined by the Chief Constable of the RUC and the commanding officer of the British Army. Members of

Table 6.1 Secretaries of State for Northern Ireland 1972–2001

Secretary of State	Duration of office	Government
William Whitelaw	1972–3	Conservative
Francis Pym	1973–4	Conservative
Merlyn Rees	1974–6	Labour
Roy Mason	1976–9	Labour
Humphrey Atkins	1979–81	Conservative
James Prior	1981–4	Conservative
Douglas Hurd	1984–5	Conservative
Tom King	1985–9	Conservative
Peter Brooke	1989–92	Conservative
Patrick Mayhew	1992–7	Conservative
Mo Mowlam	1997–9	Labour
Peter Mandelson	1999–2001	Labour
John Reid	2001–	Labour

Parliament in Northern Ireland were largely excluded from policy-making in respect of the Province. Orders in Council approved by the Secretary of State could not be amended, only approved or rejected outright (Hazleton, 1994). This process was labelled governance by 'ministerial decree' (McGarry and O'Leary, 1995: 95).

Some services, such as housing, became the responsibility of regional agencies, or joint boards. Many of these were removed from local-authority control in 1972. Whilst changes in local government were undertaken throughout Britain, the removal of powers from local authorities in Northern Ireland owed much to the association of those bodies with sectarian discrimination. Such was the emasculation of local government that it became responsible for little more than 'bins and burials'.

Greater scrutiny of legislation and government departments was facilitated by the creation of a select committee on Northern Ireland Affairs in 1994. Although favoured by the Ulster Unionist Party for some years, the decision to proceed with the establishment of the committee followed the support of Ulster Unionists for the Conservative government in tight parliamentary votes on the Maastricht Treaty. Both sides denied a deal had been enacted. In 1996, the bolstering of the Northern Ireland Grand Committee was announced. This committee would provide MPs with a mini-debating chamber, allowing certain powers of pre-legislative scrutiny.

Despite its considerable responsibilities, the job of Secretary of State for Northern Ireland was often regarded as an outpost within the British cabinet. During the 1980s, the position was awarded as a punishment to the troublesome James Prior, with Margaret Thatcher anxious to enforce an exile which meant his banishment from other policy arenas. The office holder was nonetheless granted considerable autonomy within cabinet.

6.3 'New Stormont': Northern Ireland's Executive and Assembly

The return of devolved government to Northern Ireland was always going to be on a fundamentally different basis from the form of governance seen under the previous devolved administration. New political institutions attempt to harness the rival forces of unionism and nationalism on the basis of historic compromise. Internal power-sharing with an attendant Irish dimension characterise the new politics of Northern Ireland, reflected in an interlocking set of institutions.

The type of devolved government seen in Northern Ireland is unusual. The Executive was formed using the system devised by a Belgian mathematician, Viktor D'Hondt. At the head of government are First and Deputy Ministers, elected on a cross-community basis. One cannot remain in office without the other. Two junior ministers were appointed to assist the First and Deputy First Ministers. Below these ministers is an Executive of ten ministers. These are not chosen by the First Minister, as is the norm elsewhere. Instead, parties are entitled to seats within the Executive according to the number of seats

Table 6.2　The Northern Ireland Executive 1999 (shown in running order of choice of portfolio)

Minister	Party	Portfolio
Reg Empey	UUP	Enterprise, Trade and Development
Mark Durkan	SDLP	Finance and Personnel
Peter Robinson	DUP	Regional Development
Martin McGuinness	SF	Education
Sam Foster	UUP	Environment
Sean Farren	SDLP	Higher and Further Education; Employment
Nigel Dodds	DUP	Social Development
Michael McGimpsey	UUP	Culture, Arts and Leisure
Bairbre de Bruin	SF	Health, Social Services and Public Safety
Brid Rodgers	SDLP	Agriculture and Rural Development

won in the election to the Assembly. The UUP, as the largest party with 28 seats after the 1998 assembly elections, thus chose the first executive portfolio. Its number of seats was then divided by two, giving the party 14 seats. This allowed the SDLP, DUP and Sinn Fein, in order of seats won, to select their ministerial portfolios. Each party then had its number of seats divided by two upon accepting a post. After all four parties had accepted their first ministerial post and thus had their number of seats divided by two, each still had more seats than any other parties, such as Alliance. Thus, the UUP, SDLP, DUP and Sinn Fein were all entitled to a second position in the Executive. After taking this second post, each party's remaining number of seats was again divided by two. The UUP's remaining 14 seats were thus divided again by two, leaving seven. This still left the UUP with more seats than its nearest rivals, followed by the SDLP, giving these parties the final two seats in the Executive. The running order of choices and the personnel filling the posts for the first set of ministerial portfolios are shown in Table 6.2.

The outcome of the D'Hondt system of allocation is proportionality throughout government in Northern Ireland. Unionists and Nationalists are obliged to share executive power, although the Executive is not a formal coalition. Similarly, Unionists and Nationalists, along with the two Assembly parties (Alliance and the Women's Coalition) designated 'other', are responsible for the scrutiny of Executive actions, via the committee system.

The anti-Agreement DUP rotated its ministers, as part of the party's strategy to collapse the Good Friday Agreement by undermining its institutions. Nonetheless, the Executive, by 2000, had assumed responsibility for producing programmes of legislation and drafting the budget (Wilford, 2001). The Executive is responsible for administering expenditure totalling £9 billion. With its cross-party formation, the Executive is, at most, an informal coalition and, at worst, a divided and disparate body. Inter-party tensions remain, most evident with the DUP declining to work alongside Sinn Fein. As such, concern for the good governance of Northern Ireland rests uneasily alongside historical enmity, all contained within the same government. In addition to the residual tension spilling into post-conflict government, the Executive was concerned with several problems. As examples, it had to address poor public health and a very weak public transport system. Yet the parties in the Executive have, on occasion, acted as government and opposition, appearing to support draft legislative proposals within the Executive whilst opposing them within the Assembly.

6.4 The Northern Ireland Assembly and its committees

The Northern Ireland Assembly, which met for the first time in July 1998, is extraordinarily large. The 108 members, elected under the single transferable vote system of proportional representation, represent an electorate of 1.6 million. The Assembly is nearly twice the size of the sixty-member Welsh counterpart, despite Northern Ireland having a smaller population. Given the Welsh Assembly's lack of powers, a starker example of the extent of overrepresentation is evident in the contrast with the Scottish parliament, which contains only 129 members, although it has tax-raising powers, a strength not given to the Northern Ireland Assembly. One of the reasons for the large size of the Assembly was to ensure that as many different shades of opinion as possible could be represented.

The amount of power devolved to the Northern Ireland Assembly is considerable, although power in Northern Ireland has been devolved to a wider range of institutions than in the devolved settlements for Wales and Scotland. Ironically for a party that has long desired the return of devolved government, the UUP's demands were modest in respect of the powers to be devolved. Indeed, the party proposed a devolved arrangement not dissimilar from the minimalist devolution awarded to Wales (Hazleton, 2000). The actual powers devolved are closer to the Scottish model, with the assembly possessing the capacity to initiate and pass primary legislation. The 'North Down' question, Northern Ireland's version of the West Lothian question in Scotland, could be raised. Why should Northern Ireland's MPs be able to sit in Westminster and vote on legislation affecting England, when Northern Ireland possesses its own Assembly, devoid of English representatives? The answer is that any such problem is much less acute. Northern Ireland's MPs rarely vote (or even attend debates) on issues unrelated to their country. They are somewhat more regular voters at Westminster on 'moral' issues.

From its creation, the First Minister indicted his wish for the Northern Ireland parliament to be a 'pluralist parliament for a pluralist people'. One-party Unionist hegemony had vanished with the collapse of Stormont in 1972. Decisions within the Northern Ireland Assembly can be taken on the basis of a simple majority. However, for key decisions, consociational principles, enforcing cross-community consensus, are applied. Decisions designated as 'key' items involve the election of the First and Deputy First Ministers and Assembly Chair, standing orders and budget allocations. If 30 members demand that a decision be designated as 'key', it can be added to these items.

Cross-community consensus is needed according to either of the following rules:

- *parallel consent*, in which majorities among all those voting, among Unionists and among Nationalists, must all occur; or
- *weighted majority*, in which a measure commands the support of 60 per cent of Assembly members present and voting, including at least 40 per cent of Unionists and 40 per cent of Nationalists.

The first two years of the Assembly approved only small amounts of legislation. Indeed, its early legislative programme induced a certain cynicism over how the sectarian divide was being healed. The opening two items of legislation increased financial allowances to Assembly members and political parties.

The D'Hondt system is also used for allocation of Committee Chairs and Deputy Chairs. Ordinary committee membership is allocated in proportion to party strengths in the Assembly. There are 10 Departmental Committees, and five standing committees The Departmental Committees have responsibility for scrutiny and policy development, whilst the standing committees are concerned mainly with procedures, finance and conduct. The committees perform the following main functions:

- advice on budget allocations for the Department;
- policy formulation;
- approval of secondary legislation;
- committee stage approval of primary legislation.

The committees tend to be consensual, with parties co-operating in a manner not always evident in the wider Assembly chamber. They issue reports which are usually unanimous for debate by the entire Assembly, although members of committees have on occasion returned to the party fold in opposing their own unanimous committee report. The relationship between committees and the ministers they shadow is still unfolding. One of the difficulties within the Executive–Committee structure lies in the mechanism to remove incompetent ministers. The full Assembly has the right to remove such a minister, on the basis of cross-community consensus. Given that such consensus may not be forthcoming, it may be difficult to hold ministers to account. Ministers can ignore committee proposals and be insulated from censure by sectarian, ethnic bloc voting within the Assembly. These problems notwithstanding, ministerial–committee relationships have been broadly consensual.

Northern Ireland's new political institutions are not confined to elected representatives. A consultative civic forum was also established under the Good Friday Agreement, designed to act as consultative body on social, economic and cultural issues. The Forum was supported by parties such as the Women's Coalition, which believed that it had the potential to infuse the new Assembly with fresh views. Its representatives are drawn mainly from the business, voluntary and trade-union sectors. Sinn Fein and the PUP have argued that there is insufficient working-class representation.

6.5 The North—South Ministerial Council

Established under Strand 2 of the Good Friday Agreement, the North—South Ministerial Council brings together ministers from the Northern Ireland Assembly and the Irish government on a regular basis to develop consultation, co-operation and policy implementation on agreed matters.

The North—South Council has proved a controversial aspect of the new political agenda. Its first meeting was held in December 1999, attended by 10 ministers from Northern Ireland and 16 from the Irish Republic. This and subsequent meetings were boycotted by DUP members. The Unionist case was thus presented by a mere four (UUP) representatives amongst the 26 attenders of the first all-island meeting of ministers since partition. The lack of progress on IRA decommissioning led to the First Minister, David Trimble, attempting to prevent Sinn Fein's ministers from attending meetings, a measure rejected in the courts. As required as a minimum under the Agreement, the Council agreed to establish six new North—South implementation bodies and identify six areas for co-operation between government departments and bodies, North and South. The six new North—South implementation bodies are:

- Waterways Ireland;
- The Food Safety Promotion Board;
- The Trade and Business Development Body;
- The Special European Union Programmes Body;
- The Foyle, Carlingford and Irish Lights Commission;
- The North—South Language Body.

Whatever the fears of Unionists, the North—South Council is not a freestanding expansionist body. Its position is ringfenced by the requirement in the Good Friday Agreement that any further North—South implementation bodies must be agreed by the Irish parliament and the Northern Ireland Assembly. Consent from the Northern Assembly is barely conceivable in the short and medium terms for political reasons, irrespective of any economic logic. Unionist parties will oppose such a development. Even if Nationalists were to obtain a majority within the Assembly, the requirement for cross-community consensus would prevent approval for the expansion of all-Ireland bodies. A more realistic fear is that the North—South implementation bodies adopt a broader remit than at present, due to ambiguity over their precise role. Furthermore, Unionists might fear that agreed co-operation between government bodies in the six, fairly broad, areas agreed could become incremental, leading to all-island implementation in related areas.

6.6 The British—Irish Council and British—Irish Intergovernmental Conference

Strand 3 of the Good Friday Agreement established the mildly confederal dimension of the British—Irish Council, bringing together representatives of the devolved institutions in Britain and Ireland and the British and Irish governments. The Council has no formal powers, but endeavours to reach agreement on matters of mutual interest. It met for the first time in December 1999. Five ministers from Northern Ireland, four from the Irish Republic and three from the British government were joined by three ministers from Scotland and Wales. In each case, the Prime Minister or First Minister was in attendance. Two representatives were also present from the Isle of Man, Jersey and Guernsey. The Council has identified co-operation on drugs, social exclusion, the environment and transport as initial priority areas. The Council may develop as an arena in which best practice is identified, rather than as a significant policy-maker. The British–Irish Intergovernmental conference is a significant body, as it acts as a forum for bilateral co-operation between the British and Irish governments. Ministers from Northern Ireland can attend.

6.7 The role of the European Union

Northern Ireland has been part of the European Community since 1973. Its population voted narrowly in favour of continued membership in the 1975 referendum, with the 'yes' vote of 52 per cent substantially less than the average two-thirds affirmative elsewhere in the United Kingdom. Such luke-warm support was partly explained by the disdain of the main Unionist parties for the Community, although the SDLP has always been supportive.

Subsequently, Northern Ireland has received considerable financial assistance through its status as an Objective 1 peripheral region, attracting maximum EU support. In 1987, Community funds for the regions doubled. Greater assistance for rural development, allied to agricultural support averaging £47 million annually during the first 17 years of Community membership, has aided Northern Ireland's economy. The proportion of employees working in agriculture is double that found elsewhere in the United Kingdom (Bew and Meehan, 1994).

Under the Community Support Framework, the region was awarded £550 million from 1989–93, rising to £940 million between 1994–9. The main areas of assistance thus far have been employment, industrial development, transport, agriculture and tourism. Subsidies still fail to match those found in the Irish Republic, which enjoys the largest per head benefits in the EU.

Although Northern Ireland may be included in general British representations within the Council of Ministers, the region is also reliant upon specific lobbying. This was performed by the Northern Ireland Office, but will increasingly become a feature of Executive activity. There is a European Commission office in Belfast, whilst local councils, notwithstanding their domestic weaknesses, have also begun to discover the possibilities of European networking. Significant lobbying is performed by Northern Ireland's three MEPs, drawn from the SDLP, UUP and DUP.

Each of these parties sees the potential economic benefits of EU membership. All parties lay stress on the special regional conditions which exist in Northern Ireland to attract EU funding to the area (Greer, 1996). Indeed, political co-operation produced effective lobbying to the extent that the Community's first Integrated Developments Operation was set up in Belfast (Laffan, 1994).

Nonetheless, Unionists suspect that the promotion of a federal Europe of the regions might lead to a withering of the border between Northern Ireland and the Irish Republic. These fears are heightened by European Union support for cross-border institutions. The DUP is suspicious of aspects of EU funding directed at cross-border subjects, claiming the existence of a wider agenda. The Special Support Programme for Peace and Reconciliation contains cross-border aspects (Meehan, 2000). The establishment of the EU Special Pro-grammes all-island implementation body accentuated such fears and added to the history of such concerns. In 1984, the Haagerup Report, initiated by the European Parliament and produced by a Danish MEP, advocated a greater role for the European Community in Northern Ireland. Whilst insisting that it was not the role of the Community to propose constitutional change, the Haagerup Report advocated power-sharing and increased intergovernmental co-operation (Haagerup, 1984).

Indeed, as early as 1973, the SDLP's manifesto, *A New North, A New Ireland*, had envisaged the cementing of Northern Ireland's links with the Republic in a European Community context (SDLP, 1973; McAllister, 1977). The leader of the SDLP, John Hume, argues that EU membership has provided 'a new and positive context for the discussion of sovereignty' (Hume, 1993: 229).

Elements within the DUP are also hostile to the perceived influence of the Church of Rome within the Christian-democratic traditions of the Commu-nity, a problem seemingly undetected by all other European political parties.

6.8 Northern Ireland's new consociational democracy? _____

With cross-community power-sharing, proportionality in government, equality and veto rights for the minority, the Good Friday Agreement clearly brought consociational principles to the governance of Northern Ireland (O'Leary, 1999). The new political institutions in Northern Ireland, established by statute in November 1998, got off to an uncertain start, mainly due to the prolonged dispute over paramilitary decommissioning. The diffusion of power to a range of interlocked institutions created problems, even though 80 of the 108 Assembly members were pro-Good Friday Agreement and a clear major-ity of Northern Ireland's population held goodwill towards the new political dispensation. Indeed, the electorate displayed a high level of knowledge of aspects of the Good Friday Agreement (Evans and O'Leary, 1999).

The aims of the settlement were obvious: to locate previously violent differ-ences within an exclusively political arena, to uphold the constitutional status quo whilst formally acknowledging the aspirations of Nationalists, and to cement the idea of the totality of relationships between Britain and Ireland. For a consociational deal to succeed, any lingering external threat, rhetorical or otherwise, to the status of Northern Ireland needed to be removed. Changes to Articles 2 and 3 of the Irish constitution by the Dublin government, ending the territorial claim to Northern Ireland, created space for the deal. In return, the role of the Irish government in the affairs of Northern Ireland was cemented by the establishment of new cross-border bodies, which, although in benign areas, did have executive powers. In this respect, the bi-national approach to the problem of Northern Ireland evident since Sunningdale in 1973, but cemented in the 1985 Anglo-Irish Agreement, had achieved its aim of lessening mutual suspicions of the intentions of the British and Irish governments (Needham, 1999). There were occasional returns to older forms of rhetorical republicanism from the Fianna Fail government in Dublin. The Taoiseach, Bertie Ahern, believed that Ireland would be united in his lifetime due to the 'irresistible dynamic' of the Good Friday Agreement (*Daily Telegraph*, 23 November 1998).

The main criticisms of the Agreement, that it failed to deliver a united Ireland or, more commonly, that it had almost done so, could be dismissed as mere partisanship (O'Leary, 1999). The main intellectual criticism was one hostile to the entire concept of consociational governance. It was argued that a common humanity was denied in Northern Ireland by the rigid division of its politics and parties into two ethnic blocs. Parties were obliged to designate themselves as Unionist, Nationalist or other, legitimising a form of zero-sum politics that a new political dispensation ought to overcome. Yet it was far from clear that such a segregationist approach would be needed on most decisions taken by the Assembly. Weighted majority rules assumed that either community might wish to dominate the other, an assumption which grounded Unionist and Nationalist thinking in the 1920–72 era, despite the public commitment of all parties to power-sharing. Yet many of the contentious decisions, such as policing parades and decommissioning, which impinged upon the early progress of the Assembly were outside its area of competence. Sectarian division was sometimes evident on other issues. As one example, a Sinn Fein Assembly member argued that differences in committee with the PUP on housing arose from a Loyalist 'need to defend territory' (interview with Michelle Gildernew MLA, 28 June 2000). Nonetheless, much Assembly business was characterised by a dull civility and a fair degree of consensus. Ethnic bloc politics were evident, but inter-ethnic bloc rivalries were sometimes less than intra-bloc rivalries, not that either form of competition assisted the development of a focused Executive. Supporters of the Agreement could point to the manner in which ancient enmities were played out amid the relative cordiality of the Assembly, with growing institutional and interpersonal relationships contributing to political progress, often overshadowed by continuing dispute over the decommissioning of paramilitary weapons.

6.9 Conclusion

After the Good Friday Agreement, the role of the Secretary of State was reduced, but it remains substantial. The minister retains control of reserved and excepted matters. These non-devolved functions are substantial, including policing, security and taxation. Devolved government has partly rectified the democratic deficit evident under direct rule. Although the devolved settlement established a complex set of bi-national links, Strand 1 governance, centred upon the Northern Ireland Assembly, is the most important aspect of the new political dispensation. Nonetheless, the vulnerability of Northern Ireland's political institutions was evident in their suspension by the Secretary of State from February to May 2000. Given nearly 30 years of conflict and the abnormality of the state, preliminary difficulties were to be expected.

Chapter 7

Policing Northern Ireland

Changes to the policing of Northern Ireland have been highly controversial. Most security functions are now undertaken by the Police Service of Northern Ireland (PSNI), formerly the Royal Ulster Constabulary (RUC). An Independent Commission on Policing, chaired by Chris Patten, was established under the Good Friday Agreement, leading to the creation of the PSNI. In some border areas the police are still assisted by the British Army. The Army ceased urban patrols by 1998, but is still occasionally redeployed in such areas in times of high tension. As examples, the Army returned briefly to the Shankill area of Belfast in 2000 during a Loyalist feud and was deployed in North Belfast in 2001 as a response to over 50 pipebomb attacks upon Catholics during the first month of that year.

7.1 The legacy of the Troubles

During the Troubles, policing support was provided by the Ulster Defence Regiment and, from 1992, the Royal Irish Regiment. The UDR attracted considerable hostility from some Nationalists. As the replacement for the old 'B' Specials, it was often seen as a sectarian force. Initial success in attracting Catholic members quickly subsided as the conflict escalated. Convictions for offences and alleged collusion with Loyalist paramilitaries led to calls for the regiment's disbandment. Paramilitary activity and a more general lack of support for the police and army amongst Nationalists led to a plethora of emergency security measures, outlined in Table 7.1.

'Unofficial' security-force measures contributed to hostility. Ill-treatment of suspects under interrogation was acknowledged in the Compton Report (1971). In 1976, the European Court of Human Rights found the British government guilty of using inhuman and degrading treatment. Methods included hooding, along with food and sleep deprivation. Three years later, the Bennett Report (1979) confirmed allegations of mistreatment of prisoners. The RUC claimed that injuries were self-inflicted, but the Report insisted that this was true only in certain cases.

Internment without trial proved a disastrous measure. Utilised against the advice of the Army, unhappy that its intelligence was inadequate, a trawl of suspected republicans was undertaken despite scant information. The tactic served mainly to boost recruitment to the IRA. Two-thirds of the

Table 7.1   Main emergency measures introduced

Year	Measure	Feature
1971	Internment	Detention without trial of IRA suspects (ended 1975)
1973	Trial without jury	Single judge decides court case
1974	Prevention of Terrorism Act	Extended detention: exclusion orders
1988	Broadcasting ban	Prohibition on direct television transmission of statements from paramilitary groups (ended 1994)
1998	Emergency powers legislation	Extension of powers of arrest and detention (following Omagh bombing)

2,357 detainees were released after interrogation during the first six months of internment (Hillyard, 1983).

The Diplock Report (1972) recommended the introduction of trial without jury, taking place in what became known as 'Diplock courts'. Their introduction was designed to circumvent the problem of intimidation of jurors. Four main criticisms of the courts system were levelled. Firstly, some doubted the neutrality of the judiciary. Secondly, the introduction of juryless courts produced a high conviction rate of over 90 per cent in cases involving offences related to paramilitary activity. This contrasted with almost unanimous acquittals of the security forces during the early years of Diplock courts (Boyle et al., 1980). Thirdly, there were difficulties over the admissibility of uncorroborated evidence, notably in 'supergrass' trials, in which the prosecution relied upon the evidence of informers. The conviction rate in such trials fell as 10 proceeded between 1983 and 1985, yielding an overall conviction rate of less than half the number of defendants (Greer, 1987: 525). Finally, after 1988, judges were allowed to draw negative conclusions if a defendant exercised the right to silence.

Applied nationally following the Birmingham pub bombings in 1974, the Prevention of Terrorism Act was framed to prevent the transfer of IRA activity to the British mainland. It extended the maximum detention of suspects to seven days and led to the banning from the mainland of several members of political parties linked to paramilitaries. The 1978 Emergency Provisions Act provided a further legal basis for the checkpoints and searches already used by the security forces. As early as 1973, 75,000 house searches had been conducted, amounting to a search of one in every five homes (Hillyard, 1983: 41). From 1973 to mid-1987, 574,012 such searches were conducted (Dickson, 1991: 161–2). Finally, the broadcasting ban upon the advocacy of violence removed the direct transmission of speakers from parties representative of paramilitary groups. The prohibition did not apply during election campaigns. Designed to deny the 'oxygen of publicity', the ban provided work for a number of actors whose voices were dubbed over interviews. This form of employment appeared somewhat less lucrative when Loyalist paramilitaries indicated that surrogate Sinn Fein speakers would be targets. The broadcasting ban was lifted immediately after the IRA's announcement of a ceasefire in 1994.

7.2 The critique of the RUC

One of the most obvious illustrations of the problems of Northern Ireland is the lack of consensus over policing. Most Unionists were highly supportive of the RUC and many felt change was unnecessary. The Ulster Unionist Party leader, David Trimble, pointed to the conclusion of the House of Commons Select Committee on Northern Ireland Affairs that 'there is no clear reason to make a special case of the RUC by changing its name' (*The Times*, 27 August 1999). Many Nationalists believed that drastic changes were needed. A large number of Nationalists viewed the RUC as instinctively Unionist, the armed wing of an illegitimate state. Ninety-four per cent of SDLP members desired radical reform of the RUC (author's survey, 1999); Sinn Fein demanded its disbandment. One survey indicated that two-thirds of Catholics favoured disbandment (Hadden *et al.*, 1996). The Police Authority of Northern Ireland's own figures indicated the differences in outlook between the two communities (Table 7.2). Many Unionists argued that the RUC had impossible tasks in attempting to appear even-handed and in combatting a guerilla war without alienating the community from which the IRA gathered support. The police force could hardly be anti-state. Part of the role of any police force, argued defenders of the RUC, is to uphold the state. Such supporters argued that the sensitivities accruing to normal liberal policing techniques were inapplicable to Northern Ireland.

The number of RUC officers killed between 1969 and 1999 was 303 (*see* Table 7.3). During the same period, 8,728 officers were injured (*Sunday Times*, 12 August 1999), and 70 officers committed suicide (*The Times*, 26 August

Table 7.2　Perceptions of the RUC (%)

Perception	Protestant	Catholic	Total
Treat Catholics better	8	0	5
Treat Protestants better	15	64	35
Treat both equally	69	26	51
Don't know/Refused to answer	8	9	9

Source: adapted from Police Authority for Northern Ireland, 1997: 39.

Table 7.3　Deaths in the Northern Ireland conflict 1969–99

Civilians	2,038
RUC	303
British Army	503
UDR/RIR	206
Republican paramilitary	392
Loyalist paramilitary	144
Other	158

Source: adapted from McKittrick *et al.*, 1999: 1474.

1999). The RUC was responsible for 53 deaths (*Guardian*, 26 August 1999). The RUC, however, was criticised even by some Loyalists who argued that it was 'too much a police force and not a police service' (Ervine, 1996). The difficulty, however, lay in gaining the cross-community acceptance which might allow such a development.

During the early 1980s, Nationalist distrust of the RUC increased following allegations that the force was pursuing a 'shoot-to-kill' policy against suspected Republican paramilitaries. Appointed to investigate the accusations, the Deputy Chief Constable of Greater Manchester, John Stalker, was inexplicably removed from the inquiry. Stalker's removal was followed by a concerted but unsuccessful attempt to denigrate his character (Stalker, 1988). Although the British government accepted that a cover-up had been attempted by elements within the RUC, it ruled out prosecutions.

Throughout the Troubles, the RUC was reliant upon core elements in its fight against terrorism: intelligence, informers and co-operation with the Garda Siochana (Irish police). Relations between the two police forces improved markedly, paralleled by intergovernmental co-operation on the extradition of suspected terrorists.

Anxiety to foster good relations prompted limited change by the RUC on the issue of accountability. It issued annual reports and produced a Charter in 1993. Whilst operational decisions remained the prerogative of the Chief Constable, the Northern Ireland Police Authority assumed responsibility for senior appointments, finance and scrutiny of complaints procedures. Appointments to the Police Authority were made by the Secretary of State. This led to accusations of bias. Connolly (1990) makes the point that the targeting of appointees by the IRA did not improve the balance of community representation.

Other than for a few months following the Hunt Report (1969), the RUC has always been armed. The RUC continually under-recruited Catholics, a problem partly explained by intimidation from the IRA. However, to blame IRA activity for the permanent failure of RUC to recruit Catholics in accordance with the population balance is 'simply not historically convincing' (McGarry and O'Leary, 1999: 16). Throughout the history of Northern Ireland, Catholics displayed a reluctance to join the RUC, seen as part of the apparatus of a sectarian state (Ellison and Smyth, 1999). During the first IRA ceasefire of the mid-1990s, one in five applicants to the RUC was Catholic, resulting in 16.5 per cent of new recruits being of that religion (Bew and Gillespie, 1996). This recruitment figure nonetheless represented less than half the percentage of Catholics who ought to be recruited, given the population balance. In 1998, the religious imbalance within the RUC was as acute as at any period in the history of the force: 88.3 per cent of its officers were Protestant, with Catholics amounting to a mere 8.3 per cent (Patten Report, 1999: 82). The Chief Constable of the RUC indicated his belief that a combination of threats and peer pressure were the main deterrents to Catholics joining the force (Flanagan, 1998). During the 1997 General Election, Labour promised measures to strengthen confidence in policing (Randall, 1998). Catholic applications had increased substantially by 2001.

7.3 The Patten Commission Report

The Independent Commission on Policing (the Patten Commission) established under the Good Friday Agreement was given the task of ensuring that Northern Ireland's police service attracted support and membership across the community. The Patten Commission's report, published in September 1999 after 36 meetings with the public, acknowledged that the RUC enjoyed overall high levels of public support, but that significant attitudinal variation existed between Protestants and Catholics. Many Catholics believed that the police force was too clearly associated with the defence of the state. The police force was seen by such critics as too Unionist and too Protestant. The RUC was also seen as lacking accountability.

Patten proposed measures designed to change the culture, ethos, religious balance and accountability of the force, whilst pruning its size in the new post-Troubles dispensation. The main proposed changes were:

1. the renaming of the police force, to become the Northern Ireland Police Service (later changed to the Police Service of Northern Ireland);
2. the removal of associations with Britishness or Irishness (i.e. the Crown and Shamrock on the force badge), with the force to fly its own flag, rather than the Union Jack, above buildings;
3. the creation of a new Policing Board, to replace the Police Authority;
4. the establishment of District Policing Partnership Bodies, to replace Community and Police Liaison Committees;
5. a reduction in the size of the force from 13,000 to 7,500;
6. future recruitment to be on a 50–50 Protestant and Catholic basis;
7. the integration of Special Branch within normal policing roles;
8. officers to swear an oath of commitment to human rights.

Much of the Patten Report was concerned with decentralisation, a riposte to the centralising tendencies found in respect of policing throughout the United Kingdom (McGarry, 2000). However, the Report was fervently opposed by Unionists, with their hostility supported to a limited extent by some Conservative MPs at Westminster. For Unionists, radical reform of the RUC amounted to yet more difficult emotional baggage associated with the Good Friday Agreement. Many feared the negative impact upon policing of an emasculation of the force, either through an inability to cope with any revival of paramilitary activity, or through the increase in ordinary crime likely to arise from a decline in paramilitarism. In 2000, the Ulster Unionist Council instructed the UUP not to re-enter the Northern Ireland Executive unless the title of RUC was retained. Fewer than one in five members of the Ulster Unionist Council backed full implementation of the Patten proposals (Tonge and Evans, 2001a). The lack of cross-community consensus on policing changes was such that sectarian divisions were evident even in the avowedly non-sectarian Alliance Party. Seventy-seven per cent of its Catholic members demanded full implementation of the changes proposed by the Patten Commission, but only half of the party's Protestant members supported reform (Tonge and Evans, 2001b).

Aside from religious imbalance, Patten was vexed by the lack of accountability of the force. Nationalists boycotted the Police Authority and Community Police-Liaison committees, which came to be seen as pro-Unionist and pro-RUC. The only other potential vehicle of change, Her Majesty's Inspectorate of Constabulary, tended to make only minor recommendations for change to address fundamental long-term problems. In response to the clear religious imbalance in the force, the Inspectorate proposed the 'establishment of a working group' to monitor religious representation, in response to which the RUC indicated it was 'establishing a focus group' (RUC Chief Constable's Report, 1996: 73). The Patten Commission wished to start afresh in terms of scrutiny of the RUC. The new, nineteen-member Policing Board promised a variety of political inputs, being composed of ten representatives of parties within the Northern Ireland Executive (but not Executive members) and nine members drawn from other organisations, appointed by the First and Deputy First Ministers. The District Policing Partnership Boards (DPPBs) were designed to offer local accountability. They would act as committees of district councils, from which a majority of their members would be drawn. The DPPBs would act as a consultative forum (unlike the Policing Board, which had a more formal supervisory role) and allow greater explanation of police activity, with the force requested to account for its actions on a regular basis. Patten, however, offered an imprecise description of what these new arrangements would constitute in terms of operational independence for the Chief Constable of the new force, leaving this open to interpretation and circumstance (Dickson, 2000).

7.4 Implementing Patten

The creation of local policing boards alarmed Unionists fearful of substantial input from Sinn Fein's elected representatives. Sinn Fein would also be entitled to two seats on the Policing Board, reflecting its numerical representation in the Assembly Executive. Former paramilitary members would not, however, be permitted to join the newly constituted police force. Unionists resented the symbolic removal of 'trappings of Britishness' which the new force would be obliged to endure. The Northern Ireland Assembly rejected the Patten Report by 50 votes to 42, a meaningless gesture given that policing remained a reserved power controlled by the Secretary of State. The award of the George Cross to the RUC, seen by critics as an almost posthumous tribute, did little to assuage criticism of the proposals for the new force. In January 2000, the British government announced that it accepted the Patten Report, although the name of the new force would be slightly different: the Police Service of Northern Ireland (PSNI). It was emphasised that the change of name did not mean the disbandment of the RUC. The Bill which passed through parliament, however, was sufficiently different from the original report for one member of the Patten Commission to claim that it 'dismantles the foundations on which the Patten Commission's plan was built' (Clifford Shearing, *Guardian*, 14 November 2000). The thrust of Shearing's argument was that the Patten

Report had been diluted to a police Bill rather than a policing Bill, in that it would alter operational aspects of police work without changing the ethos or accountability of Northern Ireland's police force.

Many changes to the police and modes of policing proceeded, including the merger of Special Branch and the CID, the dismantling of interrogation centres and reductions in size, with 500 officers leaving by April 2000. An independent agency was placed in charge of recruitment. A Police Ombudsman, with a staff of 105, replaced the Independent Commission for Police Complaints. However, there were large discrepancies from the Patten proposals, shifts linked to the role of Northern Ireland Office officials in drafting legislation (O'Leary, 2001). The powers of the Policing Board and the District Boards were weaker than originally envisaged. Belfast was not to be divided into four district policing boards, the original proposal under which Sinn Fein would have exercised much influence in west and north Belfast. The new oath, not requiring allegiance to the Queen, was to be sworn only by new officers. The Secretary of State was given powers over flag displays, emblems and the force's name. The reduction in numbers swearing the new oath was justified by the Secretary of State on the basis that 'existing officers have already been attested as constables and cannot be required to take the new oath' (Northern Ireland Office, 2000: 3). The Secretary of State assumed responsibility for nominations of non-elected members of the Policing Board, not the First Minister and Deputy First Ministers proposed by Patten. Sinn Fein refused to recommend that Nationalists join the force and declined places on the Policing Board. The abnormality of Northern Ireland was thus evidence by the refusal of government ministers (from Sinn Fein) refusing to back the state's police force. The SDLP backed the new force, after the British Government promised further implementation of the Patten proposals.

7.5 Policing parades

One of the more difficult problems confronting Northern Ireland's police force in the latter half of the 1990s became that of policing the 'marching season'. Between Easter and the end of August each year, nearly 3,000 parades take place. Most of these are Orange Order marches, a few of which pass through areas populated by Nationalists. Some Catholics object to what they perceive as displays of Protestant triumphalism. After initially banning an Orange parade through parts of Drumcree in 1996, the RUC reversed its decision, outraging local Catholic residents, who claimed the force had given in to the threat posed by Orange disobedience. As serious rioting erupted across Northern Ireland, the retiring Chief Constable, Hugh Annesley, declared that the RUC was in an 'impossible position'. One month later, the Secretary of State, acting on the advice of the Chief Constable, decided to prevent the Protestant Apprentice Boys' march from parading along the full length of Derry's walls, to commemorate the Siege of Derry. Operational decisions acquired a political flavour.

Appointed in 1996, the Chief Constable, Ronnie Flanagan, pledged to assist local communities in resolving disputes over contentious parades. Negotiations were impaired by suspicions on both sides. The Orange Order has been reluctant to deal with residents' groups, arguing they are Sinn Fein 'fronts' and citing the comments of Sinn Fein's president, Gerry Adams, to an internal party conference that 'three years of hard work' went into creating Drumcree and other confrontations (Haddick-Flynn, 1999: 348). Republicans stress the diverse membership of residents' groups and widespread opposition to sectarian parades.

Following the furore over parades in 1995 and 1996, the British government set up a committee of Review of Parades and Marches, comprising two members of the clergy and chaired by the vice-chancellor of Oxford University, Dr Peter North. After receiving 300 submissions and holding 93 meetings with 270 people, the North Review proposed that:

1. a Parades Commission should adjudicate disputes arising from the route or conduct of marches;
2. it should be a criminal offence if the Commission's decisions were ignored;
3. the RUC would have the right of appeal to the Northern Ireland Secretary in respect of a decision of the Parades Commission;
4. the RUC would retain the power to halt an approved parade on public-order grounds.

The North Report reduced the role of the RUC in determining which parades could proceed, but also provided a form of veto by which the RUC could make its views known in advance of a parade by appealing against a decision by the commission. The RUC would still remain in charge of the event on the day and would thus retain operational control, which by implication might involve rerouting.

In supporting the establishment of a Parades Commission, the Labour government elected in 1997 appeared keen to place the question of consent for parades on a more formal, systematic basis. Equally anxious to be relieved of direct responsibility for licensing parades, the RUC also supported the North proposals. Of the 3,160 parades in 1996, the North Report found that 20 had been banned or declared illegal; 31 were either re-routed or made subject to conditions, and 15 led to disorder. Unionists argued that the presence of a Commission would merely create a 'grievance factory' (Trimble, 1997: 15). Local accommodations would become less likely, as residents' groups would insist upon referral to the adjudicating body. Over the next few years, the Parades Commission resolved some disputes over parades through its adjudications, although a number of Orange marches and Parades Commission decisions remained the subjects of controversy.

7.6 The British Army

The presence of the British Army in Northern Ireland was symptomatic of the absence of policing by consensus. Between 1969 and 1999, the Army suffered 503 losses and inflicted 318 deaths (*Guardian*, 26 August 1999; McKittrick *et al.*, 1999: 1474). In total, the security forces were responsible for approximately 10 per cent of the deaths during the Troubles. Republicans committed 60 per cent of the killings and Loyalists were responsible for 26 per cent. The British Army's presence indicated how the problem of Northern Ireland is a product of both *endogenous* and *exogenous* factors (O'Leary, 1985; McGarry and O'Leary, 1995). Endogenous factors are problems *internal* to Northern Ireland. Thus, in 1969 the British Army was sent to the Province primarily to halt an apparent conflict between Protestants and Catholics. During this early period of the Troubles, many saw the problem as one of competing religious dominations engaged in feuding based upon religious sectarianism. This particular brand of endogenous explanation justified the peacekeeper role of the British Army.

Alternative endogenous explanations soon emerged. These emphasised that conflict was based upon the struggle between two communities over who governed Northern Ireland. Unionists wished the Province to remain British. Nationalists sought unity with the remainder of Ireland. Under such explanations the British Army could not be seen as a neutral peacekeeper. Its role was to uphold the status quo by defeating the armed rebellion against British rule within Northern Ireland. During the course of its duties, the Army was also obliged to confront Loyalist 'ultras' who waged war to defend the British presence, but this was insufficient for the Army to be perceived as neutral.

Exogenous, or *external*, explanations also undermined the neutrality argument. Such explanations frequently saw Northern Ireland as the site of a traditional British versus Irish conflict over territory. For Republicans, the Troubles were the final leg of a centuries-old colonial struggle to remove Britain from Ireland. British soldiers represented a visible foreign enemy to be confronted.

From its arrival in Northern Ireland in August 1969, the Army, under the command of General Ian Freeland, openly recognised the limits of its role as a buffer force. General Freeland insisted that a political solution was required if amiable relations with the Catholic community were to be prolonged. Within a year, the deterioration in relations was almost complete and by 1972, 22,000 British troops were based in Northern Ireland.

The number of troops was reduced substantially following the paramilitary ceasefires in 1994. Within one year, the Army ended regular patrols in Belfast and overall, army patrols fell by 75 per cent. However, the temporary fracture of the IRA ceasefire in 1996 saw the number of troops return briefly to the levels of the 1970s, before falling substantially after the renewal of the IRA ceasefire in 1997 and the 1998 Good Friday Agreement. Other personnel have supported regular units of the police and army. They include Special Branch, the intelligence services and the Special Air Service (SAS). All these bodies were engaged in gathering information regarding the activities of paramilitary organisations. In some cases covert operations were carried out as part of a 'dirty war' on a semi-autonomous basis, unknown to the Regular Army and police force. The period 1981–94 was one of active counter-insurgency. Rivalry between the Special Branch in London and the RUC's own version concerning the handling of informants created internal tensions between organisations working towards the same objectives (Dillon, 1990).

Present in Northern Ireland since 1969, the SAS supported the security forces in counter-insurgency. It participated alongside the RUC in the killing of eight IRA members at Loughall in 1987, the biggest losses sustained by the Provisionals in a single incident. Its final killings of IRA personnel occurred in 1992. One highly critical account claims various phases of SAS activity have occurred: intelligence-gathering, support for Protestant paramilitaries, a sustained offensive in South Armagh, stakeouts and shoot-to-kill (Murray, 1990).

Urban (1992) suggests that the clandestine operations of the SAS assumed greater importance following the advent of the police-primacy strategy in 1976. From this point until 1987, the SAS and the Army's élite surveillance unit, 14 Intelligence Company, killed 32 members of Republican paramilitary organisations. Despite its far greater numerical strength, the Regular Army undertook 11 such killings. No Loyalists were killed during this period. Shrouded in secrecy, members of the SAS rarely attended inquests. The Army engaged in a war of attrition against the IRA. It faced the problem of engaging in military actions against a background of a continued hybrid of normal and emergency law and within a highly sensitive political context. As the British Army and the IRA appeared incapable of scoring an outright military victory, the notion of an 'acceptable level of violence' developed, in which the non-escalation of violence was deemed a relative success. Provisional IRA violence continued until 1994, revived briefly in 1996–7. Only with the development of a political solution was the military impasse broken.

7.7 Ulsterisation and criminalisation

After the mid-1970s, the basis of government policy was to emphasise that members of paramilitary groups were common criminals. The Good Friday Agreement, however, tacitly recognised paramilitary offenders as prisoners of war, permitting their release within two years of the end of the conflict, irrespective of the actions committed. Post-ceasefire, there has also been a determined attempt to normalise policing. Even during the Troubles, the RUC had long undertaken most duties, with the Army usually operating in a supporting role. The process by which the management of security was undertaken increasingly by the local force of the RUC was known as 'Ulsterisation', or police primacy. The treatment of members of paramilitary groups as common criminals was known as criminalisation. These responses were seen as the most appropriate means of 'keeping the lid on' in terms of the security situation.

Both responses began under the Secretary of State for Northern Ireland, Merlyn Rees. He was assisted by a partially observed IRA ceasefire in 1975, which led to a decline in the strength of the organisation. During this period, contacts between the British government and the IRA were facilitated by the establishment of a number of incident centres. The IRA believed its military campaign made British withdrawal imminent. Indeed, the British government encouraged such thinking as a means of prolonging the ceasefire (Bew and Patterson, 1985).

In 'normalising' life in the Province, the British government released those detained under internment by 1975. Detention without trial was the most manifest symbol of the abnormality of the security situation. Furthermore, it had been highly ineffective and its abandonment was welcomed by the security forces. Selective detention orders ensured that individuals could be arrested according to the decree of a senior army officer and detained indefinitely.

Under the new criminalisation approach, those arrested and convicted would be treated in a manner similar to 'ODCs' – ordinary decent criminals, in the parlance of the security forces. A plethora of anti-terrorist laws was introduced. Security policy began to operate under a set of defined rules, rather than on the *ad hoc* basis that characterised the approach pre-1974. As part of the Ulsterisation process, the RUC would normally assume responsibility for undertaking arrests and processing the case against the accused. Critics argued that this was a false attempt at normalising procedures, given the presence of juryless courts and special interrogation centres.

Previously, the award of special-category status in 1972 was of considerable symbolic and practical value to the paramilitary groups. It appeared to confirm their role as 'soldiers' engaged in struggle. Special-category status also allowed detainees free association, ensuring that command structures were easily retained within prison. These features did not entirely vanish with the abolition of special status. Command hierarchies were maintained within paramilitary groups. The British government was determined to remove symbols of legitimacy to the 'armed struggle'. In 1975, the Gardiner Committee argued that the award of special-category status had been an error and its removal was swift (Gardiner Report, 1975). The removal of special-category status was followed by attempts to portray the IRA leadership as 'godfathers' and racketeers.

Ulsterisation and criminalisation were continued in yet stronger fashion by Rees' successor, Roy Mason. He was unimpressed by the calibre of local politicians and believed that there was little point in attempting to break the political stalemate which had followed the collapse of power-sharing in 1974. Mason concentrated attention upon policies designed to minimise the impact of paramilitary activity, believing that tough security measures could defeat the IRA.

There was a scant peace dividend arising from the new security approach. In 1976, there were 297 deaths related to the Troubles. Only 1972 yielded a higher death toll. The British Army suffered far fewer losses, however, as Republican violence was 'funnelled inwards into internecine feuding, sectarian murder and gangsterism' (Bishop and Mallie, 1988: 275). Although the rate of deaths fell sharply in 1977 and 1978, a series of prominent IRA atrocities in 1979 indicated the limits of strategies promoting normality. During that year, 18 soldiers were killed in a massacre at Warrenpoint. Lord Mountbatten was murdered in the Irish Republic and the Conservative Party Shadow Northern Ireland Secretary, Airey Neave, was blown up by a bomb planted by the Irish National Liberation Army, a left-wing offshoot of the IRA. Although the overall level of violence was reduced, Ulsterisation and criminalisation also revealed the durability of the terrorist campaign, despite the pledge of Mason to squeeze the IRA 'like a tube of toothpaste' (quoted in Urban, 1992: 11).

Ulsterisation and criminalisation did not offer political solutions. Furthermore, their adoption was far from total. Whilst 'normal' policing resumed, there was concurrently an increased reliance upon the undercover operations of the SAS. In addition to uncompromising security policies, Mason placed faith in economic development. He resolved to attract inward investment and provide assistance for industry, although the reality was that even heavy subsidies did little to prevent the rate of unemployment continuing to be the highest in the United Kingdom. Given the more casualised nature of unemployment amongst Catholics, considerable economic disparities remained between the two communities.

Ulsterisation was an attempt to return to internal security. By removing the army from frontline operations, it was hoped that antagonism would be reduced. It amounted to a switch from colonial counter-insurgency techniques towards an attempt to place crisis policing within a liberal democratic framework (Newsinger, 1995). Use of a local police force in place of the Army might have been a successful tactic if it were a case of policing with consent. However, mistrust of the RUC amongst sections of the Nationalist population meant that the primacy of the RUC achieved little. Numbers of troops fell from 21,000 in 1972 to 13,500 by 1978, but this was compensated by increased recruitment to the RUC and UDR. Theoretically at least, the RUC now controlled security activity in Northern Ireland.

7.8 Conclusion

Decommissioning apart, reform of Northern Ireland's police force has been as controversial as any aspect of the Good Friday Agreement. The RUC was liked and supported by most Unionists, but criticised by many Nationalists and loathed by some. Its religious imbalance and lack of accountability made change inevitable. Such changes alienated some Unionists and were too marginal to satisfy Republicans. As such, policing in Northern Ireland remains highly politicised and non-consensual, clear indicators of the insecurity of the state.

Chapter 8

The roles of religion

Religion continues to play an influential role in society in Northern Ireland. Labelling by religious denomination remains the most convenient method of identifying the division between the communities. The terms Catholic and Protestant are preferred to Nationalist and Unionist, or Republican and Loyalist, as they embrace the vast majority of people and are less problematic than other labels.

Application of the label Nationalist to a community implies that all members of that community support Irish unity. This is not necessarily the case. The use of religious labels to describe communities is also unsatisfactory. Such methodology fails to distinguish the extent of religious commitment and may include non-believers when applied to a geographical area. Other communities are also ignored, such as the Asian community in Northern Ireland, which has also endured discrimination. In an imperfect world, use of the Catholic and Protestant religious labels has remained common only through a lack of suitable alternatives.

8.1 The extent of religiosity

Although Northern Ireland has not been exempt from the trend towards secularism within western Europe, it has remained perhaps the most resistant region. Over half of the population attends church weekly. The overwhelming majority of members of the major political parties claim to practise their religious faith. Non-church weddings are rare, whilst Northern Ireland has a substantially lower rate of births outside marriage than elsewhere in the United Kingdom. The provisions of the 1967 Abortion Act permitting abortion have not been extended to Northern Ireland.

The overwhelming majority of people identify themselves as either Catholic or Protestant, as Table 8.1 indicates. Religious labels are so pervasive that the ancient joke over whether one is a Protestant or a Catholic atheist still has some resonance.

Many believe that the number of Catholics will outgrow the figure for Protestants, although there is considerable dispute over when this will occur. Higher Catholic birth rates during previous decades closed the gap. Parity of numbers might already have occurred had there not been persistently high rates of Catholic emigration. Unionists fear this demographic change, as recent

Table 8.1   Religious denominations in Northern Ireland

	Percentage
Protestant	50.6
Catholic	38.4
None	3.7
Not stated	7.3

Source: adapted from Northern Ireland Census 1991, Religion Report.

political agreements have stressed that legislation will be enacted to provide for a united Ireland if that is what the majority of the population of Northern Ireland desire.

Nonetheless, it is unlikely that a majority in favour of voting the state of Northern Ireland out of existence will emerge for at least another century. There remains a significant minority of Catholics who do not wish this scenario. It is, of course, possible that if Catholics do become a majority, these 'dissident' Catholics may support unity as they might feel it had a more democratic basis.

8.2 Protestant churches and beliefs

It is misleading to describe the Protestant Church as if it were a singular entity. Table 8.2 shows the strength of the main Protestant Churches in terms of their proportion of the entire population of Northern Ireland.

The Presbyterian Church in Northern Ireland dates back to the Scots settlers of the early seventeenth century. It began to form part of a coherent Protestant 'family' of churches in the 1800s. Loosely controlled by a General Assembly which oversees the system of synods, presbyteries and congregations, the Presbyterian Church enjoys the support of nearly half the Protestant population in Northern Ireland.

Table 8.2   Protestant denominations in Northern Ireland

Denomination	**Percentage of the population (entire)**
Presbyterian	21
Church of Ireland	18
Methodist	4
Baptist	1
Congregationalist	1
Free Presbyterian	1
Others	4
Total	50

Source: adapted from Northern Ireland Census 1991, Religion Report.

The Church of Ireland is perhaps the most liberal of the Protestant churches, in terms of religion and political outlook. According to one commentator, it is the Protestant movement most likely to overcome Unionist hostility to greater political association with the rest of Ireland (Irvine, 1991). Dr Robert Eames, head of the Church of Ireland, performed a mediation role in the construction of the peace process in the 1990s, although this task was carried out in conjunction with the Rev. Roy Magee, a representative of the more religiously and politically conservative Presbyterian Church.

Organised on an all-Ireland basis, the Church is headed by 12 bishops, the most senior of whom is the primate of all Ireland. Once the Established Church in Ireland and part of the Anglican community, its forms of worship are nonetheless distinct from the high-church Anglo-Catholicism sometimes found in England. Although sometimes associated with more prosperous sections of society, support for the Church of Ireland straddles the social classes.

Many of the Protestant churches have co-operated in the ecumenical movement designed to achieve greater Christian unity. Backed by assistance from American Presbyterian churches, a number of reconciliation initiatives have been undertaken. These began with the inter-church Corrymeela Community project in 1965 and more recently have involved neighbourhood reconciliation schemes in Belfast and Derry (Beerman and Mahony, 1993).

As a creed, Protestantism has a number of core themes. At the considerable risk of oversimplification, these might be summarised as:

1. all humans are sinners;
2. God exists and eternal salvation is possible to wipe away sins;
3. to achieve salvation, the word of God must be followed;
4. the Bible is the true word of God;
5. because the Bible is the true word, there is no need for mass, priests or 'false worship'.

Few Protestants elsewhere in the United Kingdom would have much regard for point five. Indeed, leaders of the main churches in Northern Ireland meet regularly and generally enjoy cordial relations. There exists a broad division between liberal and evangelical wings of Protestantism. In Belfast, they are fairly equally represented within the Presbyterian and Methodist churches. Smaller churches tend to contain higher proportions of fundamentalists. Such churches often base teachings upon a literal reading of scripture.

Fundamentalists within the Presbyterian Church are much less enthusiastic towards ecumenism. Their beliefs are rooted in Scottish Calvinism, in which salvation is undeserved, but may be awarded by God. Believing that the Bible is the divine work of God, they argue that only those who respond to the gospel message will be saved. Good behaviour is not sufficient as it is predestined as to whether they are to be saved or otherwise (Bruce, 1986). Fundamentalists are usually sabbatarians, placing great stress upon strict religious observance on Sunday, allied to limitation upon the pursuit of leisure. Within this creed there exists the notion of the Chosen People, destined to be delivered from hell. Fundamentalists and evangelicals differ, therefore, from the universalism

Table 8.3 Religious attitudes of Protestants in Northern Ireland

Issue	Party supported		
	DUP	UUP	Alliance
		(Percentage agreeing)	
Willing to share worship with Catholics	5	22	66
Aim for unity with Catholic Church	4	4	19
Aim for greater religious and social co-operation	21	45	64
School to be entirely Protestant	53	31	7
Happy for child to marry Catholic	2	7	41

Source: adapted from Lambkin (1996).

of liberal Protestantism under which all Christians may be saved whatever the central tenets of their faith.

Most fundamentalist of all is the Free Presbyterian Church, a tiny church even though its membership its growing. Free Presbyterianism has been described as a 'subspecies of conservative evangelicalism' (Bruce, 1986: 200). Its spiritual leader, the Rev. Ian Paisley, has denounced Catholicism and used his own church, political party and newspaper to denounce the 'false gods' of Rome.

He has declared:

> Through Popery the Devil has shut up the way to our inheritance. Priestcraft, superstition and papalism with all their attendant vices of murder, theft, immorality, lust and incest blocked the way to the land of gospel liberty' (*Protestant Telegraph*, 4 January 1967, cited in Coogan, 1995: 45).

Paisley and his followers campaign against any 'watering-down' of the principles of Protestantism and have demonstrated against co-operative ecumenical gestures. Paisleyites do not see their own approach as anti-Catholic. Indeed, Paisley believes it is his duty to represent individual Catholics within his political constituency. Instead, his religious fundamentalism is anti-Catholic Church, viewing the Pope as the Antichrist.

The ecumenical movement has had less of an impact in Northern Ireland than elsewhere in the United Kingdom. Only a minority of Protestants would be willing to share worship with Catholics, although it should be noted a majority of Protestants also disdain participation in worship with Free Presbyterians (Boal *et al.*, 1991). Attitudes amongst Protestants differ greatly according to which political party they support. The non-sectarian Alliance Party contains the highest number of liberal Protestants relatively unconcerned over integration with Catholics. The Democratic Unionist Party contains the highest number of those professing distrust of closer co-operation. These attitudinal differences are indicated in Table 8.3.

8.3 Orangeism

Religious divisions in Northern Ireland are heightened by the prominence of church-based social activity. Protestants may attend Sunday School, the Boys'

Brigade and Bible study groups, activities rarely undertaken by Catholics. Other than the churches themselves, the main Protestant institution is the Loyal Institution of Ireland, otherwise known as the Orange Order. It is headed by the Grand Master, Robert Saulters, and is organised into county, district and local lodges.

Established in 1795 following the Battle of Diamond between Protestants and Catholics, the Orange Order commemorates the victory of the Protestant King William III, Prince of Orange, over the Catholic King James in 1690. This triumph is celebrated annually on 12 July. Tens of thousands participate, with hundreds of parades feeding to 20 centres, where religious and political speeches are heard. The day is a public holiday in Northern Ireland. The Orange Order views the victory as a historic triumph for civil and religious liberty, which it pledged to defend. The main aims of the Order are:

1. to uphold belief in God;
2. to maintain the Protestant Crown;
3. to defend the Protestant faith;
4. to oppose the Church of Rome;

Orange Order members are required to oppose the 'fatal errors and doctrines of the Church of Rome' (Kennedy, 1995: 3). They must also resist any attempt by the Catholic Church to extend its power. Forbidden from marrying a Catholic, a member of the Orange Order is also barred from participating in a Catholic act of worship.

Critics argue that the Order fosters religious sectarianism, which might be defined as bigotry or narrow-mindedness in following one's denomination. One study of the Order attests that 'its references to "popery" must be seen as crudely insulting, not just to the Catholic religion but to neighbours and fellow citizens who espouse that religion' (Haddick-Flynn, 1999: 353–4). Guelke (1988: 38) argues that Orange marches are 'an assertion of the physical dominance of the Protestant community'. In refuting these charges, the Order points out that an Orangeman is required to be 'ever abstaining from all un-charitable words, actions or sentiments towards his Roman Catholic brethren'. A sympathetic account of the Orange Order argues that it is a community 'misrepresented and traduced' (Dudley Edwards, 1999: xii).

Although the Orange Order is a global institution, Northern Ireland is the only real centre of Orangeism. Elsewhere, the Order has sizeable numbers only in the west of Scotland and, to a much lesser extent nowadays, on Merseyside. It possesses 4,000 members in the Irish Republic. Membership in Northern Ireland is estimated at 80,000. There is also a small Association of Loyal Orangewomen and a separate Independent Orange Order.

Primary functions of the Orange Order have been to achieve unity across the different Protestant denominations and support amongst various social classes. The Order has traditionally attracted support amongst both Presby-terians and members of the Church of Ireland. It appeals even to those who are not churchgoers, as Douds (1995: 14) describes:

The Order still has a pivotal role within Ulster. Protestantism and all the Protestant Churches are to some extent influenced by it. The urban working-class have been lost to the main Protestant denominations for some years now and the only contact these people are likely to have with any vaguely religious body is the Order.

Two similar Protestant institutions exist. Founded in 1814, the Apprentice Boys of Derry organisation contains 12,000 members. New recruits are initiated within the walls of the city of Derry. The Apprentice Boys celebrate the lifting of the Siege of Derry in August 1689, when William of Orange arrived to relieve the 13 apprentice boys who had slammed shut the gates of Derry to keep out the Catholic King James. Six of the eight Parent Clubs within the organisation are named after leaders of the Siege.

Apprentice Boys see their parades, including the main August commemoration of the Siege, as a celebration of a victory for civil and religious liberties. Catholics, who form a majority in Derry, tend to be critical of what they see as triumphalist parades. In 1995, the Apprentice Boys revived their tradition of walking the length of the city walls, reopened for the first time since the start of the Troubles. Opposition from Nationalist residents of the nearby Bogside led to the Apprentice Boys being banned from a section of the walls in August 1996. Since then, however, an accommodation has usually been reached between the Apprentice Boys and local groups. Each December, the Apprentice Boys stage a smaller parade commemorating the closure of the gates of the city. An effigy of Colonel Lundy is burnt. Lundy attempted to negotiate a surrender of the defiant Protestants, and the term 'Lundy' is a term meaning traitor within the Protestant community. As part of an attempt to lessen the tension caused by its annual commemoration, the Nationalist-controlled Derry City Council and the Community Relations Council have encouraged cultural celebrations of the Siege of Derry. In doing so, they believed that it provided respect for the Protestant tradition. Overall, Derry has not endured the extent of sectarian tensions suffered in Belfast.

Often regarded as the 'élite' of the Orange Order, the Royal Black Preceptory is sometimes known as the Royal Black Institution, or as the Imperial Grand Black Chapter of the British Commonwealth. Membership throughout Northern Ireland is estimated at 30,000. The headquarters of the organisation is based in Lurgan, Armagh. Aims and principles of the Institution are similar to those held by the Orange Order. 'Blackmen' must also be members of the Orange Order. The Preceptory stages its main parade on the final Saturday in August.

8.4 The Catholic Church in Ireland

Organised on an all-Ireland basis, the Catholic Church is easily the biggest single institution in Ireland, as 95 per cent of the population south of the border claim membership, in addition to 40 per cent in the North. The leader of the Catholic Church in Ireland is based in the ecclesiastical capital of the island, Armagh. He is at the apex of a hierarchy of priests and bishops organised into various dioceses.

Until the 1980s, the Catholic Church enjoyed a hegemonic role within the Irish Republic. Political independence allowed the development of legislation in support of a symbol of that independence. Religious identity was seen as a central symbol of nationality and, therefore, politics. The absence of a significant party of the left, or an urban proletariat, prevented the development of the anti-clerical sentiment which developed in some European countries.

The teachings of the Church were reflected in laws prohibiting divorce, contraception and abortion. If Northern Ireland was a Protestant state for a Protestant people, so the Republic was undoubtedly a mirror image, a Catholic state for a Catholic people. In 1972 the special position of the Catholic Church was removed from Article 44 of the constitution, but the strength of the Catholic Church was acknowledged by a papal visit in 1979. One-third of the entire population of the Republic greeted Pope John Paul II on arrival. Not until the following decade did the fusion of Catholic social teaching and legislative restrictions come under serious challenge. Nor were these 'Catholic' laws swept away *en masse* by a tide of liberalisation.

In 1983, a constitutional ban on abortion was introduced, whilst the ban on divorce was upheld in 1986. Even the 1995 referendum which led to the introduction of divorce was passed by the narrowest of margins. The victory for 'yes' campaigners owed much to the scandals in which the Church had become engulfed in the 1990s, weakening its authority. These scandals involved paedophile cases and the use of Church money to pay for illegitimate children fathered by clergy. The vote to permit divorce was described as the biggest defeat for the Catholic Church since the creation of the Republic (Minogue, 1996). Opposing the change, Dr Dermot Clifford, Bishop of Cashel, stated that divorcees were heavier drinkers and smokers, recipients of higher eating disorders and even three times more likely to be involved in car accidents (quoted in Doyle, 1995: 13).

Much of the 1980s and 1990s were characterised by battles between reformers and fundamentalists. The latter often comprised lay groups, often seen as part of the Catholic Church, although they were, in defence of its stances, seen as 'more Catholic than the Catholic Church'. Indeed, the Church attempted a less overt stance in some referenda on social and moral issues, notably the final referendum on the liberalisation of the divorce laws. Increasingly, the Republic had become a liberal, pluralist society by the end of the twentieth century.

The decline in the influence of the Catholic Church in the Irish Republic was matched by a reduction in its numerical strength north and south. Between 1970 and 1989, the number of religious personnel fell from 25,172 to 15,634 (Hussey, 1995: 373). Fewer people entered vocations, resulting in an ageing clergy. Attendance at Sunday Mass, compulsory for Catholics, remains substantial but is falling, particularly in urban areas; and religiosity, if measured crudely by church-going, may be higher in Northern Ireland.

Since the Second Vatican Council of the 1960s, the Catholic Church has adopted more liberal attitudes. The alternative Christianity of Protestant Churches was recognised with participation in ecumenical projects encouraged.

In 1970, the 1908 *Ne temere* decree was relaxed. In a marriage of a Catholic and a Protestant, this was a requirement that the Catholic attempt the conversion of the Protestant and that the children of the marriage be brought up as Catholics. Whilst the demands of *Ne temere* had enormous impact upon marriages involving Catholics elsewhere, its impact in Ireland was only slight. In the South, mixed marriages were rare due to the lack of a substantial Protestant population. In the North, divisions between the Protestant and Catholic communities meant that mixed marriages were unusual even before the onset of the Troubles. Between 1943–82, only 6 per cent of marriages were mixed in Northern Ireland, less than one-tenth of the figure for marriages involving a Catholic in England and Wales (Fulton, 1991: 199).

8.5 The political influence of the Catholic Church

Whilst the Catholic Church would claim that its primary roles are spiritual and pastoral, it has sometimes been seen as performing a political role. Ironically, Unionists and Republicans have both criticised the Church, for different reasons. Militant Unionists, mainly Paisleyites, have argued that the Church is a supporter of Irish republicanism. Republicans claimed that the Church failed to support Irish unity and was too condemnatory of paramilitary attempts to achieve a united Ireland. The intervention of the Catholic Church in the Northern Ireland conflict came mainly in two forms. Firstly, it spoke against perceived injustices and was vocal in its condemnation of discrimination and violence. Secondly, it sometimes offered a brokerage role in attempts to resolve issues within the broader conflict.

Criticisms by Paisleyites have centred upon several contentions. They believe that the Catholic Church is expansionist and supportive of Irish unity. Previous cardinals, such as Thomas O'Fiaich, were indeed Nationalists. Paisleyites pointed out that the overwhelming majority of members of the IRA were Catholics. Prominent members of Sinn Fein, such as Martin McGuinness and Gerry Adams, are practising Catholics, and Adams has long argued that Catholicism and republicanism are reconcilable (Bishop and Mallie, 1988). Furthermore, the Catholic Church refused to excommunicate members of the IRA during the Troubles.

Many Republicans adopted an entirely different view. The Catholic Church was seen as a hostile critic, although friction declined markedly during the peace process of the 1990s. Given the religious allegiance of the Nationalist population, criticism from the Catholic Church was taken seriously. Although some local priests were viewed as sympathetic to Republican ideals, the Church hierarchy attracted Republican opprobrium for its vociferous denunciation of IRA violence. The Church rejected the claim that Republicans were engaged in a just war against an oppressor. Equally, the Catholic Church stressed there were no 'legitimate targets' for paramilitary action. Although critical of partition, the Church condemned the war against its maintenance. The Pope condemned violence during his 1979 visit, whilst appearing to acknowledge that its perpetrators sought justice. It was once commented that when the Catholic Church condemns violence, it becomes 'inaudible' to its flock (O'Brien, 1972: 310). Nonetheless, a majority within the Catholic community always rejected violence, although some within that community, whilst taking their religion from the pulpit, looked elsewhere for a political lead.

Catholicism has not relied upon the support of organisations straddling religion and politics. Instead, it has relied upon the strength of unity of the Church. The Catholic equivalent of the Orange Order, the Ancient Order of Hibernians (AOH), has been a very pale shadow of its Protestant counterpart. The AOH had informal links with the old Nationalist Party. Although it has organised parades for many years, lack of power and patronage have seen the AOH decline from what was always a marginal position.

In its brokerage role, the Catholic Church has attempted to mediate between different viewpoints within and between the communities. Its negotiating role means that the confidence of interested parties has to be gained. A demonstration of internal mediation within the Nationalist community was seen in the 1980–1 hunger strikes undertaken by IRA and INLA prisoners within The Maze in an attempt to obtain prisoner-of-war status. The Catholic Church refused to condemn the hunger-strikers. It also declined to label the deaths of prisoners as suicide. This refusal was important as it allowed the hunger-strikers to be buried in sacred ground. Theologically the stance was justified on the basis that it could not be ascertained that death was intended. Meanwhile, the Church, urged by some of the prisoners' families, pleaded with the hunger-strikers to end their actions, alienating some imprisoned Republicans (Stevenson, 1996). Indeed, the Church played an instrumental role in the cessation of the strike.

The stance of the Catholic Church contrasted with the attitude of the Protestant churches, which declared that deaths arising from hunger strikes were self-inflicted and, therefore, suicide. The Protestant churches claimed that there were no prisoners of conscience in Northern Ireland. The hunger strikes were an example of the Catholic Church administering the needs of its flock, whilst acting in a doubtful political role according to critics. The Church of Ireland was critical of what it saw as seeming equivocation by the Catholic Church.

In 1974, a group of Protestant clergymen met leaders of the Provisional IRA in an unsuccessful attempt to end violence. More recently, the churches combined in a negotiating role. The climax of this was the involvement of representatives of the Catholic Church and the Presbyterian Church in bringing about the peace process of the 1990s. The churches have also liaised with community groups in controversies over the routes of Orange parades.

8.6 Educational segregation

Catholic and Protestant schoolchildren are usually educated separately. This division weakens at the further education stage with the existence of integrated further education colleges and ends at university level. Catholic schoolchildren are educated mainly in primary and secondary schools established by the Roman Catholic Church. Catholic schools receive 80 per cent of their funding from grants from the state. The intake and staff of such schools are overwhelmingly Catholic. Other state schools are often labelled Protestant because few Catholics attend. Protestant clergy sit on the management boards of such schools.

Fewer than seven per cent of children attend integrated schools, the first of which, Lisnareagh College, was opened in the secondary sector in 1984. The charter of the college prevents its ratio of Protestant–Catholic enrolment from shifting beyond 60–40 (Hughes, 1994). A primary aim of the Catholic Church in the establishment of a separate system of schooling is to teach the Catholic faith to pupils. There would be little point in the creation of such schools otherwise. In defence of educational segregation, the Catholic hierarchy points out that religion is not the main source of division, whilst arguing that a Catholic education increases tolerance (Irish Episcopal Conference, 1984). Religious educational segregation is replicated in other countries, but criticism is largely peculiar to Northern Ireland. The main contentions of such criticisms are:

1. divisions in education lead to later segregation;
2. there is a lack of awareness of other faiths, creating religious intolerance;
3. differences in the curriculum, particularly in the teaching of British and Irish history, create and reinforce antagonisms.

Efforts have been made to reduce historical misunderstandings. The Community Relations Council, an organisation which replaced the original Community Relations Commission founded in 1969, exists to bring Catholics and Protestants together. It encourages the development of joint community projects. In 1994, it declared that schools in Northern Ireland 'stand separately as symbolising people's need to protect their particular brand of beliefs and history as distinct from others' (Frazer and Fitzduff, 1994: 33). Traditionally, but less so nowadays, Protestant schools emphasised British historical glories. Catholic schools tended to concentrate upon Irish history. Accordingly, schooling has been held responsible for the historical justification of Unionist or Nationalist positions.

In 1989, the Department of Education for Northern Ireland introduced compulsory cross-curricular themes of Cultural Heritage and Education for Mutual Understanding. As part of what became known as the *Opposite Religions?* project, a small number of teachers were asked to devise new teaching materials for use in all schools in the teaching of history and religious education. The aim was to produce objective, impartial material which would permit students to consider all evidence before drawing conclusions concerning the development of history and religion in Ireland. As part of the project, a survey was undertaken of the knowledge of schoolchildren concerning the 'opposite' religion (Lambkin, 1996). This concluded that:

1. religion is of great importance to schoolchildren;
2. knowledge of religion is weak and distorted;
3. a majority of schoolchildren, unlike adults, believed that the conflict was caused by religion;
4. nearly half of schoolchildren thought that the conflict could be ended by bridging the religious divide;

5. Protestant or Catholic identity appeared of more importance than jointly held Christian identity.

The survey confirmed the existence of religious and historical myths amongst schoolchildren. Many found it difficult to accept the notion of Christianity due to the extent of division between Catholics and Protestants.

In 1992, the Opsahl Commission was established to inquire into ways forward for Northern Ireland. It was an independent Commission, chaired by Professor Torkel Opsahl, designed to examine the submissions of citizens in what was known as the Initiative 92 citizens' inquiry (Pollak, 1993). Receiving 554 submissions, the Opsahl Commission presided over one of the largest consultative process ever undertaken in Northern Ireland. The remit of the Commission was to examine all aspects of life in Northern Ireland. The leadership of the three main Protestant churches responded. Responses from the Catholic Church were confined to submissions from individual priests and church groups. Submissions concerning the impact of religion varied considerably. It was argued that religion was used as a means of cultural defence and had contributed to the idea held by both communities that they were 'victims'. A process of demonisation of the other tradition had taken place, assisted by increased segregation.

A rare area of consensus amongst many of the submissions was the favouring of the extension of integrated education. Thirty-six such submissions were received, although few dealt with how to extend integration in a segregated society (Pollak, 1993). The pressure group, All Children Together, emphasised in its submission that integrated education did not simply mean that Catholic and Protestant schoolchildren were taught together in the same building for certain 'non-controversial' subjects. Religious education within schools should also be taught to integrated groups.

The Opsahl Commission made a number of recommendations designed to reduce conflict in Northern Ireland. In the intertwined areas of religion, culture and identity, the seven commissioners proposed the following measures:

1. the establishment of a public inquiry into the role of the Catholic Church in Ireland;
2. the reduction of barriers to mixed marriages;
3. the relaxation of rules concerning intercommunion;
4. the development of summer festivals as alternatives to controversial Orange marches;
5. increased integration of education and housing;
6. Protestants to recognise themselves as Irish with British citizenship; Catholics to respect cultural Britishness.

8.7 Societal segregation

Following the onset of the Troubles, the extent of residential segregation between the two communities increased. Although many areas remain mixed, it is far from uncommon for areas to be the preserve of residents of a single religion. Segregation owes at least as much to mutual hostility over political matters as religion, but the latter remains the ethnic marker. Segregation means that the two communities are often divided politically, religiously, culturally, and finally physically from each other.

In Belfast, a majority of electoral wards are segregated, in that fewer than 10 per cent of the inhabitants of an area belong to the 'other' religion. Although a majority of residents disagree with segregation, over half of the public-housing schemes in Northern Ireland are non-mixed (Boyle and Hadden, 1994). Areas are easily identified by flags, wall murals and the painting of kerbstones.

Segregation rather than reintegration has been the norm. There is periodic intimidation within these communities. Some Protestants claim that ethnic cleansing has occurred in rural border areas as Nationalists have removed local opposition. For many years, part-time soldiers in the Ulster Defence Regiment, often local farmers, were prime IRA targets. The Northern Ireland Housing Executive (NIHE) sometimes found that estates were more manageable if segregated. The NIHE did not endorse segregation, but at times of crisis favoured population movement rather than attempts at integration. The spread of segregation is common to both rural and urban areas. In outlying areas, villages have become increasingly single religion. Segregation in urban areas is much more common in working-class districts. Catholics and Protestants, Nationalists and Unionists, coexist without tension in the more prosperous districts of Belfast, particularly the south of the city, and work and share leisure in the city centre, which has long appeared prosperous.

Divisions in Northern Ireland permeate some aspects of daily life. Religious segregation in education and, to a lesser extent, work is often replicated in leisure. Catholics and Protestants play soccer and, to a lesser extent, rugby. Gaelic sports, such as camogie, hurling and gaelic football, are almost exclusively confined to the Catholic population. The playing of Gaelic games has revived amongst Catholics since the Troubles, as the community has 'turned in on itself and rediscovered its sporting heritage' (Cronin, 1994: 15). Accordingly, Gaelic games clubs have acted as centres for the community. Gaelic sports are organised by the Gaelic Athletic Association (GAA). It maintains a ban upon the security forces, a prohibition seen as sectarian by critics. The GAA views the playing of Gaelic games as an assertion of Irishness, an expression of a unique cultural identity. However, the ban upon members of the GAA playing 'British' sports, such as soccer, was ignored by members and eventually abandoned. The political beliefs of the GAA are clear. Its charter aspires to Irish unity, referring to a thirty-two county Ireland.

Spectating within certain sports is also characterised by division. The all-Ireland rugby team attracts some Protestant followers, many of whom play the sport in school. However, in soccer, sectarianism persists. The Northern Ireland soccer team is supported mainly by Protestants, although the team invariably also comprises Catholics. Sectarian chants are still audible at international home matches at Windsor Park, despite a campaign by the Irish Football Association. Catholics generally support the Republic of Ireland. At club level, sectarian rioting is not unknown. As a consequence, two clubs supported by Catholics, Belfast Celtic and Derry City, withdrew from the Irish League, in 1949 and 1971 respectively. Linfield, for many years the premier soccer team in Northern Ireland, is supported by Protestants, although the team now fields Catholics and Protestants. Cliftonville, a 'mixed' team, attracts the support of Catholic soccer fans.

Support for leading English Premiership clubs cuts across the sectarian divide. However, the main soccer teams in Glasgow, Celtic and Rangers, attract considerable support from Northern Ireland. Numerous supporters' clubs in Northern Ireland organise travel to games. Celtic has an overwhelmingly Catholic following, although the team has always been of mixed religion. Rangers, despite having signed Catholics since the late 1980s, continues to attract almost exclusively Protestant support.

8.8 Religion and conflict

It is evident that the overwhelming majority of Nationalists are Catholics. A less substantial majority of Catholics are Nationalists. Most Unionists are Protestants. These overlaps have led to the association of the Northern Ireland conflict with religion. However, these linkages do not prove that religion is central to the conflict. The importance of religion in Northern Ireland has led some to describe it as the central problem (Hickey, 1984; Bruce, 1986; Crawford, 1987). Bruce wrote (1986: 249):

> The Northern Ireland conflict is a religious conflict. Economic and social differ-
> ences are also crucial, but it was the fact that the competing populations in Ireland
> adhered and still adhere to competing religious traditions which has given the
> conflict its enduring and intractable quality.

In support of his claim, Bruce later emphasises that he perceives the problem of Northern Ireland as one of ethnic conflict (Bruce, 1994). He suggests that Protestants in Northern Ireland amount to an ethnic group rather than a nation. Central to their ethnic identity is their Protestant religion. Even moderate Unionists may be prepared to support fundamental Protestants such as Ian Paisley, a man for whom religion is foremost and politics subordinate. Marshalling his evidence, Bruce points to Moxon-Browne's 1983 survey which found that 74.5 per cent of Protestants cited fear of the power of the Roman Catholic Church as a reason for being unionist (Moxon-Browne, 1983). He also points out that it is difficult for others moving in more secular circles to comprehend the salience of religion to the lives of ordinary people in Northern Ireland.

Critics of the idea that religion is central to the conflict argue that the problem of Northern Ireland concerns claims to its territory and reluctance to be British in an Irish state, or Irish in a British state, contests unconcerned with denominational superiority (McGarry and O'Leary, 1995). They point out that Moxon-Browne's 1983 survey found that more people opposed a united Ireland because of fear of losing their British national identity than because of the fear of the Catholic Church. If the conflict was dependent upon religion, it ought to have lessened in recent years, as the power of the Catholic Church in the Republic has diminished markedly. Few, however, would attribute the development of a peace process in the 1990s to the decline of the Catholic Church in the Irish Republic. Far more would associate the reduction in tension with the willingness to compromise political principles.

The question that needs to be asked is whether the claims of Irish Republicans to Northern Ireland are in any way dependent upon religion, given that much of the conflict for three decades emanated from the violent exercise of that claim. The use of violence was condemned by the Catholic and Protestant churches. There has never been a holy war in Ireland between the rival churches. Only two clerics were killed during the conflict, one by accident. Violent Irish republicanism has always existed independently of the Catholic Church. Rival territorial claims to Northern Ireland are fundamental to the problem. These exist independently of the depth of religious fervour and thus appear impervious to co-operative or ecumenical projects. A study of attitudes at the integrated Lisnareagh College supports this argument (Hughes, 1994). It was found that most Catholics and Protestants, whilst educated together, insisted upon different national identities.

Religion is nonetheless important as a component of collective identity, even though it is not a necessary aspect, nor a modern cause, of ethno-national conflict. Republicans believe that the Northern state is sectarian and liable to discriminate against the Nationalist population. Evidence of this discrimination is usually presented in statistics using Protestant and Catholic labels. Nationalists believe that only through the creation of a unified Ireland can an Ireland be created which treats Catholic, Protestant and dissenter with equal respect.

The association of religion with political division has, ironically, reinforced division amongst Christians. According to Lambkin (1996: 193):

> One effect of the conflict in Northern Ireland has been to sustain the attachment of people to the Catholic and Protestant religious traditions. After the conflict, the 'native speakers' of Catholicism and Protestantism will be exposed increasingly to the dominant European 'language' of secularism.

Again, the impact of religion is an effect of a pre-existent conflict, not a cause. Formal legislation does exist to outlaw sectarianism, consolidated by the Good Friday Agreement. Previously, legislation was used sparingly. For example, the Prevention of Incitement to Hatred Act (1970) led to a lone prosecution following the publication of anti-Catholic lyrics in a Loyalist songbook in 1971. The trial ended in the acquittal of the three defendants.

There has always been an important link between Protestantism and unionism as a political creed. The question begged is whether unionism could transcend this. If one accepts that the most fundamental tenet of unionism is the retention of the link to Great Britain, there appears little reason why it could not exist purely as a political creed. However, the historical links with the defence of the Protestant faith illuminate unionism to many adherents and would disappear only slowly. It may be impossible for Paisleyism to achieve such a change as it does not attempt to separate politics from religion. However, Paisleyism, although popular, is a minority Unionist taste.

8.9 Conclusion

Religion may reinforce rather than create the Northern Ireland conflict. Mistreatment of the Catholic population contributed to the birth of the Provisional IRA, although such mistreatment was also due to the political aversion of unionists to Irish nationalism. The importance of religious affiliation is acknowledged even by those who deny its centrality to the conflict. It enhances a sense of community and provides unity of goals. Catholics of differing shades of Nationalist opinion may unite in opposition to Orange parades. Unionists are reminded of their Protestant heritage by the Orange Order and the fusion of religion and politics apparent in both the main Unionist political parties. It is an oversimplification to claim that the problem of Northern Ireland has nothing to do with religion. However, given the permanence and independence from religion of competing constitutional aspirations for respect of Northern Ireland, it is difficult to sustain the argument that religious differences are the root cause of modern problems.

Chapter 9

Political failures 1972–84

Following the introduction of direct rule in 1972, the search began for a political solution to the problem of Northern Ireland. Initiatives were now the prerogative of the Secretary of State for Northern Ireland. Any remedies had to be acceptable to the majority Unionist community and the Nationalist minority. Proposals, therefore, had to fuse reassurance for Unionists with some acknowledgement of the ambitions of Nationalists, scarcely an easy task.

9.1 Policy approaches

British policy between 1972 and 1984 can be divided into phases, each with its own dimensions. These are listed in Table 9.1.

From the outset, political initiatives were dominated by a belief that power should be shared between the two communities. The logical consequence of this perception was a return to devolved government, granting powers to local political parties. This did not reflect an enthusiasm for devolution within the British government, but rather an anxiety to shed direct responsibility at the earliest opportunity. Of equal importance was the recognition by the British government that there could be no return to the 'bad old days' of one-party rule at Stormont.

A new form of devolution was required, based upon cross-community co-operation, not single-party triumphalism. The decline of Unionist unity was

Table 9.1 British policy approaches 1972–84

Period	Approach	Features
1972–4	Devolution with power-sharing and an Irish dimension	Power-sharing Executive and Council of Ireland by 1974, collapsed after five months
1975	Devolution with minimal all-Ireland dimension	Constitutional Convention: unworkable
1976–9	Ulsterisation and criminalisation	'Non-politics'; normalising problem via treatment of terrorism as criminality
1980–4	Rolling devolution without an all-Ireland dimension	Northern Ireland elected Assembly: boycotted by Nationalists and ended by 1986

seen as beneficial in that it prevented the dominance of a single party from that community. A number of Unionist parties emerged in competition with each other, following the fragmentation of unionism in the late 1960s. Against this, there was little evidence that less moderate Unionists were willing to share power with Nationalists. Nationalist desires for a greater voice in the affairs of Northern Ireland were natural given their exclusion from influence throughout the previous 50 years. The British government hoped that Unionist and Nationalist parties might set aside their differences over the constitutional future of Northern Ireland, in order to govern Northern Ireland together. A workable administration was to be created which offered something for all. The failure of talks between the Secretary of State and the IRA in 1972 made the search for a solution even more crucial. Only with a durable devolved administration could the British government possess even a slim chance of marginalising the paramilitary organisations.

British policy was based upon a 'carrot and stick' approach. Unionists could enjoy a return to the devolved government they so desired, provided they were willing to countenance power-sharing with Nationalists. Nationalists could share power within Northern Ireland, provided that they accepted the state as a legitimate political entity. Nationalists were also to be rewarded with the first acknowledgement by the British government of the need for some all-Ireland dimension to any future settlement. Given this, alongside the prospect of power-sharing, it was obvious that Nationalists were the primary gainers from the new policy approach. It could hardly be otherwise, given that Nationalists were starting from a base of zero in terms of their political power and influence in Northern Ireland.

The attempt at power-sharing in 1974 represented the first effort to establish consociational democracy in Northern Ireland. Inherent within the proposals of the British government was an attempt to build a grand coalition of political élites amongst constitutional political organisations to act as a new Executive. There was recognition of the extent to which society was divided. The absence of consociationalism risked the return to the exclusionism which characterised politics in Northern Ireland under the old Stormont regime.

In October 1972, the British government produced a consultative Green Paper, *The Future of Northern Ireland* (HM Government, 1972). The Paper envisaged devolved government for Northern Ireland, power-sharing and, most significantly, some acknowledgement that the Republic of Ireland had the right to be listened to regarding Northern Ireland. It argued that it was desirable that any new arrangements for Northern Ireland be accepted by the Republic of Ireland. This was a significant step, given that three years earlier the Republic had been given short shrift by the British government when it attempted to articulate its concern for the plight of Northern Nationalists.

Formal proposals were published during the following year in the White Paper, *Northern Ireland Constitutional Proposals* (HM Government, 1973). This formed the basis of the legislation contained in the Northern Ireland Assembly Act, passed at some speed in May 1973. Two months later, the old system of governing Northern Ireland through Stormont was finally abolished. The legislative measures made provision for the following items to be enacted:

1. enforced power-sharing through the creation of a power-sharing executive – to prevent Unionist dominance;
2. arrangements for consultation and co-operation with the Irish government through a Council of Ireland – to pacify Nationalists;
3. retention by the British government of most security responsibilities – to attempt to maintain order;
4. constitutional guarantees for the status of Northern Ireland – to reassure Unionists.

9.2 Power-sharing

The elected Assembly was to:

1. contain 78 seats, making it of similar size to Stormont;
2. be elected by proportional representation, thereby ensuring adequate Nationalist representation;
3. allow for the formation of a ministerial executive, drawn from the membership of the Assembly.

Cross-community power-sharing was introduced. The new proposals for governance offered substantial numerical representation and the prospect of shares for each community in government and legislative scrutiny. These were to be achieved through the ending of straightforward majority rule and the use of an Assembly committee system. As part of an attempt to compensate Unionists for the loss of their hegemonic position, plebiscites (referenda) were conducted regularly, asking whether Northern Ireland should remain part of the United Kingdom. Given the construction of the state, 'yes' votes were inevitable. An overwhelming 'yes' vote of 97.8 per cent recorded in March 1973 reflected the in-built Unionist majority and the unwillingness of Nationalists to participate in such exercises. Only 57 per cent of the electorate voted. Only 6,000 voted against, compared to 591,000 favouring the retention of Northern Ireland's position in the United Kingdom. Such a boycott ensured that the election result acquired the appearance of a contest in the old Soviet Union. In defence of the poll, it was later claimed that up to 25 per cent of Catholics had turned out to register support for the Union (*Irish Times*, 22 February 1974). If true, this indicated that an extremely low turnout of Protestants had occurred.

Two months after the plebiscite, elections to local councils took place, the first such elections for six years. Despite calls for a boycott from the Provisional IRA and Peoples Democracy, there was a good turnout. The SDLP performed well, although anti-Unionists formed an outright majority on only one of the 26 councils, Newry and Mourne. Encouraged by levels of participation in the local contest, the British government proceeded with elections to the Assembly in June 1973. Unionists were sharply divided. The Ulster Unionist Party, led by Faulkner, supported power-sharing. Within the Ulster Unionist Party, however, many dissented and made their position clear during the campaign.

Table 9.2   Northern Ireland Assembly election results 1973

	Votes	%	Seats
Pro-power-sharing			
Faulkner Unionists	191,729	26.5	23
SDLP	159,773	22.1	19
Alliance	66,541	9.2	8
NILP	18,675	2.6	1
Others	17,053	2.4	0
Total	453,771	62.8	51
Anti-power-sharing			
Non-Faulkner Unionists	89,759	12.5	11
DUP	78,228	10.8	8
Vanguard	75,759	10.5	7
Republican Clubs	13,064	1.8	0
Others	11,660	1.6	1
Total	268,470	37.2	27

Source: adapted from Rose (1976).

Ranged against power-sharing were the Democratic Unionist Party and the Vanguard Unionist Progressive Party. The latter had been formed by William Craig as a response to his failure to ensure that the Ulster Unionist Council rejected power-sharing (Bew *et al.*, 1996). Other smaller Loyalist groups also opposed power-sharing. The Alliance Party was unsurprisingly in favour. Also supportive were the SDLP and the Northern Ireland Labour Party (NILP). Republican Clubs (the political wing of the Official IRA) opposed. The results yielded a majority in favour of power-sharing, as Table 9.2 indicates.

It was apparent that a large majority of Nationalists were in support. Nonetheless, the overall majority in favour of power-sharing was scarcely overwhelming and amongst Unionists it amounted to a minority taste. Within the Assembly itself, there was now a substantial minority opposed to its continuation.

An Executive formed from Assembly members came into being on 1 January 1974. It comprised Faulkner as the Unionist Chief Executive, the SDLP's Gerry Fitt as his Nationalist deputy and nine ministers. These nine included five Unionists, three members of the SDLP and one representative from the Alliance Party. The Unionists had pledged to share power only with those groups whose primary object was not to break the link with Great Britain (Buckland, 1981). In co-operating with the SDLP, they clearly had a perception that the main Nationalist party favoured political stability above its declared objective of Irish unification.

9.3 The Council of Ireland

Unionist opposition to the power-sharing project hardened with the establishment of the Assembly. In January 1974, Faulkner resigned from the Ulster

Unionist Party. He was defeated due to the increasing hostility of his party to the all-Ireland dimension which also formed part of the agenda of the British government. Some previous supporters of power-sharing rejected any additional arrangements which did not permit a settlement entirely internal to Northern Ireland. It was these who deserted Faulkner, who was forced to form his own Unionist Party of Northern Ireland (UPNI).

One month later, Faulkner's new party was trounced in the General Election, winning only 13 per cent of the vote. In contrast, anti-power-sharing candidates captured 51 per cent and 11 of the 12 parliamentary seats in Northern Ireland. Many of the antis were opposed to power-sharing *per se*, but it was the proposed Council of Ireland which increasingly became the focus of opposition. Although the new Labour government at Westminster supported the policy approach of its Conservative predecessor, the question begged was whether the policy could be enforced upon an increasingly reluctant populace.

In its original White Paper, the British government had left open to negotiation the precise format for the establishment of Anglo-Irish co-operation. Discussions took place at Sunningdale, Berkshire, in December 1973 between the Northern Ireland Assembly Executive and the British and Irish governments. They agreed that the Council of Ireland would contain the following elements:

1. a Council of Ministers comprising seven representatives of the British government and seven from the Republic of Ireland, to meet on 'matters of substantial mutual interest';
2. a Consultative Assembly, comprising 30 members elected by the Dail and the same number elected by the Northern Ireland Assembly.

Part of the antagonism towards the Council of Ireland lay in the mystery surrounding the extent of its remit. Bew and Patterson (1985: 57) suggest that the original proposals from the British government were 'implicitly minimalist' in respect of the Irish dimension. Operating from a position of strength following the Assembly elections and the necessity of its inclusion in arrangements, the SDLP forced the British government to concede further ground. Under revised plans, the Council of Ireland was to enjoy some executive and harmonisation functions, rather than a primarily consultative role with some executive functions. Arguably, the lack of clarity over the Council's role was deliberate, as ambiguity might lessen opposition. The Republic was to be afforded a say in policing strategies, including internment and appointments in Northern Ireland. This was ground which had to be conceded by the British government in return for increased co-operation from the Garda (Irish police) and the enactment of extradition laws, allowing IRA suspects to be handed over to the British authorities. For the constitutional Nationalists of the SDLP, the establishment of the Council of Ireland represented substantial progress. Indeed, one member of the party publicly expressed the view that the Council was 'the vehicle which will trundle Unionists into a united Ireland' (quoted in Coogan, 1995: 177).

Indeed, the Assembly and Council proposals contained most of the essential ingredients for the SDLP and provided a 'greenprint' for the approaches of the party in the peace process two decades later. A North–South dimension was provided by the consultative assembly of political representatives from the Northern Ireland Assembly and the Dail; an East–West (London–Dublin) link was provided by the instigation of regular meetings between ministers of the British and Irish governments. Satisfaction with the new arrangements within the SDLP was such that the party ended its rent and rate strike, whilst continuing to call for an end to internment.

Republicans took a far less optimistic view. According to Farrell (1980: 307) the proposals were a device to sideline rebellion:

> The White Paper was a neat summary of Westminster policy on Northern Ireland: a share in power and patronage for the Catholic middle-class and an 'Irish dimension' to satisfy Dublin, in return for support in the campaign against the IRA and acceptance of the North's constitutional position. A classic piece of neo-colonialism.

The constitutional guarantee concerning the future status of Northern Ireland contained the assertion on behalf of the Republic's government that there could be no change in the status of Northern Ireland until a majority of the people of Northern Ireland desired such a change. For its part, the British government declared that if the majority of the people of Northern Ireland were to indicate a wish to become part of a united Ireland, the British government would support that wish. The British government's declaration updated the 1949 Ireland Act which had affirmed that there would be no change in the constitutional position of Northern Ireland without the consent of its parliament. As Stormont had been abolished, a new guarantee was required.

It was just possible to view the new declaration as a tiny shift towards greater neutrality. A permanent Unionist majority was marginally less assured amongst the population than it had been within the old parliament. More important was the fact that the aspiration for a united Ireland was now acknowledged, although it was advanced little by what was on offer. Any constitutional guarantee for Northern Ireland was an anathema to Republicans. A political project which consolidated or legitimised the 'illegitimate' Northern state was bound to be opposed, given the nature of republicanism during this period.

Indeed, there were doubts over whether the constitution of the Republic of Ireland permitted any government in the Republic to accept the Northern state. Articles 2 and 3 suggested the non-existence of Northern Ireland as a distinct political entity and indicated a constitutional imperative to seek reunification. The Republic's willingness to endorse the constitutional status of Northern Ireland was, therefore, tested in the courts. To a great extent, the judges presiding over the case sympathised with the arguments of the challenger, Kevin Boland, whilst quashing his case. Their verdict was that acceptance of the Sunningdale Agreement by the Irish government was not illegal, as it amounted only to a *de facto* recognition of the existing reality of the formal existence of Northern Ireland. This did not amount to a *de jure* confirmation. Had this been the case, the judges implied that the challenge would have been upheld.

9.4 The Ulster Workers' Council strike _____

It was not a constitutional challenge in the Republic of Ireland that was to defeat power-sharing with an Irish dimension. Instead, constitutional and extra-constitutional Loyalist opposition crushed the project. Popular opposition to the Sunningdale Agreement grew rapidly in 1974, under the auspices of the United Ulster Unionist Council, a coalition of the Ulster Unionists, DUP and Vanguard Parties. This coalition was determined to bring down the power-sharing Executive, seeking its replacement in a return to Stormont and control over policing.

Although a minority within the Assembly, Sunningdale's opponents possessed external strength. This lay in the Ulster Workers' Council (UWC), a successor to the Loyalist Association of Workers (LAW). The LAW had attempted to build a mass working-class membership. The UWC was also concerned with this, but concentrated upon key industries such as power stations, It recruited shop stewards and union members in these industries which were staffed mainly by Loyalists.

By May 1974, the UWC had acquired sufficient strength to mobilise against the power-sharing Executive. A motion placed before the Assembly calling for the scrapping of the Executive was defeated. Supported by Loyalist paramilitary groups, the UWC announced the staging of an indefinite general strike, or constitutional stoppage, as it was labelled. Assisted by a combination of support and intimidation, the strike grew. The UWC controlled petrol supplies and, most crucially, the power stations. Amid a deteriorating situation, offers of compromise, such as the postponement of the executive functions of the Council of Ireland, went largely unheeded. During the strike, the UDA killed 33 people through no-warning car bombs in Dublin and Monaghan, the largest death toll of the entire Troubles.

Two back-to-work marches organised by the Irish Congress of Trade Unions (ICTU) attracted small turnouts and much derision. The ICTU perceived the strike as little more than a display of reactionary Ulster nationalism, rather than an illustration of progressive class solidarity against capitalist Unionist and British government 'masters'. Loyalists believed their actions were justifiable, as their loyalty to Britain was conditional upon Britain acting in their interests.

More significant in hardening opinion was the denunciation by the Prime Minister, Harold Wilson, of sections of the Loyalist community as 'spongers'. By no means unsympathetic to the idea, if not the practicality, of a united Ireland, Wilson had little time for militant loyalism. His adviser, Joe Haines, removed the word 'sponger' from the original transcript of the speech. The Prime Minister reinserted the label (Pimlott, 1992). Furious over the attempt to ruin the proposals and 'set up a sectarian and undemocratic state', Wilson also asked, 'Who do these people think they are?'. The Prime Minister's attack, contained in an emergency televised broadcast, caused some Loyalists to sport sponges in their lapels the following day. It achieved little in the short term, although its underlying message was that Britain's loyalty to Northern Ireland might be conditional upon 'good behaviour' from Loyalists.

In desperation, the Secretary of State for Northern Ireland, Merlyn Rees, ordered the use of troops to maintain essential supplies and, in effect, to break the strike. Ironically, this was urged by the Nationalist SDLP, critics of other forms of British military activity. Although the troops occupied a number of petrol stations, their intervention worsened affairs. The UWC threatened to cease maintenance of emergency services from power stations if the army intervened further. The British government was unwilling to sanction greater action against the strikers.

Power-sharing was supported by the British government, but some doubt whether it was a crucial part of its strategy (Bew and Patterson, 1985). Accordingly, this adjunct to policy could be ditched if it became too inconvenient. Furthermore, there was reluctance even among some members of the power-sharing Executive to support coercion of the strikers. Above all, there was insufficient consent for power-sharing both within and outside the Assembly. This was acknowledged by Faulkner when he resigned from the Executive on 28 May, along with Unionist colleagues. Power-sharing had collapsed. Faulkner had been highly critical of the obstructionist tactics of Loyalists throughout the short life of the Executive. Ian Paisley, described as the 'demon doctor, preaching goodness knows what', was a particular target of Faulkner's wrath.

Yet Paisley alone could not be blamed for the downfall of power-sharing. Although fellow Loyalists, several of the organisers of the UWC strike were critical of Paisleyite rhetoric, preferring deeds to words. Many Unionists were opposed to power-sharing and had already registered their disdain via the ballot box. There was intimidation during the strike. Workers at Harland and Wolff's shipyard were told that any cars still in the car park in the afternoon would be burnt (Bruce, 1992). As the UWC celebrated its victory, it appeared to critics that a Loyalist veto existed over the internal political arrangements and external relations of Northern Ireland.

Opponents of power-sharing had their majority position confirmed in the October 1974 General Election, when the United Ulster Unionist Council won 58 per cent of the vote. Prior to the 1998 Good Friday Agreement, Arthur and Jeffery (1996: 12) wrote that the creation of the power-sharing executive was 'the most successful of British initiatives within the Province so far'. Given the abject political failures which followed for the next two decades, this might be seen as damning with faint praise.

9.5 The Northern Ireland Constitutional Convention _____

'Son of Assembly' was soon attempted following the débacle of May 1974. This took the form of the Northern Ireland Constitutional Convention, a very pale imitation of its predecessor. Like the ill-fated Assembly, the Convention also contained 78 members. The main difference from its predecessor was that the Convention amounted to no more than a consultative elected assembly. Its remit was to discover what form of government in Northern Ireland was likely to command the most widespread acceptance (HM Government, 1974). No such discovery was made. As Quinn (1993: 32) argues, the Convention

produced a 'dialogue of the deaf'. Candidates from the United Ulster Unionist Council won 55 per cent of the vote in the first and final Convention
elections. Holding 47 of the 78 seats, they dominated proceedings, although
proceedings were scarcely worth dominating. In calling for a return of Stormont,
the UUUC remained adamant in its opposition to power-sharing and the
imposition of any all-Ireland dimension. Accordingly, there was no meeting of
minds with the SDLP, nor even the Alliance or UPNI.

One significant development did emerge, however, within the UUUC.
William Craig, the leader of the hitherto hardline Vanguard Party, surprisingly changed his view and advocated a temporary, non-statutory form
of coalition with the SDLP as part of a grand design to defeat terrorism.
Although Craig did not use the term power-sharing, this was how the plan was
inevitably interpreted. The idea had few supporters. The UUUC and Craig's
own party were openly hostile. The Vanguard Party fragmented, with many
members deserting to form a breakaway group, the United Ulster Unionist
Movement, led by Ernest Baird. Craig's political career declined and in the
1979 General Election he lost his seat as MP for East Belfast to the DUP.

By late 1975, the UUUC appeared to advocate a return to Stormont.
Modification of the old pre-1972 system of governing Northern Ireland was
offered only in respect of the allocation of some parliamentary committee
chairs to the Nationalist minority. Unsurprisingly, this plan was rejected by
non-UUUC parties. What was on offer to them was inclusion only in departmental committees, whereas the 1974 Northern Ireland Assembly offered
such parties posts in cabinet.

The minor parties issued their own minority reports, whilst the Labour
government argued that the UUUC proposals would fail to create widespread
acceptance. By this, the government meant cross-community acceptance. As
the Convention meandered aimlessly, the Secretary of State chose to end
proceedings in March 1976. As Bew, Gibbon and Patterson assert (1996:
200) the Convention was best viewed 'as a means of keeping local political
forces harmlessly occupied whilst consideration was given to a possibility of
some new departure in policy'.

9.6 Non-politics 1976–9

The British government appeared unable to think of any new political initiative between 1976 and 1979. Ulsterisation and criminalisation acted as substi-
tutes for political thought. The period was significant politically in that it
highlighted that alliances within loyalism were only temporary. Whatever the
images of the UWC strike of 1974, Loyalists were not in quite the impregn-
able position suggested by that display of strength. In 1977, an attempt was
made to repeat the Loyalist strike of 1974, this time in order to obtain a
tougher security policy from the British government. The strike was led by the
United Ulster Action Council, headed by Ian Paisley.

From its outset, the strike was doomed. It lacked the clear aims of its
predecessor. The main Unionist party opposed the action, mainly due to the

involvement of Loyalist paramilitary groups, whilst the strikers were confronting a tougher Secretary of State in Rees' replacement, Roy Mason. Many amongst the Unionist community viewed his security policy as an improvement upon those conducted by his predecessors. They were unwilling to lose income by engaging in strike action. Those reluctant to join the strike were assisted by the greater willingness of security personnel to confront those engaging in intimidation. After 10 days, the strike was abandoned.

Political impact during this period nonetheless did come from the grassroots, which attempted to fill the political vacuum created by the lack of government initiatives. The rise of the Peace People in 1976 threatened briefly to lead a citizens' revolt against terrorist activity. The catalyst was an incident in which three children were killed after a car crash involving an IRA driver shot by British troops. Huge peace demonstrations were launched throughout the second half of 1976. These included a march of up to 30,000 demonstrators in the Loyalist, working-class Shankill and Woodvale districts. Many within Nationalist areas displayed similar enthusiasm. For a time, large sections of the population publicly demonstrated their opposition to political violence.

Enjoying such large support across the political divide, the Peace People launched a document, *Strategy for Peace*, calling for the creation of a non-political assembly of community groups (Peace People, 1976). Idealism and enthusiasm straddled the social classes and the movement's leaders were awarded the 1976 Nobel Peace Prize. The award was to be the climax of the movement's success, before the onset of feuding, sparked by rows over how the prize money should be spent. Intimidation of the Peace People within both communities impaired the activities of the movement. Republicans demanded that the movement criticise the security forces; some Loyalists were suspicious of what they saw as a Nationalist tinge to the leadership. Meanwhile, the difficulty of sustaining 'non-politics' also led to the movement becoming a spent force by 1978.

9.7 The early Thatcher years

Margaret Thatcher (1993: 385) declared her instincts to be 'profoundly Unionist'. On the question of Northern Ireland, as in many aspects of her early premiership, she nonetheless took a pragmatic approach. She continued the tough line on security issues and gave few concessions to the special category status demanded by republican prisoners in the hunger strikes of the early 1980s. There was, however, recognition of the limitations of the lack of policy initiatives under Mason. A series of atrocities in 1979 sharpened this feeling. In separate incidents, killings included those of Airey Neave, the Shadow Northern Ireland spokesman; 18 British soldiers at Warrenpoint; and Lord Mountbatten, holidaying in the Irish Republic.

On non-constitutional issues, not all of the Thatcherite policies implemented elsewhere in Britain were applied to Northern Ireland. One policy analysis suggests that Thatcherism adopted a much more 'soft approach' on social and economic policy in the region (Gafikin and Morrisey, 1990: 62). This more relaxed policy style was a recognition of the hardships endured by a continuing abnormal security situation and a maintenance of the belief that better stand-ards of living might reduce terrorism.

Upon assuming office in May 1979, the Conservative government began to assess prospects for political advancement. Its election manifesto advocated the return of devolved government, but if this was not forthcoming, the possibility of the establishment of one or more regional councils had been mooted. This implied a revival of local government. Proceeding cautiously, the new Secretary of State for Northern Ireland, Humphrey Atkins, called a Constitutional Conference of the main political parties, between January and March 1980. In order to ensure at least some Unionist participation, discussions concerning an Irish dimension were confined to a parallel conference.

The DUP, SDLP and Alliance participated, but again disagreed over the most appropriate form of devolved government. In a re-run of the discussions of the 1970s, the DUP insisted upon majority rule, whilst the other two parties advocated power-sharing. The Conference was not attended by the Ulster Unionists, on the ground that it would achieve little, a view which proved correct as the Conference was abandoned. Atkins suggested a replace-ment Advisory Council comprising local politicians, but the idea floundered.

A more important development occurred in December 1980. Thatcher and Charles Haughey, the Irish Prime Minister, agreed to set up joint Anglo-Irish studies on matters of common concern. The studies would examine the 'totality of relationships within these islands'. The phraseology was significant as it heralded the onset of intergovernmentalism which would characterise later political initiatives. Indeed, the report of the studies in November 1981 pro-posed the establishment of an intergovernmental council of ministers to examine policy in Northern Ireland. If Thatcher was 'profoundly Unionist', Haughey was 'profoundly Republican' at least in terms of rhetoric, arguing that Northern Ireland was a 'failed political entity'. He too possessed a pragmatic streak. Intergovernmental studies provided a means by which he could be seen to expound his republican credentials.

Politics in Northern Ireland became even more polarised during the following two years. Buoyed by success in the European elections in 1979, the DUP had been a willing player in initiatives in 1980. Following the Thatcher–Haughey declaration, its position hardened. Ian Paisley indicated the willingness of his supporters to physically resist removal into a united Ireland. Amongst Nation-alists, sympathy for the IRA swelled with the development of the hunger strikes, indicated by the by-election victory of the imprisoned hunger-striker, Bobby Sands. After his death through starvation, Sands' election agent, Owen Carron, triumphed in the ensuing by-election. Such was the impact of the action that hunger-strikers even won seats in the Irish parliament.

Intergovernmentalism was temporarily reversed. This was in part due to the conflict of opinion over the resolution of the hunger strike, as the Irish government, along with several international organisations and the Catholic Church, demanded concessions from the British government. It was exacerb-ated by the friction between Thatcher and Haughey over the latter's neutrality in Britain's war with Argentina over the Falkland Islands.

9.8 Rolling devolution

Given the unpromising background, it was perhaps surprising that any political initiative emerged. Less startling was the realisation that the 'new initiative' was merely a variation on an old theme. James Prior became Secretary of State in September 1981 with some reluctance, fearing (correctly) that his selection was a form of internal exile.

Gradual or rolling devolution was the policy that emerged from Prior's deliberations. If politicians within Northern Ireland were prepared to co-operate, they were to be granted a restoration of devolved government. Introduced through the Northern Ireland Act 1982, the plan contained the following elements:

1. the election of a 78-seat consultative Assembly;
2. scrutiny powers would be given to the Assembly;
3. selected legislative powers would be transferred to the Assembly if 70 per cent of members approved.

Many Unionists had opposed devolution with an all-Ireland dimension in the 1970s. Now it was the turn of the Nationalist SDLP to boycott proceedings, given the absence of any such dimension. Equally, the SDLP was concerned over the lack of formal power-sharing contained in the proposals. The development of the Assembly in legislative terms was dependent upon consensus, but this did not equate fully with formal power-sharing. By now the SDLP was cooling slightly on the idea of power-sharing. Under the leadership of Hume, it was moving away from the idea of any internal settlement and towards the embryonic intergovernmentalism developing in Anglo-Irish talks.

Elections to the Assembly took place in October 1982. Both the main Unionist parties participated in the elections and the Assembly. This approval came despite their unhappiness about the 70 per cent weighted majority voting required for the acquisition of powers. Unionists believed such an arrangement was tantamount to power-sharing. The more integrationist Ulster Unionists won 26 seats although the party was more reluctant than the DUP, winner of 21 seats, concerning the overall plan. The DUP hoped that the provision of scrutiny powers might herald a return to genuine devolved government. Whilst contesting the elections, the SDLP and Sinn Fein, winners of 14 and five seats respectively, made clear that they had no intention of taking their seats. Sinn Fein's vote of 10.1 per cent, amounting to a third of the Nationalist vote, alarmed the British and Irish governments, which pondered how to bolster the constitutional nationalism of the SDLP.

Devoid of Nationalist input, devolution failed to roll. The Assembly became little more than a Unionist talking shop. Its committees did provide the first serious scrutiny of legislation under direct rule undertaken by elected politicians. In this task, the committees provided a means of Unionist and Alliance Party co-operation. Beyond this, the limitations of the Assembly had been exposed long before its disbandment in June 1986.

The main legacy of the rolling devolution plan was that it amounted to a rejection by the Conservative government of the integrationist approach held by some Ulster Unionists and elements within the Conservative Party. The White Paper introducing the proposals made this clear, declaring that 'Northern Ireland's divided community, its geography and the history of its politics all make it impracticable to treat the Province as though it were in all respects identical to the rest of the United Kingdom' (HM Government, 1982: para 6).

In accepting that Northern Ireland was indeed a place apart, the British government paved the way for later agreements which would attempt its governance through novel mechanisms. The 1982 declaration was designed to pave the way for devolved government in Northern Ireland. Its effect, along with the Nationalist boycott, was to provide the death knell for attempts at purely internal solutions to the problem of Northern Ireland.

9.9 The New Ireland Forum Report

For many years, the policy of successive governments in the Irish Republic consisted mainly of hoping that Ulster Unionists would one day wake up and realise that they had been misguided all along in wanting to be British citizens. Calls for reunification regularly provoked the loudest cheers at Fianna Fail conferences, although all present knew that little was to be done in practical terms. Strident demands for a 'nation once again' were surrogates for political thought.

Encouraged by the brief and unlikely Thatcher–Haughey co-operation, the government of the Republic of Ireland became more confident in asserting its views concerning Northern Ireland through recognised Anglo-Irish channels. This development continued under the Fine Gael government led by Garret Fitzgerald, but went further in the establishment of the Forum for a New Ireland.

The Forum invited all interested parties in Ireland to discuss their positions in respect of the constitutional position of the island and attracted over 300 submissions. Boycotted by Unionist parties in Northern Ireland, the Forum enjoyed participation from the main parties in the Republic, in addition to the SDLP in the North. Its creation reflected the desire of Fitzgerald to produce a positive agenda for unification, rather than the green Nationalist rhetoric of old, which paid little more than lip-service to the fears of Unionists. Establishment of the Forum coincided with Fitzgerald's constitutional crusade, designed to rid the Republic of those elements of Catholic theocracy unattractive to Unionists. Critics believed that the project was an irrelevance in respect of prospects for unity. Even if Catholic influence was reduced, Unionists would not be enticed into a unitary state.

Partly due to differences amongst participants, the *New Ireland Forum Report*, published in 1984, had a muted impact (New Ireland Forum, 1984). It criticised the British government for reinforcing Unionist supremacy in Northern Ireland, stressed the need for recognition of the existence of two traditions of equal validity on the island of Ireland and recognised the Britishness of Unionists. Yet, whilst claiming a consensual approach to Irish unity, none of the conclusions of the Forum was likely to be acceptable to Unionists. Indeed, its proposals were seen by some as a reassertion of old-style nationalism, whatever the original ambitions of Fitzgerald (O'Halloran, 1987). It was argued that the proposals were unrealistic, but emerged as a consequence of a political background shaped by concern over the rise of Sinn Fein in Northern Ireland (Boyle and Hadden, 1984).

Three options were offered by the Forum Report:

1. a united Ireland, achieved through consent;
2. a federal or confederal state;
3. joint authority.

A united Ireland was the favoured option, but there was no sign of the required 'agreement and consent' unless the majority view on the entire island was used as the means of measurement. The federal solution offered the prospect of devolved, largely autonomous, governments which might leave Unionists in charge of most of their own affairs. Guarantees for different traditions would have been reinforced by a wider confederation of Britain and Ireland, in which the two countries were loosely linked. Joint authority involved the control of Northern Ireland by both Britain and Ireland on the basis of equal, shared responsibility.

A brusque response followed from Margaret Thatcher. The reply to 12 months of effort and consideration was more succinct than the weighty Forum Report. Speaking at a press conference in December 1984, she insisted:

> I have made it clear . . . that a united Ireland was one solution that was out. A second solution was confederation of two states. That is out. A third solution was joint authority. That is out (quoted in Connolly, 1990: 147).

9.10 Conclusion

The search for political agreement amongst politicians in Northern Ireland between 1972 and 1984 proved fruitless as the recurring theme was a lack of consensus on the issues of enforced power-sharing and the all-Ireland dimension. All parties agreed that there could be no return to the bad old days of Stormont, but for Nationalists, the suspicion remained that this was the closet project envisaged by Unionists, especially those within the DUP, in their demand for devolution. Unionists feared that the all-Ireland dimension demanded by Nationalists amounted to a trojan horse for a united Ireland. If the brevity of Margaret Thatcher's dismissal of the Forum Report appeared a setback for Anglo-Irish relations, the reversal was to prove only temporary. By 1985, the British government had decided to bypass local political forces by using an intergovernmental Anglo-Irish Agreement.

Chapter 10

The 1985 Anglo-Irish Agreement

The 1984 New Ireland Forum Report confirmed the view of most parties in the Irish Republic that a purely internal settlement in Northern Ireland was impossible. The British government believed a limited role was possible for the Irish government in the affairs of Northern Ireland. Yet these conclusions were set against the rejection by Unionists of any interference by the Irish Republic. Political paralysis appeared the certain result of any attempt to seek agreement on this issue amongst local politicians. In response, the British government decided to bypass local politics in favour of an intergovernmental agreement in 1985. Accordingly, the Anglo-Irish Agreement was signed at Hillsborough Castle, County Down, on 15 November 1985. The Agreement effectively went over the heads of local politicians and placed the problem of Northern Ireland within a co-operative Anglo-Irish intergovernmental framework.

10.1 Origins

A bomb which exploded at the Grand Hotel in Brighton during the Conservative Party conference in October 1984 might have killed many members of the cabinet. The event emphasised the need for adequate security responses to the problem of terrorism. The British Army and the RUC continued to exert maximum pressure upon Republican paramilitaries in Northern Ireland. Yet the Irish Republic continued to be viewed as a relatively safe haven for IRA personnel. Greater co-operation between the British and Irish security forces was required. In return, the Irish government could be awarded input to policy-making in Northern Ireland.

Such calculations partly explain the origins of the Anglo-Irish Agreement. The British government was prepared to shift its position from its 1969 declaration at the onset of the Troubles that the affairs of Northern Ireland were purely a matter for domestic consideration. It was prepared to accept the Irishness of the minority in Northern Ireland in the hope that the Irish government would help ensure that expressions of minority interests were non-violent.

Yet, following the publication of the New Ireland Forum Report in 1984, it appeared initially that the British government was prepared to make few concessions. Unionists were adamant in their opposition to not only the Forum Report but also the findings of the Kilbrandon Report (1984). Chaired by Lord Kilbrandon, the Report was an unofficial response to the New Ireland

Forum Report and Unionist counter-proposals, produced by a committee of interested individuals, including academics and politicians. It released its proposals on the constitutional future of Northern Ireland a few days before Thatcher's withering rejection of the New Ireland Forum. The Kilbrandon Report rejected the models of a unitary or confederal state produced in the New Ireland Forum Report. It also refused to endorse the option of joint authority.

Nonetheless, the Kilbrandon Report did countenance the notion of a definite say for the Irish Republic in the affairs of Northern Ireland. Although the Committee disagreed over conclusions, its majority report argued for a co-operative devolution within Northern Ireland. At the head of government would be a five-person executive, comprising the Secretary of State for Northern Ireland, the Irish Foreign minister and three locally elected politicians. Co-operation between each party was to be encouraged by the risk that a boycott would be overridden by joint London–Dublin rule, by the two ministers on the executive. Other measures favoured included a Bill of Rights, modification of the juryless Diplock courts, and joint authorities in areas of economic co-operation, such as tourism and transport.

Unionist rejection was unsurprising. In addition to opposition to a role for the Dublin government at the apex of decision-making, Unionists objected to the proposed reduction in the size of the Ulster Defence Regiment and the legalisation of the flying of the Irish tricolour. The DUP was particularly scathing over the origins of the Commission Report in the findings of the Forum Report. Its deputy leader, Peter Robinson, argued: 'If you have to comment on a document that is absolute nonsense – as the New Ireland Forum Report was – then naturally your document will be nonsense' (quoted in Kenny, 1986: 81).

A more influential set of proposals came from Boyle and Hadden (1985). The authors argued for the exercise of authority in both Britain and Ireland by joint authorities in certain instances. In proposing a draft Anglo-Irish treaty, they advocated recognition of the following:

1. that a special relationship exists between Britain and Ireland;
2. that both communities in Northern Ireland need to be able to express their identity;
3. that the only democratic way of determining to which state Northern Ireland should belong is via the votes of its population.

The authors went on to propose many of the specific measures which would give effect to these principles. They included rights of Irish citizenship and cultural expression, joint parliamentary memberships and greater formal police co-operation. Such features were to form an integral part of the Anglo-Irish Agreement.

10.2 Terms

The Anglo-Irish Agreement was registered as an international treaty under United Nations Charter 102, although it referred to the internal workings of a sovereign state. It contained the following main themes within its 13 Articles.

10.2.1 Constitutional guarantees for the status of Northern Ireland

Article 1 of the Agreement was designed to reassure Unionists. It affirmed that any change in the status of Northern Ireland would only come about with the consent of a majority of its people. Further, it acknowledged that the 'present wish of a majority of the people of Northern Ireland is for no change in the status of Northern Ireland'.

Simultaneously, Article 1 attempted to offer hope to Nationalists that future demographic changes, leading to a Nationalist majority, would produce a united Ireland. Paragraph (c) promised to introduce legislation in the British and Irish parliaments to give effect to that wish if there was clear majority in favour.

An important aspect of the Agreement was that it did not define the state purely in territorial terms. Instead, its existence was conditional upon the consent of its people (Guelke, 1988). Normally, such a condition is applied only to a particular government, not the state itself.

10.2.2 A limited role for the Irish government in certain affairs in Northern Ireland

By far the most controversial section of the Anglo-Irish Agreement was the establishment of an intergovernmental conference. This was set up under Article 2, within the framework of the Anglo-Irish Intergovernmental Council created in 1981. The Intergovernmental Conference was to deal with the following:

(i) political matters;
(ii) security and related matters;
(iii) legal matters, including the administration of justice;
(iv) cross-border co-operation.

In accepting that the Irish government was entitled to put forward views and proposals in respect of each of the above, it insisted that there was 'no derogation of sovereignty'. Either country was to remain the ultimate arbiter of decisions taken within its own sovereign territory.

The British government suggested that the activity of the Conference would be confined to matters not already the responsibility of a devolved administration in Northern Ireland. As no such administration existed and would not be created within the immediate future, this was scarcely a reduction in the extent of intergovernmentalism. Insertion of this provision in the Agreement was a hint to politicians in Northern Ireland that they needed to co-operate if powers were ever to be restored locally.

Subsequent Articles in the Agreement attempted to define what the Intergovernmental Conference would comprise and clarify what it would discuss. Serviced by a secretariat, based at Maryfield near Belfast, the Conference was to meet at ministerial level, jointly chaired by the permanent Irish Ministerial Representative and the Secretary of State for Northern Ireland. This emphasised that the Conference would not be confined to low-level discussions.

Articles 7 and 8 dealt with security and legal matters. There was a Conference review of existing extradition procedures, under which terrorist suspects could be transferred from the Irish Republic to the United Kingdom. More contentious was the possibility raised in Article 8 of the introduction of 'mixed courts' to contain judicial representatives from both countries. Article 9 dealt with cross-border co-operation between the police forces, stressing that operational responsibilities would remain with the respective forces of the RUC and the Garda Siochana. Article 10 referred unspecifically to cross-border arrangements in other spheres of activity. Article 12 mooted the possibility of an Anglo-Irish parliamentary body, containing representatives of both parliaments.

10.2.3 Recognition of the minority tradition within Northern Ireland

The Intergovernmental Conference was to concern itself with the 'rights and identities of the two traditions in Northern Ireland'. This included matters such as cultural heritage and election arrangements, in addition to economic and social discrimination. Most significantly, there was an acceptance that the government of the Irish Republic was to be given a guaranteed role in respect of the Nationalist community. It would be permitted to put forward views in proposals for major legislation and policy issues 'where the interests of the minority community are significantly or especially affected'.

10.3 The Unionist dilemma

In a critique of the Anglo-Irish Agreement, Aughey (1989) outlines the four assumptions of the British government upon which it was predicated:

1. Northern Ireland is different from any other part of the United Kingdom and must, therefore, be treated differently;
2. the problem of Northern Ireland need not form part of debate in the British parliament, as the Province is a place apart;
3. the logic of history suggests Irish unity;
4. stability will only be achieved by a balance of political forces.

Aughey goes on to outline the assumptions that underpinned the Irish Republic's approach to the Agreement. These can be condensed to two. Firstly, Irish unity was both inevitable and desirable. Secondly, it was not imminent, nor was imminent change desirable, as the Irish government did not wish to inherit one million dissident Unionists.

To these underpinnings needed to be added the realities of politics in Northern Ireland in the mid-1980s. Attempts to achieve devolved government had been an abject failure. There was scant prospect of achieving a purely internal settlement within Northern Ireland. What was needed, therefore, was an arrangement which would provide the assurances required by Unionists without demolishing the aspirations of Nationalists.

Unionists were enraged by the Agreement. Opinion polls indicated that only 10 per cent of Protestants supported a decision-making role for the

Dublin government in the affairs of Northern Ireland (Cox, 1987: 339). Opponents saw the influence afforded to Dublin as a prelude to Irish unity. British sovereignty over Northern Ireland could no longer be absolute, as the Irish government was to be given a say in the internal affairs of Northern Ireland. Accordingly, the constitutional reassurances provided within Article 1 were seen as meaningless, as the constitutional position of Northern Ireland had been altered without the consent of the majority.

For many Unionists, allowing the Irish government a defined role in the governance of Northern Ireland was tantamount to joint authority, even though that had been rejected by Margaret Thatcher after the New Ireland Forum Report. Unionist responses were described as 'outrage, panic and hysteria' (Harkness, 1996: 109). Others criticised Unionist reaction to an 'eminently reasonable and minimalist' Agreement (Kilby, 1996: 18). The difficulty for Unionists lay in the fact that the Agreement appeared 'impervious to boycott' (Arthur, 1996: 119). The political strike which ended the power-sharing Executive of 1974 meant that the Loyalist community 'believed it could literally pull the plug on any political arrangement constructed by the British government which did not suit them' (Arthur and Jeffery, 1996: 14).

The power-sharing Executive had amounted to a failed attempt by local politicians to govern on the basis of consensus. As no consensus had been found, the policy-making base had shifted. The Anglo-Irish Agreement was an accord between two governments. The Agreement also enjoyed international backing from interested parties, notably the United States government, which provided financial support for Northern Ireland during the implementation of the Agreement. Such support was approved by the American Congress in March 1986, provided that human rights were respected in Northern Ireland (Coogan, 1987). The Agreement was devised partly due to pressure from the Irish-American lobby and the European Community, not least upon British and Irish civil servants (Connolly and Loughlin, 1986).

If local political parties and the wider population did not like it, they could protest but their dissenting actions need not be heeded. Meetings between government ministers and officials would continue apace. Violence might have produced a rethink, but the Loyalist paramilitaries instead looked to constitutional politicians for their lead. Unionist MPs possessed little clout. With a majority of over 100 in the House of Commons, the Conservative government did not require their support on domestic political issues. Support for the Anglo-Irish Agreement was cross-party, reflected in the overwhelming House of Commons approval by 473 votes to 47.

Whatever the strength of their historic links, few inside the Conservative Party had much sympathy for the position of Ulster Unionists. Amongst those taking exception to the Agreement on the right of the party was Ian Gow, a Treasury minister later murdered by the IRA, who resigned from the government over the signing of the accord. Committed since 1981 to a policy of Irish unity by consent, the Labour opposition gladly endorsed the principles of the Anglo-Irish Agreement and in 1988 promised to enlarge the work of its secretariat (Labour Party, 1988).

Overwhelming parliamentary approval for the Agreement heightened the problem for Unionists of determining a strategy of resistance which would not further undermine the Union with Great Britain. As loyal citizens, they felt obliged to accept the will of the sovereign parliament. Indeed, the demand for equal citizenship under the laws of parliament was central to their protest. Yet Unionist loyalty was conditional upon that parliament acting in the best interests of Northern Ireland. Unionist loyalty was conditional, in the same manner that loyalty from the United Kingdom appeared conditional. If Unionists were to engage in protest which enraged the remainder of Britain, the Union might be undermined to an even greater extent. Unionists believed that they were being pushed to the edge of the Union and that the Agreement represented their deeds of transfer.

Fearful for their future in the United Kingdom, Unionists were unhappy in regard to the logic of the Agreement. Britain, in effect, had given up on being a persuader for Nationalists to accept that they were British citizens. Recognition of the cultural heritage and identity of the minority exacerbated the problem of Northern Ireland by encouraging loyalty to be transferred elsewhere. A foreign state was to be the overseer of their rights. This willingness to allow influence from another state was seen as advancing the Irish Republic's territorial claim to Northern Ireland. Whatever the official insistence that there was to be no reduction in British sovereignty over Northern Ireland, the Republic had not been obliged to withdraw its claim to the six counties.

Unionists' outrage was heightened by the fact that they had been willing players in the Northern Ireland Assembly established in 1982. Politicians often seen as obstructive, such as Ian Paisley, had been strong supporters of the Assembly. Sinn Fein and the SDLP had boycotted proceedings and had appeared to rule out the prospect of devolved government in Northern Ireland. Now it appeared to Unionists that the SDLP was to be rewarded with the ending of attempts at rolling devolution. The abandonment of a party-led approach in favour of government-based initiatives appeared, in Unionist eyes, to treat the co-operative forces of unionism with contempt.

10.4 Unionist responses

Despite the problems of mounting a campaign of opposition, a huge peaceful mobilisation nonetheless occurred, through overlapping organisations. The Ulster Clubs began the co-ordination of opposition, provided by a network of local protest groups. They demanded full British citizenship and defence of the Protestant heritage. Aughey (1989) acknowledges that the two demands appeared contradictory, in that the latter created an unnecessary condition of citizenship.

The Ulster Resistance movement was formed, designed to provide disciplined opposition to the implementation of the Agreement. As with his pursuit of the Carson Trail in the display of firearms certificates in 1981, so Paisley again offered the prospect of civil disobedience, with the implied threat of even greater militancy. Paisley's sense of betrayal was such that he urged redress from another quarter. Addressing his congregation in November 1985, shortly after publication of the Agreement, he implored:

> We pray this night that Thou wouldst deal with the Prime Minister of our country. We remember that the Apostle Paul handed over the enemies of truth to the Devil that they might learn not to blaspheme. In the Name of thy blessed Self, Father, Son and Holy Ghost, we hand this woman Margaret Thatcher to the Devil, that she might learn not to blaspheme. We pray that thouds't make her a monument of Thy divine vengeance; we pray that the world will learn a lesson through her fall and will learn a lesson through the ignominy to which she will be brought . . . O God, in wrath take vengeance upon this wicked, treacherous lying woman . . . take vengeance upon her O Lord and grant that we shall see a demonstration of thy power. (quoted in Smyth, 1987: 192).

In the event, vengeance upon Margaret Thatcher came exactly five years later, although her removal from prime ministerial office has been more closely associated by most commentators with a devilish poll tax and divisions over Europe rather than celestial forces.

The extent of anger within all sections of the Unionist community was visible on 23 November 1986 when an astonishingly large turnout of 200,000 attended an 'Ulster Says No' protest rally at the City Hall in Belfast. The rally was attended by 20 per cent of the entire Protestant population. A similarly proportional demonstration in England would have produced a turnout of four million.

Unionists emphasised the need for a united protest. To this effect, all 15 Unionist MPs resigned their seats and contested by-elections in January 1986. In a number of seats, a dummy candidate called Peter Barry, the name of the Irish Foreign Minister, was entered. The device was used to give the impression of a referendum, in which those in favour could vote for a pro-Agreement candidate.

In the event, the impact of the referendum policy was muted for several reasons. From a Nationalist perspective, the in-built Unionist majority in Northern Ireland gave all electoral contests an air of unreality. More specifically in this case, the tactic backfired as the Unionists were returned in only 14 of the 15 seats from which they had resigned. Media focus was concentrated upon the loss of Newry-Armagh to Seamus Mallon of the SDLP.

Overall, the total number of votes against the Agreement cast for Unionist candidates totalled 418,230. This amounted to three-quarters of those polled, although less than half of the electorate. Even if the votes of Sinn Fein were added to the 'anti' cause, a highly dubious proposition given the entirely different basis of its opposition, less than half of the electorate bothered to record a vote against the Agreement. Unionist hostility to the Agreement was indeed intense, but the referendum device was perhaps not the clearest means of its expression.

Unionist disaffection was now translated into actions which affected the governance of Northern Ireland. With the exception of Enoch Powell, Unionist MPs boycotted proceedings at Westminster. A petition of protest attracted over 400,000 signatures. Disruption of council business, a protest begun after the election of 59 Sinn Fein councillors in May 1985, was now extended to each of the 18 councils controlled by Unionists.

Not all councillors were happy over the withdrawal from public duty. The decision of Unionist councils not to set a rate and to adjourn meetings indefinitely prompted some disquiet. Ulster Unionist Party councillors in North Down chose to ignore the party edict and continued to conduct council business. There was division over whether councillors should resign or simply refuse to conduct certain aspects of council activity. Generally Unionists remained united. Most thought that withdrawal tactics would be persuasive in eliciting a change of heart from the British government, but the Thatcher government remained unmoved and rates for dissenting councils were set by the Northern Ireland Office. There was some official recognition of the need to appear to implement the Agreement with sensitivity. For example, no action was taken against those councillors failing to set a rate. This contrasted with actions pursued against councillors engaging in political strikes on the mainland, as disqualified and surcharged councillors in Liverpool and Lambeth could testify.

The Taoiseach (Irish Prime Minister), Garret Fitzgerald, argued that the main impact of the Unionist response was to force the British government to play down the importance of the Agreement, thereby underselling to Nationalists the 'remarkable number of changes effected through its mechanisms' (Fitzgerald, 1991: 575). The refusal of the British government to budge on the Anglo-Irish Agreement held firm even when Unionists modified their negotiating position to call for its suspension, rather than entire abandonment, pending talks about devolution. A new difficulty for Unionists was deciding what political stance to adopt as the new reality dawned. The affairs of Northern Ireland would never again lie in the exclusive domain of the British government, nor would they reside solely amongst politicians in Northern Ireland.

A general strike on 3 March 1986 also failed to move the British government. There were numerous allegations of intimation made against the organisers of the strike. As RUC officers attempted to remove barricades, attacks by Loyalists increased upon 'their' police force. In the six months following the Agreement, 300 attacks on the homes of officers had occurred, causing 50 officers to be rehoused away from staunchly Loyalist areas, previously considered relatively safe.

Unionists feared correctly that violence would increase as a result of the Agreement. For all their criticisms of the content of the accord, Sinn Fein believed that any political gains were nonetheless all their work. The IRA campaign had forced the British government to concede a permanent political role for the Irish government. This gave effect to the Republic's constitutional claim to the North and moved the prospect of Irish unity a little closer. The British government appeared to shift towards an assumption of the inevitability of Irish unity, whilst conceding that it was impossible to achieve at present.

In their desperation to get rid of the Agreement, two Unionists even challenged its validity in the Irish Republic. They argued that it violated the constitutional claim to Northern Ireland found in Articles 2 and 3 of the

Republic's constitution. In rejecting the case, Mr Justice Barrington declared that Article 1 of the Agreement amounted merely to a recognition of the existing political reality in Northern Ireland, in that consent for a united Ireland was not immediately available. It was not tantamount to a renunciation of the Republic's claim that the Irish nation consisted of the entire island of Ireland. Pursuit of this constitutional imperative was unimpaired. The verdict echoed that recorded after the challenge to the Sunningdale Agreement a decade earlier.

10.5 Nationalist responses

The SDLP was delighted by the introduction of the Anglo-Irish Agreement. It mollified the desire of the party for an intergovernmental approach which reflected that the Northern Nationalist minority was Irish, not British. This minority saw the Republic as a guarantor of its rights, an aspiration recognised in the accord. The Irish government claimed a 'special relationship' with Nationalists in Northern Ireland (Connolly, 1990: 68). It had now secured an Agreement which 'reflected the upward trajectory of Dublin influence' (Coogan, 1995: 183).

From the outset, the SDLP had proposed that the Anglo-Irish Intergovernmental Council established in 1981 should deal with issues of security and nationality. Conflict resolution needed to be institutionalised in a British-Irish context (White, 1984). The Anglo-Irish Agreement provided a suitable framework. The SDLP's enthusiasm outshone even that held by the Irish government. Aughey (1989: 59) describes this as the 'SDLP tail wagging the Irish dog'.

Two other aspects of the Agreement delighted the SDLP. Firstly, the Agreement had a 'green tinge' in that it acknowledged the aspiration of Irish unity, without immediately advancing its implementation. This was sufficient for constitutional Nationalists, who recognised that an 'agreed Ireland' could only be achieved with the consent of a majority in the North. What was needed was explicit reassurance that the British government would facilitate a united Ireland when sufficient consent arrived. Few in the South desired an immediate transfer of overall responsibility for the problem of Northern Ireland. This further annoyed Unionists who believed that the Agreement gave the South power without responsibility.

Secondly, pending the arrival of Northern consent for unity, what was required was a welding together of institutions in the island of Ireland. By providing a framework of co-operative relationships, the SDLP hoped that the border might wither as an irrelevance. Optimistically, there was a belief among some Nationalists that Unionists might be dissuaded of the necessity of the preservation of the British link by an economic rationale, if trading links were developed with the Republic and Europe.

A deliberate aim of the Agreement was the bolstering of the constitutional nationalism of the SDLP at the expense of the militant republicanism of Sinn Fein. Both the British and Irish governments had been concerned by the electoral rise of the latter. In the 1983 General Election, Sinn Fein achieved only 4.5 per cent fewer votes than the SDLP. Whilst it remained unlikely that support for the constitutional variation of nationalism would be relegated to a minority taste within the Nationalist community, it was now a possibility.

Sinn Fein's support was not merely a product of increased Nationalist political support for the IRA's 'armed struggle'. Residual sympathy from the hunger strikes and the involvement of Sinn Fein councillors in community work also boosted the party's following. After the Anglo-Irish Agreement was signed, Sinn Fein's electoral support waned for a time, although it is difficult to identify with precision the extent to which this decline can be attributed to the treaty. In the 1987 General Election and 1989 European contest, Sinn Fein trailed the SDLP by 10 per cent of the vote.

Sinn Fein saw little merit in an Agreement which it believed consolidated the six-county state and provided a Unionist veto over change. The party saw the main motivation underpinning the Agreement as the formation of an anti-Republican consensus (Ryan, 1994). In allowing the aspiration of Irish unity or even joint authority to be quashed by the British government, the Irish government had settled for a pale imitation, based around periodic consultation. The Agreement appeared to recognise British sovereignty over Northern Ireland. Concurrently, increased British influence upon the activities of the government in the Republic amounted to a partial recolonisation of Ireland.

Republicans viewed the main role granted to the Irish government as the prevention of terrorism. The Irish government was being asked to do the 'dirty work' of the British government in propping up the Northern state. Cross-border policing initiatives were designed as a counter-offensive against the IRA. Even some constitutional Nationalists within the island of Ireland did not favour the Agreement. In the Republic, Charles Haughey, the leader of Fianna Fail, the main opposition party, condemned the accord. He shared the view of Gerry Adams, the president of Sinn Fein, that the Agreement 'copper-fastened partition', through its refusal to change the status of Northern Ireland without majority consent. For Haughey, the 'failed political entity' of Northern Ireland was illegitimate and artificial. Haughey's party forced a close vote in the Dail, but the Agreement was passed by 88 votes to 75. Faced with political difficulties arising from the popularity of the Agreement amongst the electorate of the Republic, Haughey subsequently toned down his opposition.

10.6 After the Anglo–Irish Agreement

Whilst the intensity and extent of protest against the Agreement was considerable in the short term, by mid-1986 the campaign was already in decline. Although it was to be some time before all councils resumed normal business, Belfast City Council narrowly voted to end its protest and resume business in May 1986. A 1988 review of the Agreement amounted to little more than a renewal (Cochrane, 1993). A search was underway amongst Unionists for political alternatives.

One such alternative was *Common Sense*, published by the UDA in 1987. The UDA's abandonment of the idea of an independent Ulster in favour of a retention of British control was received favourably in Unionist circles. Whilst the UDA supported independence, it was seen by fellow Loyalist critics as some kind of 'Prod Sinn Fein' (Bruce, 1994: 104). Now the UDA was seen as 'sound' on the constitution and its ideas of devolved government, with all parties represented according to electoral support, steered an acceptable course between enforced power-sharing and majority rule.

In order to continue the campaign against the Agreement and search for alternatives, the Unionist Task Force was established in February 1987, again emphasising unity between different strands of unionism. Such unity was reinforced in the June 1987 General Election in which the Ulster Unionist Party and Democratic Unionist Party did not fight each other in parliamentary constituencies.

One Unionist disturbing this common approach was Robert McCartney, the Head of the Campaign for Equal Citizenship (CEC) and later the leader of the United Kingdom Unionist Party. The CEC was established in the wake of the Anglo-Irish Agreement to campaign for full electoral integration, McCartney refused to accept the 'no contest' edict and was expelled from the Ulster Unionist Party. It was the view of the CEC that the Anglo-Irish Agreement highlighted the need for full integration. Only by allowing the citizens of Northern Ireland to participate fully in selecting a British government would they be treated equally within the United Kingdom. Ulster unionism also needed to shed its sectarian image and embrace Catholics to a greater extent. At odds with the devolutionist DUP, McCartney went much further than the seemingly integrationist approach of the Ulster Unionist leader, James Molyneaux. McCartney wanted total integration, rather than the 'minimalist unionism' of compromise between the integrationist and devolutionist wings of the Ulster Unionist Party practised by Molyneaux (Bew and Patterson, 1987).

The Joint Unionist Manifesto devised for the 1987 General Election concentrated most of its efforts upon a scathing critique of the Anglo-Irish Agreement, exemplified by the title of the document *To Put Right a Great Wrong*. Unsurprisingly, the document demanded the suspension of the Agreement as a precursor to the formation of a viable alternative. The electoral pact yielded 380,000 votes, over half the total cast. Most coverage nonetheless centred upon the ousting of the Ulster Unionist Enoch Powell by the SDLP in South Down.

In an attempt to move forward after the Anglo-Irish Agreement, Unionists produced the report *An End to Drift* (Joint Unionist Task Force, 1987). Whilst favouring devolution as the long-term option, the Report rejected this as a means of abolishing the Anglo-Irish Agreement. It argued that the Agreement had placed too many constraints upon a devolved settlement, through the workings of the Anglo-Irish Conference. More surprisingly, the Report appeared to suggest a doomsday scenario, hinting that Unionists should prepare for devolution outside the United Kingdom, a defeatist notion which alarmed other Unionists (Aughey, 1989).

10.7 Lasting significance

The Agreement had huge implications for the conduct of Northern Ireland policy, henceforth bi-national. In the shorter term, there were legislative items arising as a consequence of the Agreement, such as the repeal of discriminatory legislation and changes in security structures. One such change was the abolition of the Flags and Emblems Act which forbade the display of the Irish tricolour. Another was the merger of the Ulster Defence Regiment (UDR) with the Royal Irish Regiment. Whether this made any impact within Nationalist communities is doubtful. Many Nationalists viewed this force, whatever its title, as a successor to the old 'B' Specials. Other measures were rehousing schemes, promotion of the status of the Gaelic language and the initiation of fair employment legislation (Cochrane, 1993). Part of the fair employment legislation was based upon the 'MacBride Principles' named after the Nobel Prize winner, Sean MacBride. Firms investing in Northern Ireland were monitored in an attempt to eliminate religious discrimination in recruitment and workplace policies.

Unionists believed that the Agreement did not succeed in eliciting substantial progress on extradition procedures. The 247 deaths arising from the Troubles in the three years immediately following the Agreement represented a 27 per cent increase on the total for 1983–5. Republican violence increased as the electoral gains of Sinn Fein were halted. Loyalist paramilitaries revived.

Little change was effected internally in the Irish Republic. Optimistic constitutional crusaders, such as Fitzgerald, believed that reform would make the Republic a more attractive proposition for Unionists. These campaigners received a rebuff in 1986, when a referendum on whether to overturn the constitutional ban on divorce introduced in the 1937 Constitution produced a two-to-one majority in favour of the status quo. The victory was welcomed by the Catholic Church but it disappointed the Church of Ireland, which argued for greater separation of church from state policy. A further nine years elapsed before this result was overturned.

Few in Northern Ireland saw the Anglo-Irish Agreement as a panacea. In 1988, a very substantial majority in both communities believed that the Agreement had failed to benefit Nationalists or Unionists. Despite their protests against the principle of the Agreement, only 28 per cent of Protestants claimed that it benefited Nationalists (Boyle and Hadden, 1989: 19). What, therefore, was all the fuss about?

Perhaps more important than the specific measures produced was the model of intergovernmental co-operation which underpinned the Agreement. In attempting to resolve the Northern Ireland conflict, the Anglo-Irish Agreement was the undoubted forerunner of the peace process of the 1990s. Parties were no longer the main arbiters of politics in Northern Ireland, until they could agree to co-operate. Governments were now the key players. Agreements produced in the peace process of the 1990s were framed by governments, and then shaped, in terms of detail, by political parties. Britain's relationship with Ireland was now much more crucial to the immediate future of Northern

Ireland than local politics. As Arthur and Jeffery (1996: 2) noted, the implication was that 'a much greater onus is placed on the British political process than heretofore'.

Equally, even non-Unionist commentators acknowledged that the Anglo-Irish Agreement 'signalled a decline in British enthusiasm for the Union' (Ryan, 1994: 3). This lack of enthusiasm was to become further evident in future. Each recent agreement, beginning with the Anglo-Irish accord, was to indicate that the future of unionism had no more solid base than the demographics of the time. If they were to change and a Nationalist majority were to emerge, the British government would end its involvement in Northern Ireland. Such demographic change was nonetheless a remote prospect.

10.8 Conclusion

The Anglo-Irish Agreement provided a forerunner to the peace process which developed in the 1990s. Notwithstanding his party's official stance of opposition, a senior member of Sinn Fein conceded in private that 'as a result . . . the British government position has changed and changed irrevocably' (Mitchel McLaughlin, quoted in Mallie and McKittrick, 1996: 36). The changes were thus. Firstly, any lingering prospect of a return to a pre-1972 Unionist veto over internal change in Northern Ireland was ended. Secondly, Britain had declared herself broadly neutral on the future of the Union. Thirdly, the Irish government was the new custodian of the rights of Nationalists in Northern Ireland.

Constitutional guarantees that the formal status of Northern Ireland could not be changed without the consent of Unionists meant that the Anglo-Irish Agreement was unacceptable to Republicans, who also rejected its cross-border security measures. What Republicans sought was some discussion of the notion of self-determination for all living on the island of Ireland, not merely a requirement for Unionist consent to constitutional change. If the IRA was to be weaned away from violence, such 'green language' was required in future agreements. With gathering momentum, the search began for nuanced phraseology.

Chapter 11

The logic of the peace process: changes in republicanism

By the mid-1980s, there was a military stalemate in Northern Ireland. Outright defeat of the IRA appeared unlikely. Equally, it was apparent that the IRA could not force a British withdrawal. To end its campaign, the IRA needed to be convinced that Britain had no particular desire to stay in Northern Ireland and might withdraw at some point in the future. If Britain gave a strong indication of withdrawal, there was a risk of Loyalist violence. Could this dilemma be resolved and a peace process created?

Given the IRA's assessment throughout the Troubles that it was fighting an anti-colonial war, persuading the organisation that violence served no positive function in the cause of Irish unity would not be easy. Nonetheless this was the task upon which constitutional Nationalists embarked in the late 1980s. This persuasion was designed to create a logic of peace. It represented the informal stage one of what became known as the peace process. Stage two, based upon formal government declarations, was to follow. Stage three brought about multi-party negotiations, culminating in the Good Friday Agreement. This chapter analyses the development of the first stage, arguing that the peace process was built mainly upon changes within Irish republicanism. This is not to underplay the roles of other actors, notably the British and Irish governments, the United States government, the SDLP and the Unionists. Each nuanced their stance in respect of Northern Ireland, but remained committed to the core principle of consent for change in Northern Ireland. All groups shifted, but Sinn Fein shifted most, in developing a peace process.

Republicanism has never been entirely cohesive. Indeed, throughout the history of the IRA, Brendan Behan once remarked, the first item on the agenda was the split. After the Official IRA called a ceasefire in 1972, it was the Provisional IRA which soon became *the* IRA, continuing a military campaign against British rule. Some former supporters of the Official IRA became strident critics of the Provisionals within the Workers Party or the Democratic Left. Others took a different course and joined the Irish National Liberation Army (INLA), or its political wing, the Irish Republican Socialist Party. The INLA was committed to violence as a means of establishing a thirty-two-county Irish Republic. It engaged in a murderous feud with remaining members of the Official IRA during the 1970s. Avowedly socialist and non-sectarian, the INLA nonetheless engaged in a high number of sectarian acts and committed several of the worst atrocities during the Troubles. If a peace process was to develop, it was important, firstly, that most Republicans, notably Sinn Fein and the IRA, were 'onside' and, secondly, that a serious Republican split did not emerge. Any peace process which failed to deliver the traditional goals of republicanism risked splitting the Republican movement.

11.1 Militarism versus politics

The initial belief of the Provisional IRA that Britain could be rapidly ejected from Ireland through force peaked in 1972. It appeared that the organisation had bombed itself to the negotiating table. A delegation of IRA members met the Northern Ireland Secretary William Whitelaw for talks. A straightforward 'Brits out' policy characterised the IRA's approach. The non-negotiability of this demand contributed to the rapid collapse of the talks, as did alleged infringements of the ceasefire called during their duration.

Yet, by the time of the fruitless 1972 talks, the IRA campaign had already peaked. Under increasing pressure from the security forces, the offensive waned under a series of ceasefires, internecine feuds, a descent into sectarian killings and the lack of a political outlet for activity. By the late 1970s, the IRA was not beaten, but it had been contained.

During the era that paramilitary activity was seen as likely to triumph, politics were subordinate. The only political strategy that existed was based upon the form a new Ireland would take when the British withdrew. Politics as a route towards achieving the removal of the British presence was regarded by many with contempt. A new Ireland was to develop along the lines of the socialist romanticism of Eire Nua, the policy of Sinn Fein. This was based upon the following ideas:

1. the creation of a federal Ireland;
2. the establishment of four federal parliaments, based upon the historic four provinces of the island;
3. the development of industrial and farming co-operatives.

In effect, what was proposed was a garrison Ireland, which would, for example, withdraw from the European Community. Outside the Provisional IRA and its supporters, the proposals attracted little interest. Within Ireland, power would be devolved to each parliament. According to supporters, a particular advantage would be that Unionists would remain largely in control of their own destiny within a nine-county Ulster parliament (O'Bradaigh, 1996).

As the limitations to its military strategy became apparent, Sinn Fein sought to bolster its political role. In 1981, it rejected the Eire Nua strategy in favour of a unitary Irish state. This did not represent the adoption of a more moderate political approach. Rather, Eire Nua was abandoned because, according to Sinn Fein, 'any solution that left power in the hands of Loyalists would not have succeeded in breaking the political presence of the British in this country' (Morrison, 1985: 87).

Sinn Fein began to campaign much more actively in elections following the hunger strikes by Republican prisoners in 1980 and 1981. As Nationalist sentiment was aroused, so election successes began for Republicans. The election of the IRA's Bobby Sands in a Westminster by-election was followed by the election of his agent, Owen Carron, in the by-election caused by Sands' death from starvation. Republican prisoners were also elected to the Irish Parliament.

Within Sinn Fein, these developments led to greater parity for a political approach, alongside the IRA's continuing military campaign. This strategy was indicated by the director of publicity for Sinn Fein, Danny Morrison, at the 1981 *ard fheis*:

> Who here really believes that we can win the war through the ballot box? But will anyone here object if with a ballot paper in this hand and an armalite in this hand we take power in Ireland?.

Sinn Fein's difficulty was, of course, that a great many people outside the conference hall would have objected. Nonetheless, the party's dual strategy proved successful in mobilising support. A resurgent IRA, organised into cells, was capable of launching countless 'spectacular' operations, even if the overall level of activity was reduced from that of the early 1970s. Political support for armed republicanism, if measured in terms of votes for Sinn Fein, was at its highest level since partition.

Despite this, the Republican movement faced two particular difficulties by 1986. Firstly, it had a lack of a decisive mandate amongst the Nationalist population. Following the signing of the Anglo-Irish Agreement, the SDLP's electoral support had stabilised and it appeared that Sinn Fein would remain the minority voice of Irish nationalism. A senior party figure, Mitchel McLaughlin, wrote in 1985, in an internal party document, that there were positive aspects to the Anglo-Irish Agreement and that it marked a change in British policy. McLaughlin later claimed that his document was designed as a polemic to 'stimulate debate' (interview with author, 28 June 2000). He achieved his objective, as Republicans considered alternative strategies. In the Irish Republic, Sinn Fein secured only woeful election results. Secondly, the IRA was coming under considerable pressure from the security forces and from revived Loyalist paramilitary groups. Under new leaderships, the latter concentrated upon the removal of suspected Republicans.

Politically stalled, there was a realisation amongst many leading figures within Sinn Fein and the IRA that military pressure alone would be insufficient to remove Britain from Northern Ireland. Whilst the IRA had enough weaponry to continue its campaign for the foreseeable future, it was prepared to countenance a shift in political direction. After the bombing of a Remembrance Day commemoration in Enniskillen by the IRA, there was even a brief period when English public opinion was so enraged that it favoured keeping troops in Northern Ireland (Hayes and McAllister, 1996). Sinn Fein's political message was having little impact, a problem worsened by the broadcasting ban imposed upon supporters of paramilitary activity in 1988. A strategic rethink was begun. This involved three developments: acceptance of the twenty-six-county Irish Republic, dialogue with constitutional Nationalists and a reduction in immediate political demands.

11.2 Recognition of the Irish Republic _____

A central problem for Sinn Fein was how to assert its demand for a united Ireland in the face of the persistent assertion from the British government that there could be no change in the constitutional future of Northern Ireland without the consent of a majority of its population. For Sinn Fein to significantly advance its position, it might mean movement from seeing itself as the sole 'liberator' of Ireland. This is itself would be a significant step, given that the term *Sinn Fein* means 'ourselves'.

Coogan (1995) suggests that the origins of the 1990s peace process date back to the first indication of Sinn Fein's abandonment of the 'go-it-alone' strategy. This shift began shortly after the papal visit to Ireland in 1979. During his visit, the Pope condemned violence. Exasperated by the refusal of the Catholic hierarchy, in Rome and Ireland, to support what he regarded as a just war, Gerry Adams engaged in dialogue with church leaders, seeking clarification of their position.

During the latter half of the 1980s, a more substantial alignment of political forces began to take shape, through the development of a so-called 'pan-nationalist' front. The term was often used in a derogatory sense by Unionists. It meant that Nationalists of differing shades of green were to come together to try to achieve constitutional change in respect of Northern Ireland. The leadership of Sinn Fein perceived that the best way to advance its cause might be to end political isolation. If this meant that the formerly despised Dublin government should act as a voice for Northern Nationalists, so be it. The development of a coalition of forces would be based upon incrementalism. If it became apparent that one set of constitutional Nationalists were prepare to engage in discussions with Sinn Fein, it was assumed that others would follow.

A first major step away from political wilderness came in 1986. At the party's *ard fheis*, Sinn Fein delegates voted by 429 votes to 161 to end the policy of abstentionism in elections to the Dail. From now on, in the event of Sinn Fein candidates being elected to the parliament of the Irish Republic (an unlikely prospect at the time) they would take their seats. Crucially, the move was supported by the General Army Convention, the ultimate authority of the IRA. Its meetings are extremely rare, stressing the importance of the 1986 decision. Similar events have been staged in 1969 at the formation of the Provisionals; in 1996, when future strategy was debated after the end of the IRA ceasefire; and in 1998 in respect of the decision to enter Stormont. The General Army Convention elects the Army Executive which in turns chooses an Army Council of seven members. General Headquarters Staff, below the Army Council in the hierarchy, co-ordinates paramilitary action.

The decision to end abstentionism had considerable symbolic importance. Having been founded partly as a result of their ideologically pure abstentionist stance, the Provisional IRA was reversing policy. No longer was it claiming that the short-lived 1918 parliament created after the Easter Rising was the only legitimate Irish parliament. On election to the party presidency in 1983, Gerry Adams denied that he sought an end to abstentionism (*An Phoblacht/*

Republican News, 17 November 1983). However, change appeared logical and Adams moved swiftly in this direction, not least because he acknowledged that the citizens of the Irish Republic accepted their state institutions as legitimate. Indeed, it had already been acknowledged that failure to recognise this was to 'blinker republican politics' (*An Phoblacht/Republican News*, 23 June 1983). The end of abstentionism enraged traditionalists, with a number leaving to form their own organisation, Republican Sinn Fein, proclaiming that it was the direct lineal descendant of the 1918 Dail Eireann.

In effect, Sinn Fein was recognising the Southern, twenty-six-county state, which until this point it had denounced as a neo-colonial 'puppet'. Recognition of the state made it easier for the Irish government to embrace some of the aspirations of Sinn Fein. Shortly after the *ard fheis* decision, the Irish government began limited contacts with Sinn Fein.

11.3 Dialogue with constitutional Nationalists

By the late 1980s, Sinn Fein's search for allies was gathering pace. Gerry Adams argued that 'the politics demanded the building of a consensus. Sinn Fein had by that point developed a position which saw dialogue as the main vehicle for resolving this problem' (quoted in Mallie and McKittrick, 1996: 72). The SDLP had always taken this view. Its leader, John Hume, believed that dialogue with Sinn Fein might move the IRA away from violence. In 1988, the Hume–Adams talks began.

Facilitated by figures within the Catholic Church, including a Belfast priest, Father Alec Reid, a series of meetings between the leaderships of the SDLP and Sinn Fein took place in 1988. The dialogue took place amid growing debate among Republicans, although publicly their demands remained unaltered. A policy document issued by Sinn Fein in May 1987, *Scenario for Peace*, offered an uncompromising reassertion of the basic principles of armed republicanism:

1. Britain must withdraw from Northern Ireland;
2. the use of armed force to eject Britain is legitimate;
3. the 'armed struggle' is a war against a colonial aggressor;
4. British security forces, namely the RUC and UDR, must be disbanded;
5. all Republican prisoners must be released unconditionally;
6. Unionists must accept a united Ireland.

Whatever *Scenario for Peace* was, it was not a basis for negotiation. Arguably, it was the last gasp of uncompromising republicanism from Sinn Fein. Despite this, the Hume–Adams talks began in April 1988 and exchanges of policy documents continued until September 1988. Hume attempted three things. First, he strove to persuade Adams of the futility of continued violence. Second, he attempted to convince Sinn Fein of British neutrality. Finally, he argued that Sinn Fein needed to develop much greater consideration of the Unionist position.

Although the initial Hume–Adams dialogue ended without agreement, the fact that the meetings occurred at all was perhaps more significant. Sinn Fein was no longer a political leper and other furtive political contacts could begin within the 'Nationalist family'. Whilst Hume had been unable to convince Adams that abandonment of violence by the IRA was the appropriate way forward, there was agreement upon the idea that the Irish question could only be resolved through national self-determination. In other words, all the people on the island of Ireland must be involved in the resolution of the political future of the island. The debate was to move on to the question of how that self-determination could most fairly be exercised.

Acknowledgement of some of Hume's arguments was apparent within Sinn Fein thinking by 1992. During that year, Sinn Fein produced a document more conciliatory than *Scenario for Peace*. Instead, *Towards a Lasting Peace in Ireland* appeared to indicate a shift in Republican analysis, which did not envisage the role of the British government merely as one of 'surrender and withdrawal' (Bean, 1995: 3). Significantly, the document urged Britain to become a persuader to Unionists to accept the need for a united Ireland. Suddenly, Unionist attitudes, as distinct from the British presence, appeared to be the central problem. Republicans hoped that Britain would adopt the position of, for example, de Gaulle in permitting self-determination for Algeria, despite the presence of a French minority within the country. Others argued that there were fewer similar strategic advantages for Britain in adopting a 'persuader' role (Wright, 1987).

Urging Nationalist unity, *Towards a Lasting Peace in Ireland* outlined the need for Irish self-determination. All the people on the island of Ireland were to determine their future together in a process of national reconciliation. There was a downgrading of emphasis upon the need for 'armed struggle' and less stridency over the need for immediate British withdrawal. *Towards a Lasting Peace in Ireland* amounted to an appeal to all of Nationalist Ireland to form a common approach towards constitutional change. At the same time, the role of armed struggle was being reconsidered, with a leading Republican, Jim Gibney, urging Republicans not to be 'deafened by the deadly sound of their own gunfire' (quoted in Patterson, 1997: 240).

As republicanism moved tentatively towards constitutionalism, it aimed to achieve two things. First, Unionists would be left as an even smaller minority waged against the combined Nationalist forces of the Irish government, Irish America and Northern Nationalists. British neutrality would be insufficient to shore up their position, particularly as the attitude of the British public was unsympathetic to the Unionist position. Secondly, it was hoped that Republicans would then enter into a 'historic handshake' with the British government in a manner reminiscent of that between the South African President de Klerk and Nelson Mandela in 1989 (Toolis, 1995: 329).

11.4 The Brooke Initiatives

In appearing to endorse the idea that Britain should join the persuaders, Sinn Fein was encouraged by the attitude of Peter Brooke, appointed Secretary of State for Northern Ireland in July 1989. Brooke encouraged the IRA to call a ceasefire, promising 'imaginative steps' in response. In a speech in his constituency in November 1990, the Northern Ireland Secretary gave perhaps the baldest assertion of British neutrality thus far when he insisted that Britain had no 'selfish strategic or economic interest' in Northern Ireland. Brooke's statement was based upon his exasperation from reading copies of *An Phoblacht* (*Republican News*) which 'did go on and on and on about it being a colonialist struggle and the motivation of the British Government being imperialist' (quoted in Mallie and McKittrick, 1996: 108). The minister also engaged in two initiatives, one public, the other private. Public politics were based upon a tentative search for a replacement for the Anglo-Irish Agreement. Any replacement would need to incorporate the three dimensions of Northern Ireland's politics: intercommunity relationships, intergovernmental negotiations, and co-operation between Northern Ireland and the Irish Republic. Talks involving the main constitutional parties on the internal government of Northern Ireland (Strand 1 talks) were to be followed by discussion of North–South relationships (Strand 2) and intergovernmental arrangements (Strand 3). As a concession to Unionist sensitivities, the Intergovernmental Conference enshrined in the Anglo-Irish Agreement was suspended temporarily whilst an agenda for talks was framed.

Whatever the potential for such talks, they broke down before progressing beyond arguments over agendas. Disputes over the timetable for each Strand and the choice of a chairman for the Strand 2 talks undermined the Brooke Initiative. The public Brooke Initiative, therefore, withered by mid-1991. Acrimonious debates over procedural matters had, in effect, left the political parties in Northern Ireland powerless.

Whilst acknowledging the possibilities raised by the Brooke Initiative, Arthur (1992: 114) nonetheless describes the attitudes of the participants of the 1990–1 non-discussions as the 'equivalent of two bald men fighting over a comb'. A similar form of initiative instigated by Brooke's successor, Patrick Mayhew, floundered in similar circumstances a year later. More significant was Brooke's private sanctioning of a secret line of communication to the Republican leadership, known as the Back Channel. Established in 1990, the Back Channel was not new, in that lines of communication to the IRA had existed during previous crises. Its role now was to establish the conditions under which the IRA might call a ceasefire. Discussions took place between authorised British intelligence personnel and Republican leaders. The contacts took place on a basis that their existence could be denied.

The precise extent and content of the Back Channel discussions was disputed. Sinn Fein's account argued that the British representatives agreed that Irish unity was inevitable (Sinn Fein, 1994). The British government claimed that the IRA had initiated the contacts by asserting that the conflict was effectively over. Whatever the veracity of either account, the existence of the Back Channel was embarrassing for the Prime Minister, John Major, who had publicly insisted that he was unwilling to talk to Sinn Fein.

What was apparent was that both sides were serious in their intent to end political stalemate. Secret discussions continued after Brooke left his post. The

departure followed a bizarre incident in which he was admonished by Unionists for being lured into singing 'My Darling Clementine' on the Gay Byrne
show on Irish television, in the sensitive aftermath of a Republican atrocity.
Contact with the IRA survived even the revulsion felt after the organisation's
killing of two young boys in Warrington in 1993. A mortar bomb attack
upon Downing Street and a large bomb attack upon the City of London also
occurred during the period of secret communications.

11.5 The revival of Hume–Adams

Whilst the Back Channel continued secretly, the Hume–Adams talks were
resuscitated and this time produced a more substantial outcome. In April
1993, the two leaders issued a joint statement reiterating their commitment to
the achievement of self-determination for the Irish people. Part of the statement declared:

> . . . we accept that an internal settlement is not a solution because it obviously does
> not deal with all the relationships at the heart of the problem. We accept that the
> Irish people as a whole have the right to national self-determination. This is a view
> shared by a majority of the people of this island, though not by all its people. The
> exercise of self-determination is a matter for agreement between the people of
> Ireland.

Assisted by changes within Sinn Fein's strategy highlighted in *Towards a
Lasting Peace in Ireland*, the talks gathered momentum. The two party leaders
were prepared to engage in a Nationalist-led initiative which looked to the
London and Dublin governments for brokerage. The tortuous attempt to
build a ceasefire appeared threatened in October 1993 when an upsurge of
violence claimed 25 lives, including nine deaths in an IRA bombing of a fish
shop on the Shankill and a Loyalist machine-gunning of seven people at
Greysteel. Adams bore the coffin at the funeral of the Shankill bomber, killed
in the explosion.

Surviving these crises, the Hume–Adams dialogue and embryonic peace
process continued apace. The two leaders produced a draft document, an
amended form of which was to form the basis for the Downing Street Declaration in December 1993. Eight Articles were contained in the draft. Article 5
declared:

> the democratic right of self-determination by the people of Ireland as a whole must
> be achieved and exercised with the agreement and consent of the people of North-
> ern Ireland . . . (quoted in *Sunday Tribune*, 28 August 1995).

That Sinn Fein was prepared to discuss consent in respect of the unit of
Northern Ireland was a significant step. Until this point, the existence of
Northern Ireland was not recognised. Nonetheless, the phraseology masked
continuing differences between the constitutional nationalism of the SDLP
and the republicanism of Sinn Fein. Debating the Downing Street Declaration at Sinn Fein's national internal conference at Letterkenny in July 1994,
Sinn Fein passed the following motions:

1. the exercise of national self-determination is a matter for agreement between the people of Ireland;
2. the consent and allegiance of Unionists are essential ingredients if a lasting peace is to be established;
3. the Unionists cannot have a veto over British policy or over political progress in Ireland.

11.6 Changes in the Republican agenda

To what extent had the agenda of Sinn Fein and the IRA really changed? Nationalists of different shades of opinion were united in their insistence that the Northern Ireland state had failed in its previous and present forms. The peace process therefore needed to be predicated upon the assumption that the pursuit of an internal settlement within Northern Ireland was futile.

In arguing that the consent and allegiance of Unionists were 'essential ingredients for a lasting peace', Sinn Fein was not stipulating that Unionist consent was a precursor for the exercise of self-determination. Rather, Sinn Fein was, in effect, acknowledging that the outcome of the exercise of self-determination could only be successful once it enjoyed the allegiance of Unionists. In refusing to sign up to the principles of the Forum for Irish Peace and Reconciliation in 1995, Sinn Fein confirmed its refusal to accept that Unionist consent was a prerequisite for Irish unity. Sinn Fein's historical view appeared to remain intact, namely that Unionist consent and allegiance would be a *consequence* of the creation of Irish unity. For the SDLP, such consent was a *prerequisite* for the establishment of a united Ireland. What had softened was the language of Republicans. Demands for 'Brits Out' had been superseded by calls for 'constructive disengagement' (Sinn Fein, 1995a: 7).

Sinn Fein had changed its view in calling on Britain to act as a persuader for Unionists, although the goal of the party, the exercise of national self-determination, remained constant. The more explicit statement of the need for Unionist consent in the Downing Street Declaration, contained in the reference to self-determination exercised on a North and South basis, was more than Sinn Fein could accept.

Aside from the important question of Unionist consent, debate over the extent of genuine change rested upon whether the IRA now believed in a tactically unarmed strategy or a totally unarmed approach. A briefing paper circulated by the Republican leadership in 1994 argued that it was possible to create a dynamic which might lead to a totally unarmed struggle. Sinn Fein believed that for the first time all Nationalist forces were rowing in the same direction. This consensus aimed at dividing Ulster Loyalists from the British government. For Sinn Fein, British involvement breached the principle of national self-determination.

The aim of Republicans was to enter into accommodation with Unionists, but still within a unitary framework The notion of covenantship was raised, with Sinn Fein insistent that Republicans:

will do everything possible to ensure full consultation and equal citizenship for Protestants in a new Ireland . . . We covenant that we will insist on full recognition of the Protestant identity in the new Ireland. The right of those in Ireland who wish to retain a British passport must be guaranteed (Hartley, 1994: 3).

Acceptance of dual citizenship represented a new departure in Republican strategy in that it gave a limited form of opt-out for individual Unionists in a united Ireland. Nonetheless, the central problem remained of how entry into a covenant would be possible with Unionists diametrically opposed to the ambitions of Irish republicanism. Sinn Fein continued to insist upon 'respect for the integrity of the land mass of Ireland' (Sinn Fein, 1995b: 4). Effectively this meant that the achievement of self-determination could be based only upon a territorial, all-Ireland basis.

Sinn Fein also argued that it was 'only in the context of the absence of Britain that the problem can then be reduced to a question of rival attitudes being given equal respect and treatment' (Sinn Fein, 1995b: 6). An obvious difficulty here was that the rival (pro-Union) attitude would have been overlooked by the establishment of a united Ireland, not given equal treatment. Unionists were invited to 'join with the rest of the people of Ireland in formulating an agreed future' (Sinn Fein, 1995c: 4).

11.7 Entering Stormont

If the end of abstentionism from the Dail marked a fundamental change in Sinn Fein in 1986, this was minor compared to the willingness to enter Stormont as part of the Good Friday Agreement in 1998. Republican purists, such as Ruairi O'Bradaigh, had long argued that entry to the Northern 'partitionist' parliament would inevitably follow the 1986 decision, as the two horses of abstentionism and constitutionalism could not be ridden simultaneously. The debates in 1998 indeed mirrored those of 1986. There were denials from the leadership of entry to the parliament, exemplified by Sinn Fein's mobilisation of supporters in 1997 in a 'no return to Stormont' campaign. When entry became a live issue, the justification took two forms. One was the practical electoral value of participation, increasing the mandate for Sinn Fein and allowing Republicans a voice in parliament. Second, the point was made that abstentionism had been elevated to a fundamental Republican principle when it was a mere tactic. For Mitchel McLaughlin, even abstentionism from Westminster is 'not a fundamental Republican principle. It is simply that there is no strategic value in taking seats there' (interview, 28 June 2000).

By 1997, it was evident that Sinn Fein's 'persuader' strategy of the early 1990s had run its course. The new Labour government was not going to act as a public persuader to Unionists for a united Ireland. It would not declare that it favoured Irish unity as a long-term solution, a stance which had been Labour party policy from 1981 to 1994. Pan-nationalism would not shift the British government from a rigid adherence to the claimed neutrality of the consent principle. The best deal on offer to Sinn Fein was, therefore, an agreement offering some institutional persuasion to Unionists that a united Ireland need not be feared and might even be economically attractive. Hence, a number of cross-border bodies with executive powers formed part of the Good Friday Agreement. Non-expansionist, they amounted to a minimalist all-Ireland dimension, but at least one which would not be reduced. Sinn Fein's other hope was to continue to maximise its vote to become the largest Nationalist party in Northern Ireland. With a swelling aggregate Nationalist vote due to demographic change confronting a divided unionism, Nationalist parties could effect change within Stormont. Concurrently, an increase in the number of Sinn Fein TDs in the Irish Republic could leave the party holding the balance of power. At its 2000 *ard fheis*, the party held its first debate on whether to enter into coalition in the event of such a scenario. If electoralism could not achieve a united Ireland, neither could militarism, nor even a combination of the two. A deal involving the pain of entering Stormont was sweetened by prisoner releases. This legitimised the IRA's claim to have been an army fighting a war and assisted those otherwise facing incarceration for participating in what appeared to many to be an unwinnable conflict.

11.8 Interpretations of changes in republicanism

The changes within republicanism have brought competing interpretations. According to some Unionists and, ironically, Sinn Fein, there has been no dilution of principles, merely tactical adjustments. The core goals of Sinn Fein remain unchanged: British withdrawal and Irish unity. The Provisional IRA remains, with its weaponry intact. Occasional bursts of unreconstructed republicanism could still be heard from the Provisionals. Thus, one prominent Republican, Brian Keenan, told his audience in February 2001:

> Those who say the war is over, I do not know what they are talking about. The revolution can never be over until we have our country, until we have British imperialism where it belongs, the dustbin of history (quoted in *Daily Telegraph*, 27 February 2001).

Even this speech, however, designed as reassurance that goals remained intact, was an appeal for *political* strength.

Others insist that the republican agenda has changed substantially and what Sinn Fein offers is, in effect, no longer republicanism. For example, Ryan (1995) suggests that the softening of approach heralds the death of republicanism, as Sinn Fein and the IRA have 'repudiated their key principles' (Ryan, 1995: 27). He claims that the downgrading of emphasis upon a united Ireland, the agreement that the consent of Unionists is vital, and the calls for parity of esteem between the Nationalist and Unionist traditions amount to a historic compromise with Britain, out of step with the traditional Republican approach. Ryan's argument is that Sinn Fein has, in effect, become a mere Nationalist party, representing no more than a minority in Northern Ireland. Against this argument, Sinn Fein, undoubtedly now a constitutional and electoral force, is the only party with a significant vote in both parts of the island and clearly required a fresh mandate rather than the eighty-year-old claim to legitimacy that underpinned 'fundamental' republicanism.

Ryan's view that republicanism has been blurred by pan-nationalism finds some sympathy in the writings of Bean (1995; 2001) and McIntyre (1995). The latter offers a slightly different emphasis in arguing that the Republican movement has always been vulnerable to changes in British state strategy. It is scarcely surprising, therefore, that the movement became enmeshed in a peace process devoid of exit strategies. Breen (2000a) argues that Sinn Fein have accepted the type of Agreement previously scorned:

> Certainly the Agreement represents advancement in many areas for Catholics in the North – but within the existing constitutional arrangements. What is sad is that this deal was on offer in 1974 but the Provos categorically rejected it and rejoiced when the Sunningdale power-sharing executive was brought down. In the intervening years, around 2,000 people died . . . If it wasn't for the appalling loss of life, it would be side-splittingly funny that it was SF recently demanding 'Bring Back Stormont'.

Although the limitations of 'armed struggle' had long been exposed, the formulation of alternative approaches was difficult. Sinn Fein's peace strategy of the 1990s could be derided, but the alternatives, of continuing IRA activity or Northern abstentionism, were equally problematic. This was apparent from the comments of a member of Sinn Fein's *ard chomhairle* (executive):

> Some in our own movement have been less than welcoming to the current strategy . . . My reply to those in our movement who are critical of our strategy is to say: 'Well find another one . . . give me a better one' (Alex Maskey, quoted in *Labour Left Briefing*, June 1996: 16).

11.9 International influences

Republicans were also influenced by external forces. The Clinton administration in the United States facilitated the development of a pan-nationalist alliance, gave respectability to Sinn Fein and acted as an honest broker for the British and Irish governments. Cox (2000) attributes a significant amount of the change in republicanism to the end of the cold war, although, as he points out, the end of the Northern Ireland conflict is not reducible to a single factor. Cox argues 'it was inevitable that as the tide of global radicalism began to retreat after 1989, this would feed into republican thinking' (2000: 251). Undoubtedly Sinn Fein dropped much of its left-wing agenda, a fusion of radical socialism with lingering Gaelic Irish nationalism and republicanism, during the early 1990s. The counter-argument is that two of the most fundamental shifts from fundamental to pragmatic republicanism, the ending of abstentionism from the Dail and the search for pan-nationalist alliances, occurred before the collapse of the Berlin Wall. Guelke (1994: 106) argues that the end of the cold war has 'less significance for Northern Ireland than for South Africa or the Middle East as the main source of assistance for the IRA was ethnically based support in the superpower that survived, the United

States', not Soviet Russia. Sinn Fein was encouraged by the success of peace processes elsewhere, notably in South Africa and the Middle East, as evidence that historic goals can either be achieved or continue to be pursued, within a new political framework. The collapse of the peace process in the Basque country and the return to violence by the IRA's erstwhile allies, ETA, offered a less auspicious example.

11.10 The influence of Loyalist paramilitaries

Loyalist paramilitary groups also had an input to the development of the peace process, albeit not on the scale of the changes in republicanism. The nature of Loyalist violence changed in the late 1980s, with members of Sinn Fein often the targets. From the late 1980s until the late 1990s, Loyalist paramilitaries set aside differences of political emphasis. The growth of pan-nationalism raised new fears amongst the Ulster Volunteer Force (UVF) and the Ulster Freedom Fighters (UFF). The latter group was, in effect, the Ulster Defence Association (UDA) operating under another name. The UDA insisted that both the SDLP and Sinn Fein formed part of a 'pan-nationalist' front.

Claiming ancestry as the defenders of Ulster earlier this century, the UVF had none of the mass support enjoyed by its historical predecessor. Arising from the citizens' defence committees of the 1970s, the UDA claimed a shorter history, but attempted, through a more political role, to develop into a broader social movement (Bruce, 1994). Nonetheless, politics was subordinate to violence during the 1970s, partly at the insistence of the UDA's leader during that period, Andy Tyrie (Nelson, 1976).

Despite the political overtures to Nationalists contained in the policy documents of the UDA, Loyalist paramilitaries nonetheless engaged in frequent random killings of Catholics during the Troubles. The idea that 'any Taig [Catholic] will do' appeared to underpin many of the murders, on the basis that it was within the Nationalist community that support for the IRA could be found. Most notorious of all killings were those undertaken by the Shankill Butchers in the 1970s.

The IRA claimed it was waging a war against 'Crown Forces', although these forces only accounted for slightly over half the deaths attributed to the IRA. Loyalists had less visible targets at which to aim. As a result, of over 500 Catholics killed by Loyalist paramilitaries, only a handful were members of Republican paramilitary groups. It is claimed that targeting of the latter has been abetted by periodic bouts of collusion with the security forces (Newsinger, 1995).

By 1993, the Loyalist paramilitaries were killing at a faster rate than the IRA. Gangsterism and racketeering had been displaced in favour of a paramilitary 'offensive' against the new threat of a combined all-Ireland nationalism. The targeting of Republicans led to 13 deaths of members of Sinn Fein between 1989 and 1992 (O'Muilleoir, 1999). The UDA and UFF believed they were 'winning the war' (Crawford, 2001: 16). Meanwhile, the upsurge in sectarian attacks against Catholic targets was matched by more progressive political developments and left-wing political reasoning. In one sense this was nothing new. As McAuley argues, Loyalist paramilitary organisations have 'provided an important channel for articulating social grievances and for reproducing sectarian ideology within the Protestant working-class' (McAuley, 1991: 45).

Despite the upsurge in Loyalist violence, there were also hints of conciliation. At the outset of the Brooke Initiative military activities were suspended for the duration of the talks. The resumption of hostilities was countered by a statement in 1992 by the combined paramilitary groups offering Nationalists full participation in a reconstructed Northern Ireland. By 1994, as the IRA moved towards a ceasefire, it became obvious that the Loyalist paramilitaries would respond with their own military cessation. It was in any case regarded as easier for Loyalist groups to cease activity. Firstly, for all the outrage amongst some Unionists over Britain's disinterest towards Northern Ireland, it remained part of the United Kingdom for the foreseeable future. Second, Loyalist violence had traditionally been seen mainly as reactive, activated primarily as a response to Republican paramilitary activity. This is an oversimplification, in that Loyalist offensives, or the threat of such, have been important ever since the prospect of partition developed. Nonetheless, it appeared a logical step for the Loyalist paramilitaries to call a ceasefire in response to the suspension of IRA activity. Satisfied that no secret deal had been done between the British government and Irish Republicans, Loyalists have held their ceasefire since 1994, feuds and dissidents apart. Loyalists sold the Good Friday Agreement as a reasonable deal, securing the Union to their constituency, and the Progressive Unionist Party, linked to the UVF, sits in the Northern Ireland Assembly.

11.11 Conclusion

The logic of the peace process of the 1990s was based upon three main factors. Firstly, there was growing recognition of the futility of IRA activity. Secondly, the limitations of Sinn Fein's political approach, constructed in 1918 and largely unchanged, were visible. Thirdly, a coalition of Nationalist forces emerged, ending the political isolation of Republicans. These forces combined in an attempt to create the momentum for an Irish-led peace initiative, based upon an informal Nationalist alliance. However, the success or otherwise of any peace process would also clearly depend upon the formal agreements and activity undertaken by the British and Irish governments.

Chapter 12

The development of the peace process

If political agreement was to be achieved in Northern Ireland, it was evident that this would occur only in the context of paramilitary ceasefires. A unique coalition of Nationalist forces embracing the Irish government, the SDLP, Sinn Fein and Irish America was now in place, allowing a series of peace initiatives to develop. The British and Irish governments embarked upon a peace process, headed by prime ministers who both declared a personal interest in resolving the problem of Northern Ireland. A heady phase of politics began, marked by a joint governmental declaration for peace in 1993 and Republican and Loyalist ceasefires in 1994. Even if prospects for a permanent resolution of the conflict remained uncertain, many welcomed what appeared to be the first substantial political progress for two decades. This chapter concentrates upon the attempts at conflict resolution which created a peace process.

12.1 The Downing Street Declaration

By December 1993, sufficient common ground was found for the British and Irish governments to produce a Joint Declaration for Peace, otherwise known as the Downing Street Declaration. The Declaration, made on 15 December by the British Prime Minister, John Major, and the Irish Taoiseach, Albert Reynolds, formalised the peace process by outlining the approach of the two governments to the removal of conflict and represented the start of a series of initiatives, outlined in Table 12.1.

Input to the Downing Street Declaration came from a variety of sources. The Hume–Adams discussions on the principles of national self-determination, by which all the Irish people would determine their own future together, provided early drafts. The Irish government added its formulations. Although concerned that the origins of the document in Hume–Adams discussions would amount to a 'kiss of death' in terms of Unionist responses, the British government acted as a rewriter of the numerous drafts. With Protestant churchmen acting as intermediaries, even representatives of the main Unionist party and Loyalist paramilitary groups had some input (Coogan, 1995; Mallie and McKittrick, 1996).

Table 12.1 Chronology of the peace process 1993–9

Year	Event
1993	Downing Street Declaration (Joint Declaration for Peace) issued by the British and Irish governments.
1994	Republican and Loyalist paramilitary groups announce ceasefires.
1995	Joint Framework Documents issued by the British and Irish governments.
1996	Mitchell Principles of Non-Violence declared, with all parties pledging their support. IRA ceasefire temporarily ends. Elections to a Northern Ireland (Peace) Forum, designed to produce preliminary party negotiating teams.
1997	IRA ceasefire restored.
1998	Good Friday Agreement is forged after months of multi-party negotiations, supported in referenda in Northern Ireland and the Irish Republic. Elections to the new Northern Ireland Assembly take place. Six new cross-border bodies are agreed.
1999	Power is devolved to a cross-community Northern Ireland Executive and Assembly. The North–South Ministerial Council and British–Irish Council meet for the first time.

Within the Declaration, the British government pledged the following:

1. It would 'uphold the democratic wish of a greater number of the people of Northern Ireland on the issue of whether they wish to support the Union or establish a sovereign united Ireland'.
2. It had no 'selfish, strategic or economic interest in Northern Ireland'.
3. It is 'for the people of the island of Ireland alone, by agreement between the two parts respectively, to exercise their right of self-determination on the basis of consent, freely and concurrently given, North and South, to bring about a united Ireland'.

For its part, the Irish government acknowledged the following:

1. 'It would be wrong to attempt to impose a united Ireland, in the absence of the freely given consent of a majority of the people of Northern Ireland'.
2. The 'presence in the constitution of the Republic of elements which are deeply resented by Northern Unionists'.
3. 'In the event of an overall settlement, the Irish Government will, as part of a balanced constitutional accommodation, put forward and support proposals for change in the Irish constitution which would fully reflect the principle of consent in Northern Ireland'.

Both governments also declared their recognition of the validity and rights of the different traditions in the island of Ireland. Expression of these rights was perfectly acceptable, provided that they were exercised by 'peaceful and legitimate means'.

The British government was also anxious to emphasise what was *not* included in the Declaration. A list of omissions, or Not the Downing Street Declaration, was attached to the real thing, with the contents of the non-Declaration reiterated by John Major in the House of Commons. The British government declared in this context:

1. that it would not act as a persuader for a united Ireland;
2. that it did not set any timescale for a united Ireland, nor assert its value;
3. that it did not contemplate joint authority over Northern Ireland shared by the British and Irish governments;
4. that it had not reduced British sovereignty over Northern Ireland.

12.2 Interpretations

The Downing Street Declaration had to appeal to both communities in Northern Ireland. It was designed to give hope to Nationalists and reassurance to Unionists. Accordingly, it was bound to represent a mass of 'necessary ambiguities' (McGarry and O'Leary, 1995: 414). An opinion poll conducted immediately after the Declaration found that 87 per cent of Nationalists welcomed its assertions, compared to only 43 per cent of Unionists (*Irish News*, 22 December 1993).

Effectively, the Irish government acted as the spokesperson for the Nationalist coalition forged since the 1980s. As in the Anglo-Irish Agreement eight years earlier, the legitimacy of the Nationalist tradition in Northern Ireland was recognised. The Declaration went somewhat further in giving vent to Nationalist aspirations. It contained the first explicit guarantee from the British government that the expression of Irish self-determination was legitimate. Political structures in Northern Ireland and the Republic were to be determined through agreement amongst the people of Ireland.

Overall, the tone of the Declaration was one of British neutrality concerning the future of Northern Ireland. The British government declined to act as persuaders to Unionists that their true interests lay in a united Ireland, an act which would in any case have needed a selling feat surely beyond the smoothest salesperson. Britain's lack of interest in Northern Ireland was nonetheless confirmed. It rated equally the aspiration for a united Ireland and the status quo of the lack of majority in Northern Ireland for such a constitutional change.

However, the number of rejoinders added to the document from the original drafts of Hume–Adams meant that Republicans could not formally accept its contents. Sinn Fein rejected the Unionist consent elements of the Declaration at a special conference at Letterkenny in 1994. Whilst welcoming the seeming embrace by the British government of the concept of Irish self-determination, there were too many qualifications to this for Republicans. The phrase requiring that consent for a united Ireland must be 'freely and concurrently given, north and south' meant to Republicans that a 'Unionist veto' over the national exercise of self-determination might continue. Republicans sought clarification of the Declaration, not least over how national self-determination ought best to be exercised. For Republicans, national self-determination was not the same as the dual national self-determination (North *and* South) on offer in the Downing Street Declaration.

The Ulster Unionist Party offered a mild reaction to the Declaration and acknowledged the stress upon the need for consent within Northern Ireland for constitutional change. Whilst concerned by the green tinge to the document, the main Unionist party was also reassured by the production by the British government of its list of exclusions from the Declaration. Less sanguine was the Democratic Unionist Party, which argued that the Declaration was a further move towards the expulsion of Unionists from the United Kingdom. The leader of the DUP also denounced the British government's attempt to clarify the Declaration for the benefit of Sinn Fein as amounting to a 'twenty-one page love letter to Gerry Adams'. Critical Unionists pointed to the lack of specific guarantees from the Republic for any replacement of Articles 2 and 3 laying claim to Northern Ireland. The Republic had still to play its hand in respect of its constitutional claim.

12.3 Paramilitary ceasefires

Although Republicans were lukewarm in their response to the Downing Street Declaration, the ambiguity of its content, allied to the momentum for peace created elsewhere, provided enough grounds for a ceasefire. On 31 August 1994, the IRA announced a 'complete cessation of military operations'. Briefly, there appeared to be a mood of euphoria in Republican areas. The question begged was what response would now follow from the British and Irish governments. From the British government, Sinn Fein demanded inclusion in all-party talks on the constitution. From the Irish government, the party sought backing for this entry. Sinn Fein also sought the early release of Republican prisoners.

Sinn Fein envisaged a procedure in which various shades of political opinion in Northern Ireland would be invited to round table talks, after preliminary bilateral talks in which each party met government official and ministers on a separate basis. Two stumbling blocks were immediately apparent. First, the British government was unhappy over the exclusion of the word 'permanent' from the IRA's ceasefire announcement. Second, the British government preferred to operate a 'quarantine' period, delaying entry into talks with Sinn Fein whilst waiting to be convinced on the durability of the ceasefire. It appeared that all-party talks were a distant prospect. Bilateral discussions were less problematic. In December 1994, a Sinn Fein delegation held its first meeting with government officials at Stormont to discuss aspects of the peace process.

The Irish government was much more forthcoming. Within a week of the IRA ceasefire, the Irish Taioseach shook hands with Gerry Adams outside the Mansion House, the Taioseach's office. It was a moment pregnant with symbolism, the first such meeting between militant and constitutional Irish Republicans since the Irish civil war. Following the Downing Street Declaration, the Irish government lifted its broadcasting ban on Sinn Fein. After the announcement of an IRA ceasefire, the British government lifted its prohibition. As indicated in the Downing Street Declaration, the Irish government also established the Forum for Peace and Reconciliation in October 1994. It invited submissions from all parties interested in resolving the constitutional problem in Ireland. However, the only non-nationalist party in Northern Ireland prepared to contribute was Alliance. In December 1994, the Irish government ordered the early release of nine IRA prisoners.

Upon the announcement of an IRA ceasefire, graffiti appeared in Loyalist areas 'accepting the unconditional surrender of the IRA', although Loyalist paramilitaries were slightly more cautious. Forty-three days elapsed before the Combined Loyalist Military Command, representing the UDA, UFF and UVF, announced its own indefinite suspension of violence, emphasising that it was conditional upon Republicans desisting from the use of force. Loyalist paramilitaries had been influenced by the argument of their representatives in the UDP and PUP that no deal had been struck with the IRA by the British government. Accordingly, the continuation of violence was pointless. The PUP saw the ceasefires as a shift away from armed conflict towards dialogue, but not necessarily as part of a process of conflict resolution, declaring that 'the implacable opposites of nationalism and unionism are irreconcilable' (Rowan, 1995: 157).

By December 1994, the UDP and PUP were engaged in exploratory dialogue with British government officials at Stormont. Initially, the British government appeared reluctant to concede formal involvement on peace talks to the two parties, although they were to be informally consulted. However, the importance of maintaining a Loyalist ceasefire meant that the two parties were indeed consulted on a regular basis, despite their small electoral support. In the first year of the ceasefire, the PUP met with British ministers and officials on 15 separate occasions (McKittrick, 1995).

12.4 The Framework Documents: Part I

The Downing Street Declaration provided only a broad political framework within which it was hoped that the problem of Northern Ireland might be solved. What was now required were the mechanics of any such settlement. Formal proposals were put forward in February 1995, in the form of two framework documents entitled *Frameworks for the Future*. They were sometimes referred to as the Joint Framework Documents although it was only Part II that represented a joint effort (HM Government, 1995).

The first framework document was entitled *A Framework for Accountable Government in Northern Ireland*. This contained the proposals of the British government for the most appropriate means of governance within Northern Ireland. It favoured increasing local accountability 'as part of a comprehensive political settlement embracing relations within Northern Ireland, between Northern Ireland and the Republic of Ireland and between the two Governments' (HM Government, 1995: 3). This section of the Framework Documents concentrated upon internal political institutions in Northern Ireland. The Republic of Ireland was mentioned only fleetingly, mainly in the closing two paragraphs of the twenty-eight-paragraph document.

Part I of the Framework Documents advocated:

1. the creation of a Northern Ireland Assembly of 90 members, elected by proportional representation, for a period of four or five years;
2. the new Assembly should hold the same legislative powers as that given to the last such cross-party Assembly in the 1970s;
3. an Assembly committee system, consisting of party representatives proportionate to electoral strength, should scrutinise legislation;
4. weighted voting, requiring majorities between 65 per cent and 75 per cent, should be used in Assembly committees to ensure that legislative measures have considerable support;
5. a panel of three members, elected by proportional representation, should adjudicate on controversial issues.

There was a stress upon the need for checks and balances to ensure adequate representation for the Nationalist minority and full participation by all political parties. Such checks and balances were based mainly upon qualified majority voting and the extensive use of a panel. The following conditions were suggested:

1. panel decisions must be unanimous;
2. the panel might nominate committee chairs and deputy chairs;
3. weighted voting should be used for confirmation of appointments or dismissals;
4. there must be majority support for legislation in the Assembly and its committees.

Overall, Part I of the Framework Documents concentrated upon the avoidance of monopoly power, devising electoral and institutional procedures designed to facilitate the sharing of authority. Lijphart (1996: 247) argues that in seeking this solution, the British government, supported by its Irish counterpart, had 'firmly nailed its colours to the consociational mast' by advocating or allowing:

1. a grand coalition of heads of departments, along with panel members, to form a cabinet sharing power;
2. proportionality in government;
3. a veto of controversial proposals by the Nationalist minority.

Part I of the Framework Documents contained a number of problematic aspects. Firstly, it sought to counter the power of any one group through a system of checks and balances, whilst appearing to concentrate power in an élite of panel members and key Assembly figures. Secondly, what was proposed was a form of diluted proportionality. A majoritarian form of government appeared to be most heavily qualified by the demand for panel decisions to be unanimous, a safeguard against the reality that Unionists would have the greater numerical representation in such an Assembly. Even more problematic was the proposed composition of the panel. As it was to be directly elected by the people of Northern Ireland as an entirety, its election would be similar to those conducted for the European Parliament, in which Ian Paisley tops the poll. A panel would almost certainly comprise two Unionists, one each from the UUP and DUP, working alongside a Nationalist from the SDLP. This begged the question of whether sufficient degree of consensus existed to move from mundane co-operation to mutual power-sharing. The risk was of lowest common denominator decision-making, in which consensus and 'grand coalition' amounted to little. Worse, Sinn Fein's likely exclusion from the panel would antagonise Republicans.

Annex A of Part I repeated some of the themes of British neutrality on the future of the Union evident in the Downing Street Declaration. Annex A declared the following:

1. there was unlikely to be change in the constitutional status of Northern Ireland in the foreseeable future;
2. the aspiration for a united Ireland was of equal validity to that for retention of the Union;
3. there could be no return to one-party rule in Northern Ireland.

In effect, Annex A declared that there could be no such thing as disloyalty to Britain within Northern Ireland, as there was parity of esteem for the ambitions of Irish nationalism and Ulster unionism. The government was anxious to stress that an interim settlement did not require either side to abandon basic political principle. This appeared to be designed especially for Republicans as it attempted to offer them some hope that they could 'compromise with honour' without betraying their fundamental goal of outright independence.

Part I nonetheless also stressed the limits of British neutrality. A neutral match referee might not declare before kick-off that he 'cherishes' a particular result. Yet, in the Foreword to the *Frameworks for the Future* documents, John Major declared: 'I cherish Northern Ireland as part of the United Kingdom' (HM Government, 1995: iv).

12.5 The Framework Documents: Part II

The second section of the Framework Documents was a joint paper by the British and Irish governments entitled *A New Framework for Agreement*. Paragraph 10 laid out the guiding principles for the Agreement. They were:

1. self-determination, of the variety set out in the Downing Street Declaration;
2. consent;
3. non-violence;
4. parity of esteem.

In adopting the principles of the Downing Street Declaration, *A New Framework for Agreement* advocated:

1. the creation of a North–South body to discharge executive, harmonisation and consultative functions;

Table 12.2 The 1995 Framework Documents' proposals for a North–South body

Function	Definition	Suggested areas
Executive	Agreement and implementation on an all-Ireland basis	EU, tourism, culture
Harmonising	Agreement on common policy	Most policy areas
Consultative	Agreement not required	Not defined, but e.g. policing

2. compulsory membership of this body for key Northern Ireland assembly members;
3. the creation of a parliamentary forum comprising representatives from new political institutions in Northern Ireland and the Irish parliament;
4. permanent East–West (London–Dublin) structures, including an inter-governmental conference and secretariat.

As much of the East–West dimension reiterated the workings of the 1985 Anglo-Irish Agreement, the novelty lay mainly in the North–South proposals. It was proposed that the new North–South body should contain heads of departments from the Irish government and a new Northern Ireland Assembly. The British and Irish governments would determine in the first instance which matters should be subject to the executive, harmonisation or consultative roles of the North–South body. In an attempt to remove some of the ambiguities over the extent of the all-Ireland dimension which had dogged the 1973 Council of Ireland, the Joint Framework Document was more explicit. It defined the different remits and likely areas of competence of the North–South body as in Table 12.2.

The Joint Framework Document provided the usual assertion that there would be no change in the constitutional status of Northern Ireland without the consent of a majority of its people, whilst again promising legislation in the event of such a development. Paragraph 18 gave official recognition to the existence of two dissident groups on the island, one already a reality, another which would be created if forced into a united Ireland. The paragraph asserted that 'the option of a sovereign united Ireland does not command the consent of the unionist tradition, nor does the existing status of Northern Ireland command the consent of the nationalist tradition' (HM Government, 1995: 26).

In an often ambiguous document, there was a warning to Unionists of the possible implications of the failure to agree to the Framework Proposals. Direct rule from Westminster would be reintroduced, but with a commitment to 'promote co-operation at all levels between the people, North and South, representing both traditions in Ireland, as agreed by the two Governments in the Joint Declaration' (HM Government, 1995: 34). Given that the Joint (Downing Street) Declaration had provided only the loosest outline of the mechanics of this North–South co-operation, the passage again puzzled readers. Despite British denials, many agreed that a willingness to impose joint authority was implied (Bew and Gillespie, 1996).

The Irish government moved a little closer towards introducing proposals for an amendment to Articles 2 and 3 of its constitutional claim to Northern Ireland. Paragraph 21 of the Joint Framework Document declared that the Irish government would introduce constitutional amendments reflective of the lack of majority consent for a united Ireland in Northern Ireland. This remained conditional upon an overall intergovernmental constitutional agreement, whilst the Irish government would maintain the right of people North and South to 'be part of, as of right, the Irish nation' (HM Government, 1995: 28).

12.6 Political responses

According to one commentator, what was remarkable about the Joint Framework Document was the 'success of its ambiguity' (Smyth, 1996: 14). Unlike the Downing Street Declaration, however, the document met with a hostile reception from the Ulster Unionist Party. Its leader James Molyneaux resigned in 1995. Whilst this resignation was not directly due to the publication of the documents, he was unimpressed at the manner in which the Framework had been devised with scant input from Unionists. His successor, David Trimble, hardened resistance, claiming that the documents were simply not viable. The main fears of Unionists were:

1. the undermining of British sovereignty through the influence given to the Republic in policy formulation;
2. the use of the European Union to undermine the border;
3. the likely ineffectiveness of the Northern Ireland Assembly;
4. the use of the North–South body and failure of the Assembly as devices to impose joint authority.

Unionists were especially concerned by their inability to sideline the proposed North–South body. Heads of departments in the Northern Ireland Assembly were obliged to participate in this all-Ireland institution. In other words, Unionists could have some internal power returned within Northern Ireland, provided that they were also prepared to concede power to an external force. It would be impossible to boycott the North–South body. It would be possible to boycott the Northern Ireland Assembly, but this might mean that Unionist influence would be removed almost entirely from political arrangements.

Of equal concern was the extent of the remit of the North–South body. The British and Irish governments would determine the opening extent of the remit of the North–South body. As this did not appear to be ringfenced (prevented from expanding), it seemed likely to grow. The Framework Documents declared:

> . . . the British Government have no limits of their own to impose on the nature and extent of functions which could be agreed for designation at the outset, or subsequently, between the Irish Government and the Northern Ireland administration' (HM Government, 1995: 30).

Part II of the Framework Documents provided for a substantial cross-border dimension in relation to European Union programmes. These would automatically be referred to the North–South body and those with a cross-border dimension would be implemented by that body. The European Union was thus feared by Unionists as a potential eroder of sovereignty. Unionists feared the cross-border momentum generated by the Framework Documents. Such fears were exacerbated by paragraph 24 which spoke of 'present and future political, social and economic inter-connections on the island of Ireland, enabling representatives of the main traditions, North and South, to enter agreed dynamic, new, co-operative and constructive relationships' (HM Government, 1995: 28). Against this, any expansion of the North–South body required Assembly approval, allowing Unionists to prevent its development.

Unionists agreed with the Framework Documents that the return of local political functions was desirable, but argued they must be locally controlled, devoid of external interference. In 1996, the UUP produced a policy document, *The Democratic Imperative*. This acknowledged the value of establishing a 'proper and appropriate' relationship with the Irish Republic for the 'mutual exploitation of economic benefits' (Ulster Unionist Party, 1996: 12). It expressed a willingness to discuss the relationship between Belfast and Dublin and acknowledged the empathy of northern Nationalists with the Irish Republic, whilst arguing that this should not affect Northern Ireland remaining an integral part of the United Kingdom.

In dismissing the 'framework of shame and sham', the DUP argued that it was a sell-out to Dublin. Claiming vindication for its hardline opposition to the peace process, the party held the earlier conciliatory approach of the UUP partly responsible for the difficulties faced by Unionists. Thus, Ian Paisley (1997: 16) argued that it was 'strange to relate those who prepared the womb of the Declaration have now rejected its offspring – the Framework Document'. The DUP argued that the Framework Documents amounted to joint authority 'between Dublin and the representatives of the proposed new Ulster assembly' (Democratic Unionist Party, 1995: 11). It insisted that the British government should not negotiate with the Irish government until the latter removed its constitutional claim to Northern Ireland. The party perceived the North–South body suggested by the Framework Document as an embryonic all-Ireland parliament.

Amongst supporters of the Union, only the Alliance Party welcomed the Framework Documents. On the Nationalist side, the SDLP endorsed much of their content, scarcely surprising given that they largely reflected SDLP thinking. The SDLP supported the substantial intergovernmental framework and dynamic of cross-borderism consistent with the party's approach.

Having refused to accept the Downing Street Declaration, Sinn Fein could scarcely endorse its mechanics as laid out in the Framework Documents. There was the encouraging assertion of the validity of Irish self-determination, but the manner of its exercise would provide a 'Unionist veto' over change. Preoccupied with insisting upon entry into all-party talks, Sinn Fein provided a muted response. Gerry Adams even endorsed the overall approach of the

Framework Documents as 'a clear recognition that partition has failed, that British rule in Ireland has failed . . . The ethos of the document and the political framework envisaged is clearly an all-Ireland one' (Adams, 1995: 229). Although significant, the advancement of cross-border co-operation proposed in the Joint Framework Document conceded only part of the traditional Republican agenda. The absence of Republican antipathy to the Framework Documents was a clear hint that henceforth they envisaged further gains through the dynamic of co-operative cross-borderism.

After the Framework Documents were issued, the pace of the peace process slowed for two years. Intergovernmental declarations and documents had acknowledged the right of the Irish people to achieve their own destiny and not distinguished which would be the better destiny. Paramilitary ceasefires offered the possibility that the resolution of that destiny might be by peaceful methods. However, by this point, Sinn Fein had not yet come in from the cold in terms of the British political process. This was in contrast to its rapid inclusion in dialogue in the Irish Republic. The United States Government also offered great encouragement for the switch from armed conflict to potential dialogue.

12.7 The Irish–American lobby

Given that 44 million Americans claim to be of Irish origin, it is scarcely surprising, therefore, that electoral candidates in America, including prospective presidents, are anxious to emphasise their interest in Irish affairs. Given the strength also of America's historical links with Britain, it was always a possibility that in any peace process requiring a broker, the American government might play a significant role.

Irish-America provided the fourth dimension of the pan-Nationalist coalition, embracing the SDLP, Sinn Fein and the Irish government. The American government was obliged to be somewhat more circumspect, anxious to develop the peace process, whilst publicly being obliged to appear neutral over the outcome of developments.

Once caricatured as an ignorant, shamrock-wielding group, the Irish-American lobby has always been much more diverse. Indeed, the sheer range of Irish-American groups had been described as a case of 'hyper-pluralism' (Dumbrell, 1995: 112). Nonetheless, there was some residual sympathy for the 'armed struggle' amongst many members of the larger groups. Indeed, the Irish Northern Aid Committee (NORAID) was run as a welfare adjunct for the families of imprisoned IRA members. With considerable crossovers of membership, groups such as the Ancient Order of Hibernians contained many passive or tacit supporters of the Provisional IRA, although few had subscribed to its socialism of the late 1970s and early 1980s. Instead, romantic nationalism and Catholicism produced such favourable dispositions.

Most of these organisations were nonetheless outsider groups, screened from political influence by Irish-American moderates who held political sway. Constitutional Irish nationalism was favoured by Irish-American political élites. At the apex of this lobby were senior figures known as the 'Four Horsemen'.

Tip O'Neill, Edward Kennedy, Daniel Moynihan and Hugh Carey were experienced politicians of considerable standing in the Irish-American community. During the 1970s, they encouraged the American president, Jimmy Carter, to develop a more proactive stance on Northern Ireland, whilst denouncing the activities of militant Irish Republicans. The Dublin government and the SDLP were also instrumental in persuading lobby groups such as the Friends of Ireland that support should only be given to non-violent expressions of Irish nationalism (Wilson, 1995). The Irish National Caucus, led by the Irish Nationalist, Father Sean McManus, and containing Irish-Americans with a somewhat broader range of sympathies than NORAID, enjoyed some success in securing the establishment of a Congressional Ad Hoc Committee on Northern Ireland in 1977. Its members were instrumental in persuading Congress to ban the sale of weaponry to the RUC.

The Irish-American lobby also laid considerable stress upon the need for American states to assert the MacBride Principles, despite the reservations of even many constitutional Nationalists in Ireland. These principles insisted upon minimum quotas for Catholics. Individual US states with companies based within their region could enforce compliance upon those locating in Northern Ireland. Increasingly, American companies were investing in the Province. Since DuPont became the first to locate there in 1959, 45 other companies had followed by 1995, providing 10,000 jobs and £500 million worth of investment (*Financial Times*, 30 November 1995).

British lobbying of the US State Department was effective in reducing the impact of more strident demands for American involvement in the affairs of Northern Ireland. A reassertion of the special relationship between Britain and America during the Thatcher premiership and Reagan presidency during the 1980s ensured that American involvement was kept to the minimum necessary to proceed without alienating Irish-America, despite Reagan's shock discovery of Irish roots in a visit to the Republic in 1984. American support for the Anglo-Irish Agrement was primarily financial and satisfied more moderate elements within the lobby.

12.8 The role of the American government

In the 1990s, American involvement finally extended towards political mediation. Bill Clinton enjoyed large support from the Irish-American voters in his 1992 presidential triumph. Clinton's approach to the problem of Northern Ireland was to be different in several respects from that of his predecessors, a shift prompted partly by an interest in Northern Ireland held by Clinton since the civil rights campaign began back in the 1960s whilst he studied at Oxford.

Firstly, Clinton was prepared to criticise aspects of British policy in Northern Ireland. During the 1992 campaign, he criticised the 'wanton use of lethal force by British security forces'. Differential rates of unemployment between Protestants and Catholics and earlier collusion between the security forces and Loyalist paramilitary groups had also attracted Clinton's attention (Coogan, 1995).

Secondly, the new president was prepared to use a peace envoy to attempt to hasten moves towards political accommodation in Northern Ireland. The official manifestation of this approach was the deployment of Senator George Mitchell as a peace 'broker' in December 1994. Mitchell's task was to become even more crucial within a year, as disputes over the principle and timetable of decommissioning of weapons deepened.

Thirdly, Clinton was not hidebound by the sympathies of the State Department towards Britain. Instead, he preferred to use National Security Council advisers to develop his strategy. The main adviser, Nancy Soderberg, was particularly anxious that members of Sinn Fein be given the opportunity to develop their credentials as constitutional politicians. It was her influence that persuaded Clinton to award an entry visa to Gerry Adams after the Downing Street Declaration, despite the absence of an IRA ceasefire at that stage and the strong opposition to the award expressed by the British government and US State Department. The US ambassador in Ireland, Jean Kennedy Smith, hailed the visa award as a 'wise and courageous move', indicating how the forces of Irish America and much of the American government were rowing in the same direction as other elements of the Nationalist coalition. At the White House St Patrick's Day reception in 1995, numerous shades of opinion, including Republicans and Loyalists, were represented.

Finally, a different coalition of Irish-American forces had emerged by the 1990s. Groups of Republican sympathisers had fragmented. In 1989, NORAID split, the fracture caused mainly by the end of abstentionism by Sinn Fein in the Irish Republic. Diehards such as Michael Flannery quit the organisation. The annual fundraising abilities of NORAID fell from $1 million in the early 1980s to less than one-fifth of that figure 10 years later (*Financial Times*, 30 May 1994). By the mid-1990s, small groups, such as the Friends of Irish Freedom and Republican Sinn Fein, were attempting to build up a network of hardline Irish Republicans in the United States from a small remaining base. The huge bulk of Irish-Americans had instead feted Adams. The granting of his entry visa led to the development of the Friends of Sinn Fein organisation, with a $200,000-a-year office in Washington. The second visit of Adams, after the IRA ceasefire announcement, proved a huge fundraising success. To a considerable degree, support for Sinn Fein was seen as part of mainstream Irish-American politics whilst the IRA ceasefire held.

President Clinton's visit in late November 1995 was the first made to Northern Ireland by a sitting US president. It was a political *tour de force* which raised optimism that the peace process, which had appeared increasingly stalled, might yet be moved forward. At this point, the politics of the process had been like 'watching a glacier move' according to O'Leary and McGarry (1996: 329) although perhaps without so much excitement.

The presidential visit revived the excitement provoked by the paramilitary ceasefires during the previous year. At the time, scarcely anyone knew that, according to one authoritative source, the IRA's Army Council had already taken the decision in October, in principle at least, to return to violence (Holland, 1996). In stressing the benefits of peace, Clinton managed to satisfy the overwhelming majority of citizens in Northern Ireland. Even-handedness was the underlying theme of the visit, along with the need for advancement of political dialogue. He asserted that the terrorists' 'day was over'.

For Nationalists, the visit contained a handshake with Gerry Adams on the Falls Road in Belfast and a demand that those who move away from violence should be included in political dialogue. American emphasis was upon a twin-track approach. This was based upon substantive all-party political talks, to be staged in parallel with talks about the decommissioning of weapons. The Democrat Senator, George Mitchell, was appointed by the British government to chair a three-man commission to discuss whether weapons should be decommissioned as part of the peace process. It was on this issue that the peace process stalled, despite the apparent revival of momentum produced by American enthusiasm for its continuation.

12.9 Conclusion

The early to mid-1990s saw the development of an 'official' peace process, in which joint British and Irish government declarations and documents indicated the basis of a future political settlement. The politics of the conflict remained unresolved and there was little movement towards all-inclusive dialogue at this stage. For a peace process to be sustained, it was apparent that two conditions would need to be fulfilled. Firstly there was a need for a commitment to a long peace by republican paramilitaries in the manner in which they had prepared for a long war. Secondly, the peace process would only survive if Sinn Fein was included in all-party talks.

Whilst achieving a remarkable transformation, the first 18 months of the 'official' peace process were about creating a peaceful background, prior to the attempted reconciliation of the seemingly irreconcilable in terms of the political problems of Northern Ireland. A non-violent situation at least offered the prospect of permanent dialogue rather than increased polarisation.

In many ways the Downing Street Declaration and Framework Documents were masterpieces of ambiguity, in that both sides could comfort themselves with their reading of the nuances contained within. Yet the publication of clever documents could not act as a permanent substitute for the hard decisions which would be required in multi-party talks conducted in an absence of consensus. As progress towards these talks slowed in 1995, Northern Ireland stood in limbo between peace and conflict, awaiting decisive movement towards a fully inclusive negotiated settlement.

Chapter 13

War and peace: the long road to negotiations 1995–7

The peace process fluctuated in pace. Rapid progress towards peace from 1993 to early 1995 was followed by a period of stagnation and temporary collapse. The peace process developed problems with the delay over Sinn Fein's entry into multi-party talks. This delay led to the fracturing of the IRA's ceasefire in 1996, before the rapid revival of the process under the Labour government elected in May 1997. The issue of weapons decommissioning remained unresolved, but was overridden by the anxiety of the Labour government to move towards multi-party talks including Sinn Fein. In response, the IRA revived its ceasefire. The peace process was renewed and movement towards the negotiated outcome of the Good Friday Agreement began in earnest. This chapter examines the stalling of the peace process and the reasons why it revived after May 1997.

13.1 (Non)-Movement towards multi-party talks 1995–6 _____

The IRA ceasefire at the heart of the peace process was predicated upon the idea that its political representatives in Sinn Fein would quickly become engaged in inclusive dialogue with the British and Irish governments and other political parties in Northern Ireland. Although Republicans would articulate the case for Irish unity, the broad outline of any settlement was apparent from the 1995 Framework Document. Subsequent multi-party talks would change the details, not the three-stranded approach. Negotiations would centre upon the details of:

1. internal government within Northern Ireland;
2. the relationship between the North and South of Ireland;
3. the relationship between the British and Irish governments.

As delays to the starting date of these talks emerged, the peace process came under increasing strain. Bilateral talks between British government officials and each of the major political parties were commonplace. However, serious negotiations concerning the future of Northern Ireland were only likely to develop when all the parties met. Given the DUP's hostility to the conduct of the peace process, it was unlikely that it would wish to be involved. As such, multi-party rather than all-party talks would be the most inclusive form attainable. Aside from DUP non-involvement, the most obvious difficulty confronting the British government was when to allow Sinn Fein into negotiations. The IRA ceasefire raised several questions:

1. Was it permanent or tactical?
2. What would happen to IRA weapons?
3. Should prisoners be released?
4. How long must Sinn Fein wait before being permitted to enter multi-party talks?

Raising the questions was easier than providing the answers. In its ceasefire announcement in August 1994, the IRA had urged everybody 'to approach this new situation with determination and patience'. Its own patience snapped after 18 months of prevarication by others, in what the IRA perceived as an eight-hundred-year conflict. Delays in Sinn Fein's entry to peace talks were created by two main obstacles. Firstly, the exclusion of the word 'permanent' from the IRA's ceasefire announcement meant that the British government sought clarification of the intentions of the organisation. Secondly, the British government insisted upon the decommissioning of IRA weapons.

In the event, all-party talks did not take place during the 1994–6 peace process. The breaking of the IRA ceasefire in February 1996 ensured that Sinn Fein was excluded when multi-party talks went ahead in June that year.

13.2 The Mitchell Principles of Non–Violence

One of the central stumbling blocks in the peace process concerned whether paramilitary groups should be required to get rid of their weapons and armaments. Although decommissioning has been an important element of peace processes elsewhere, McGinty (1999) makes several arguments concerning the exceptionalism of Northern Ireland. Decommissioning has tended to occur after larger conflicts, with the demobilisation of large armies, not small paramilitary groups, with peace deals often brokered by the United Nations.

Unionists and the British government wished to see the IRA begin to disarm before any entry into multi-party talks. The paramilitaries were insistent that no decommissioning should take place in advance of a negotiated political settlement. The abandonment of weapons would arise from a political settlement rather than precede such a development. Any prior decommissioning would amount to a 'surrender'.

The IRA's ceasefire declaration had stressed that the organisation remained undefeated. During the 1990s, the IRA had proved, particularly via attacks on targets in London, that it retained the capacity to inflict considerable damage. It was far from certain whether the IRA would accept decommissioning even if talks took place, but, even in an era of shifting Republican tactics, it stretched credulity that decommissioning would precede talks. Sinn Fein's Martin McGuinness insisted that there was not a 'snowball's chance in hell of any weapons being decommissioned this side of a negotiated settlement' (quoted in the *Guardian*, 21 June 1995).

The Irish government also insisted that decommissioning was not a pre-requisite for entry to all-party talks, pointing out that the Downing Street Declaration made no reference to the surrender of arms. According to the Taoiseach, Albert Reynolds:

> Everybody clearly understood that the ceasefire of August 1994 was about getting a place for Sinn Fein at all-party talks. And there was never any question of decommissioning being set as a pre-condition for those talks. So decommissioning became the poisoning factor (*Irish World*, 11 October 1996).

As the longest-serving Secretary of State for Northern Ireland ever, from 1992 to 1997, Patrick Mayhew clung to a belief that IRA decommissioning had to take place before Sinn Fein's entry to multi-party talks (Elliot and Flackes, 1999). His three principles, outlined in Washington in March 1995 and henceforth known as 'Washington 3', demanded: (1) a willingness to disarm in principle, (2) agreement upon the method, and (3) acceptance that some weapons must be given up before Sinn Fein's entry to talks (Bew and Gillespie, 1999). The British government argued that decommissioning had always been on the agenda and that Nationalists had collective amnesia concerning this condition. For example, the Secretary of State for Northern Ireland had appeared on Irish television in 1993 to indicate such a requirement (Bew, 1995). Mayhew was criticised by Unionists and Nationalists. Unionists argued that a token surrender of weapons by the IRA was useless. Nationalists insisted that expectations of any advance decommissioning amounted to a new and unrealistic impediment to all-party talks.

There were three main options to consider on decommissioning:

1. *Prior decommissioning.* The IRA (and Loyalist paramilitaries, it was assumed) should be required to surrender all or part of its weaponry in advance of entry into all-party talks.
2. *Parallel decommissioning.* Known as the twin-track approach, this would require the paramilitary groups to give up some of their weapons as all-party talks proceeded. All-party talks might be preparatory or full. There would be no requirement for a surrender of any weapons in advance of the start of talks.
3. *No decommissioning.* The British government would be obliged to continue to maintain its 'working assumption' that the IRA ceasefire was permanent.

In an attempt to solve the problem, a Commission of three members was appointed, chaired by the US Senator George Mitchell. It took submissions from a number of interested parties, although the DUP declined to cooperate in its deliberations, pointing out that it had 'nothing to give up'. Sinn Fein wished the Commission to extend its remit beyond the considerations of paramilitary weapons. The party argued for the removal of the legal weaponry held by the British Army and RUC. In its report published in January 1996, the Mitchell Commission found in favour of parallel decommissioning. All-party talks could start, with decommissioning of weapons to take place along-side the talks, rather than in advance of negotiations (Mitchell Report, 1996).

These conclusions appeared to provide a rebuff to the demands of the British government. It had insisted all along that the IRA must begin to destroy its weapons in advance of talks, but this was no longer a requirement. The Mitchell Commission did, however, insist that all negotiating parties be committed to peace. To this effect, the Commission produced six principles of non-violence. All parties were obliged to subscribe to the following principles:

1. to use democratic and exclusively peaceful means of resolving political issues;
2. total disarmament of paramilitary organisations;
3. disarmament to be verifiable to the satisfaction of an independent commission;
4. to renounce for themselves, and to oppose any effort by others, to use force, or threaten to use force, to influence the course or the outcome of negotiations;
5. to agree to abide by the terms of any agreement reached on all-party negotiations and to resort to democratic and exclusively peaceful methods in trying to alter any aspect of that outcome with which they may disagree;
6. to urge that 'punishment' killings and beatings stop and to take effective steps to prevent such actions.

These six principles were endorsed by the constitutional parties, but appeared likely to pose problems for Sinn Fein and the IRA, not least if the outcome of any multi-party negotiations failed to advance the cause of a united Ireland. Nonetheless, Sinn Fein's president claimed that his party was willing to sign up to them. The Mitchell Principles made multi-party talks possible by sidelining the problem of decommissioning as a prerequisite for entry for parties still linked to paramilitary organisations. Additionally, the Mitchell Report insisted that all parties abide by the principles of any agreement reached at all-party negotiations.

All-party talks, thought likely to start at the beginning of 1996, were deferred. The earlier row over decommissioning and much of the Mitchell Report itself were sidelined by two events: the insistence upon the staging of elections to a peace forum and the temporary collapse of the IRA ceasefire.

13.3 The Northern Ireland Forum elections 1996

Whilst accepting the idea of parallel decommissioning, the British government also seized upon a much more tentative suggestion contained within the Mitchell Report. This referred to the possibility of elections to confirm a mandate for representatives within a peace forum. These elections could take place, the report argued, if there existed sufficient consensus for the idea.

The idea of elections rather than talks caused much disquiet. Despite his public optimism, Mitchell suspected that the increasingly impatient IRA was about to end its ceasefire (Mitchell, 1999). Despite the bipartisanship at Westminster, at least one member of the opposition Labour Party's frontbench Northern Ireland team believed that the Conservative government should have moved towards talks, whilst emphasising the need for adherence to the

Mitchell Principles. However, the Labour leadership continued to refuse to 'play politics' with the peace process and offered support for the government's approach, on the basis that elections were 'the only show in town' (Mo Mowlam, quoted in the *Irish Post*, 27 April 1996).

Unionists supported the idea of elections to an elected forum in Northern Ireland. Within the UUP, the proposal had strengthened with the election of David Trimble as leader and increased further with Mitchell's refusal to insist upon prior decommissioning. The UUP argued for elections to establish the 'democratic *bona fides*' of participants in talks, given the non-surrender of weapons. This represented something of a compromise. After earlier insisting upon prior decommissioning, the Ulster Unionist Party was now prepared to talk to Sinn Fein if that party participated in an assembly, even if the IRA had not surrendered any of its weapons in advance.

In an attempt to entice Nationalists to participate in the electoral process, the UUP and the British government insisted that the elections were not designed to institute forms of governance within Northern Ireland. The legislative proposals for the Northern Ireland Forum insisted that it would be deliberative only and that it 'shall not have any legislative, executive or administrative functions, or any power to determine the conduct, course, or outcome of the (peace) negotiations' (HM Government, 1996: ch. 11, para. 3). The purpose of the elections was, therefore, to produce teams of negotiators for the promised multi-party talks, drawn from parties successful in elections to the peace forum. The forum itself would last for one year, with the possibility of an extension for another year by the Secretary of State for Northern Ireland.

13.4 Nationalist objections

Nationalists of differing shades of opinion were enraged by the proposals for elections. They saw the plan as a dangerous stalling device, produced by Unionists and supported by the British government to avoid the need for all-party talks in February 1996. Aside from the stalling allegation, there were other Nationalist objections.

First, neither of the main Nationalist parties endorsed the idea of 'peace' elections. As such, there was not the consensus for the idea which the Mitchell Report suggested should be a prerequisite for the creation of an elected peace forum. This lack of consensus appeared confirmed by a poll of Catholics in Belfast, which indicated that four-fifths were opposed to elections as a means of choosing representatives at all-party talks (*Daily Telegraph*, 19 February 1996).

According to Nationalist critics, the British government had deliberately distorted Mitchell's findings. This approach appeared suspiciously pre-determined. Stories indicating an outcome of elections after the Mitchell Report had begun to appear in the British press during early January, before the Mitchell Commission had concluded its deliberations (*see*, for example, *Daily Telegraph*, 12 January 1996).

Second, the support of the Conservative government for elections appeared to confirm to Nationalists that parliamentary arithmetic rather than concern for the peace process dominated politics. Returned in 1992 with a seemingly comfortable majority of 20 in the House of Commons, the Conservative government enjoyed the slenderest of majorities by 1996. Support from the Ulster Unionists was more than welcome for a Conservative government anxious to avoid a premature General Election. Nationalists perceived the favouring of peace elections as part of a series of favours to Unionists for their usual support of the Conservative government in parliament. Other favours included the award of a select committee on Northern Ireland, granted after initial denials of a deal following a close vote on the Maastricht Treaty and the establishment of a grand committee to scrutinise legislation relating to the Province.

A third Nationalist criticism was to ask what purpose elections would serve. The SDLP and Sinn Fein already possessed electoral mandates, consistently attracting a large number of votes and enjoying substantial representation on local councils. As such, they did not see the need to elect either peace forum representatives or a team of negotiators, many of whom would already enjoy a local electoral mandate. Elections were thus seen as another needless obstacle placed before all-party talks. The leader of the SDLP, John Hume, advocated the staging of an alternative, all-Ireland referendum, asking whether electors wished all sides to commit themselves to peaceful and democratic methods of conflict resolution.

Finally, the introduction of elections appeared to confirm to Nationalists that the peace process was no longer an Irish-led initiative. Instead the British government, under Unionist urgings, was now seen as the prime mover of the process. This was reflected even in the format for elections. The British government determined which parties were eligible to stand and shaped the outcome of the election through use of a peculiar form of electoral system.

Despite these objections, Nationalists grudgingly took part in elections. In January 1996, Sinn Fein dismissed the idea of any forum as a 'non-runner'. Four months later, the party agreed to contest the forum elections. Sinn Fein pledged that it would not take its seats in the forum, but it would participate in all-party talks, for which participation in the forum was not required. The SDLP also considered an outright boycott of the electoral process, but eventually decided to take part in elections, promising participation in the peace forum on an 'à la carte' basis, depending upon the agenda for each day.

13.5 The Forum election results

The elections took place on 30 May 1996, designed to produce negotiating teams for all-party talks due to open on 10 June 1996. Twenty-three parties or individuals contested the elections. The electoral system was a complex affair. It briefly united the political parties in condemnation. 'Dog's breakfast; pig's breakfast; monster raving loony idea; and rubric-cube (*sic*) type election' were perhaps four of the more flattering descriptions (*Irish Times*, 22 March 1996).

The UUP wanted a ninety-seat forum, with five representatives elected from each parliamentary constituency. The DUP and SDLP formed an unusual alliance in advocating a party list system. This would see Northern Ireland treated as a single constituency, a method which favoured those two parties in European elections. A hybrid system was the actual type chosen, mixing constituency representation with party lists and 'top-up' seats, to produce a 110-member forum. Electors cast a single vote for the party of their choice. Five candidates were elected from each of Northern Ireland's 18 parliamentary constituencies.

Candidates were elected via an order-of-preference list supplied by each party for each constituency. The first two seats in a constituency were filled using the 'droop' quota system. A party's vote had to equal or exceed a set quota. This quota was determined by dividing the total number of votes plus one by six. After the first two seats were filled, the D'Hondt system was used, whereby each party's vote was divided by the number of seats it had already filled, plus one. The number of votes for each party without a seat at that stage was left unaltered, with the party with the biggest total being elected.

The aim of this constituency election method was to ensure that adequate representation was given to each of the main parties attracting a significant vote in a constituency. The system produced occasional anomalies. For example, in Fermanagh and South Tyrone, the DUP obtained one forum seat, an identical figure to that obtained by Sinn Fein, although the latter gained almost twice as many votes. Overall, however, the percentage share of forum seats for the five biggest parties in Northern Ireland was not markedly distinct from their percentage share of votes. Indeed, a study of the results indicated that the contest was 'one of the most proportional ever held in Northern Ireland' (Mitchell and Gillespie, 1999: 82).

A 'top-up' system was grafted on to the constituency list elections. In addition to the 90 constituency members, 20 additional candidates, drawn from party lists, were elected to the forum, two each for the 10 parties attracting the most votes in the constituency list election. The aim of this system was to guarantee places for the UDP and PUP. As representatives of the Loyalist paramilitaries, their presence in talks was important. They did not possess sufficient electoral strength to be elected under the constituency format, but were almost certain to gain sufficient support to be in the top 10 parties. On a 65 per cent turnout, the most striking aspect of the elections was the high level of support for the hardline variants of unionism and nationalism, as represented by Sinn Fein and the DUP. Sinn Fein's support exceeded its normal figure of around 10 per cent. Support for the UUP fell by 10 per cent from the 1992 General Election, whilst the DUP saw its share rise. As a gateway to round-table talks, the results achieved their aim for the representatives of the Loyalist paramilitaries. Improving from a poll rating of around 1 per cent in the 1993 local elections, the PUP and UDP scored sufficient votes to confirm a place in the forum, from which they could select a team of negotiators for multi-party talks (see Table 13.1).

The election outcome was in one sense bizarre. The fringe Loyalist paramilitaries, women's coalition and Labour all now had negotiating teams in multi-party talks of equal size to those of the main Nationalist and Unionist

Table 13.1   Northern Ireland Forum election results 1996

Party	Vote	Percentage share	Seats
UUP	181,829	24.2	30
SDLP	160,786	21.4	21
DUP	141,413	18.8	24
SF	116,377	15.5	17
APNI	49,176	6.5	7
UKUP	27,774	3.7	3
PUP	26,082	3.5	2
UDP	16,715	2.2	2
NIWC	7,731	1.0	2
Labour	6,425	0.9	2
Others	18,083	2.3	0

Source: adapted from *Guardian*, 1 June 1996.

parties, despite attracting a mandate from a tiny percentage of the electorate and each holding only two forum seats, gained under the 'top-up' system.

The talks came under the overall chairmanship of Senator George Mitchell, to whom all committees reported. Strand 1 talks on internal governance in Northern Ireland were chaired by the British government, whilst Strand 2 talks were chaired by the Canadian General John De Chastelain. The British and Irish governments jointly chaired the committee looking at relations between Britain and Ireland. Procedural wrangles and discussions of agendas characterised the talks. Substantive progress was not forthcoming.

13.6 Stagnation, sectarianism and IRA violence

With Sinn Fein's entry to fully inclusive talks delayed, the IRA called off its ceasefire in February 1996, killing two with a huge bomb at Canary Wharf in London. As the 1997 British General Election loomed, the Conservative government had other priorities, the language of negotiation all but disappearing. The Major government, hamstrung by the lack of a Commons majority, contained its share of cabinet doubters over the entire peace process (O'Kane, 2001). The Secretary of State for Northern Ireland now denounced the IRA as 'criminal gangsters' (*Independent*, 2 January 1997). The concessionary noises to Republicans proffered in the early 1990s by the former Secretary of State, Peter Brooke, seemed a distant memory.

Following the IRA's return to violence, the fragile 'pan-nationalist' coalition temporarily disintegrated. The alliance had been strained ever since the removal of Albert Reynolds as Irish Prime Minister over a domestic political row in December 1994. His replacement, John Bruton, led Fine Gael, a party much less ideologically welded to republicanism than Reynolds' Fianna Fail. Bruton's reliance upon the coalition partners of the Democratic Left, hostile to Republicans, ensured that during his period in office the Irish government took much less of a vanguard role in the peace process (Ruane and Todd, 1996).

The Forum elections produced a managed outcome designed to facilitate multi-party talks amongst the 'key players'. However, one of these, Sinn Fein, was not admitted when multi-party proceedings finally got underway on 10 June 1996. With the IRA having ended its ceasefire, Sinn Fein was excluded from the political process. A limited talks process continued and the Loyalist ceasefire remained. As with all else in the peace process, the forum elections and subsequent negotiations had been predicated upon the maintenance of an IRA ceasefire. Instead, the talks took place without the political representatives of Irish republicanism and against a backdrop of renewed IRA activity. As Fergus Finlay, an adviser to the Irish government from 1992–6, put it, talks without Sinn Fein were 'not worth a penny candle' (Finlay, 1998). Given the party's 'special relationship' with the IRA, only Sinn Fein might be able to deliver a peaceful settlement. The IRA had continued to function as an organisation. Supporters had been reminded by Gerry Adams in 1995 that it had 'not gone away'. Nonetheless, the IRA offered hope that the peace process could be revived despite the Canary Wharf bomb. Its statement announcing the end of the ceasefire insisted that the 'blame thus far for the failure of the Irish peace process lies squarely with John Major and his government'. The IRA argued that the 'selfish' parliamentary interests of the Conservative government had led to intolerable delays over the entry of Sinn Fein into talks. The Conservative government was viewed as over-reliant upon Unionist support to preserve its narrowing majority in the House of Commons. Republicans claimed that Major's promised 'risks for peace' had evaporated due to fear of an early, highly losable, General Election.

IRA activity during 1996 remained sporadic and, until October, concentrated outside Northern Ireland. Five further bomb attacks, all in London, were carried out in the two months after the Canary Wharf explosion. In June, the IRA detonated the largest bomb ever in mainland Britain, wrecking part of Manchester city centre. In October, the IRA bombed the British Army barracks at Lisburn, killing a soldier. With such displays of strength, the IRA's main purpose in returning to 'war' was to achieve a place for Sinn Fein at the negotiating table, not to achieve a united Ireland. Republicans achieved their aim, as the sheer scale of destruction made the inclusion of Sinn Fein an imperative for the Labour government elected during the following year.

The Lisburn bombing apart, IRA activity within Northern Ireland centred mainly upon 'punishment' attacks, carried out against individuals whom the IRA deemed guilty of 'anti-social behaviour'. By December 1996, Republicans had carried out 164 such attacks during the year, including three shootings. On the Loyalist side, 121 beatings and 18 shootings of this type had been recorded. The brutal attacks may have a deterrent effect, although this is difficult to measure. Northern Ireland has the lowest 'ordinary' crime rate of any country in the United Kingdom.

In returning to violence in 1996, the Provisional IRA was conscious of the demand for military action which had prompted its foundation in 1969. Now Sinn Fein members were sensitive to the jibe asking what was the difference between a 'stickie' (a member of the old official IRA which gave up violence) and a 'Provo'? Answer: 27 years. In 1996, the temporary return to violence appeased those Republicans who feared the IRA had compromised or 'gone soft'. Yet there were also doubters in the movement who regarded the deployment of violence as futile. This debate would come to a climax in 1997 with the formation of the 'Real IRA'. Meanwhile Gerry Adams made it clear that there would be no return to the days of Sinn Fein subordination to the IRA, nor even a prolonged revival of the armalite and ballot box strategy, when he told an internal Sinn Fein conference at Meath in 1996 that 'This party is not going back to the days when we were cheer-leaders for the Army [IRA]' (quoted in O'Brien, 1999: 369).

The separate Republican group, the Irish National Liberation Army, committed itself to the peace process in March 1996, via the announcement of a 'tactical suspension of operations'. The organisation had long held maverick status (Holland and McDonald, 1994). INLA did return briefly to its violent past, killing the leader of the Loyalist Volunteer Force, Billy Wright, in the Maze Prison in December 1997.

To the surprise of many, the Loyalist ceasefire held. Hardline mid-Ulster UVF members formed the Loyalist Volunteer Force in 1996, in opposition to the more concessionary approaches of the political representatives of the UVF and UDA. The PUP and UDP were anxious to maintain a Loyalist ceasefire in order to remain in the multi-party talks at Stormont.

13.7 Sectarian boycotts

Accompanying the problems of the political development of the peace process was a deterioration in inter-community relations. This developed partly through the revival of IRA activity, but increased substantially following the tensions created by the parades of Ulster's 'marching season'. The insistence of the Portadown Orange Order upon marching through a Nationalist area of Drumcree, despite protests from local residents, took on huge symbolic influence as a contest involving fundamental claims of territory, rights and liberty.

The 1996 decision to allow the Drumcree parade through a contentious area produced a strong reaction from Nationalists, as the authorities reversed their ban on the marchers in the wake of Loyalist violence. Relations were temporarily soured between the British and Irish governments. The SDLP withdrew from the Northern Ireland Peace Forum, whilst continuing to attend multi-party negotiations. 'The present is Orange' asserted *The Independent* (12 July 1996). An alternative view was that the parades were the 'last hurrah' of Orangeism, a declining force facing an uncertain future. For example, revisionists such as Eilis O'Hanlon, from a Nationalist background, derided the use of 'Orange state clichés' as entirely unrealistic (*Sunday Independent*, 14 July 1996). Although willing to re-route some contentious parades, the Orange Order insisted that its *right* to march could not be impeded by what it saw as Republican groups. Advocating that lodges march quietly through contentious areas, the Orange Order insisted that:

negotiations prior to parades . . . are to be welcomed . . . However Orangemen must not be given the feeling that the community groups are just fronts for the IRA. If these groups are serious about reaching accommodation they should consider carefully who they appoint as their spokesmen. Orangemen are not afraid to talk but there are some people with whom they cannot in conscience discuss these matters (Montgomery and Whitten, 1995: 34).

After the controversial parade was staged at Drumcree the previous year, the 'Spirit of Drumcree' group was formed, calling for a hardline approach to be taken on marching rights. The group ended the deferential tradition within the Order. It called for the resignation of the Grand Master of the Orange Order, the Reverend Martin Smyth, and the severing of links with the UUP. In the event, Smyth quit at the end of his term in office at the end of 1996. His replacement, Robert Saulters, denounced the Labour Party leader Tony Blair as a 'traitor to his religion' for attending Catholic mass and receiving Catholic communion.

Unionists argued that the increased concern of Sinn Fein to redirect Orange parades was merely a device to increase the party's legitimacy within the Catholic community. Convicted IRA members did indeed front some of the residents' groups. Nationalists pointed to the broad coalitional nature of such groups, arguing that antagonism to displays of Orange triumphalism was longstanding throughout the Nationalist community. The tensions over Orange parades reflected a shift in the paradigm of Northern Ireland politics. Constitutional issues were not dead, but the old certainties of the Republican agenda of a united Ireland were being matched, or even displaced, by 'softer' demands based upon equality and cultural agendas. Previously, Sinn Fein had seen Orangemen as merely unthreatening, deluded Irishmen clinging to traditions which would disappear or be unthreatening in a united Ireland. As Sinn Fein now became increasingly concerned with equality for Nationalists within the existing state, displays of Orange sectarianism were challenged.

Tensions were exacerbated further as Loyalists intimidated Catholics attending mass in Harryville, Ballymena. The Protestant Unionist mayor joined Catholic worshippers to display opposition to such sectarianism. The new Grand Master of the Orange Order also demonstrated his support of the right of Catholics to worship unfettered. Arson attacks upon Catholic schools and churches increased. Arguably, the extent of sectarian polarisation matched that at the outset of the Troubles. The prolonged 'marching season' in Northern Ireland, although a sideshow to the peace process, highlighted divisions. By 2001, however, there were some signs that the parades issue was fading. The British government, Parades Commission and the RUC made it clear that the Drumcree march would not be allowed to proceed in 1998 and similar rulings followed in subsequent years. The Parades Commission, with isolated exceptions, no longer allowed Orange parades to travel through mainly Nationalist areas.

13.8 New Labour: new peace process

From 1981 to 1994, Labour Party policy was that of support for 'Irish unity by consent'. This policy was dismissed as 'platitudinous' by one critic, given the absence of that consent (Bennett, 1996: 153). According to Bew and Dixon (1994: 154–8) it was based upon three things: the redefinition of consent, from 'majority' to a 'significant' level; the achievement of working-class unity; and the reform of Northern Ireland, the lattermost resting uneasily alongside the long-term goal of its abolition in favour of a united Ireland.

The sacking of the pro-Nationalist Kevin McNamara as Labour's Northern Ireland Spokesman in October 1994 confirmed that, under Tony Blair, Labour's approach would move towards that of the Conservatives (Tonge, 1997). After the removal of McNamara, it became evident that a Labour government would not try to act as a persuader to Unionists that their better interests lay within a united Ireland. Henceforth, Labour would emphasise that consent for Northern Ireland's place in the United Kingdom was paramount and that the party's position was not to have a preferred outcome, be it the Union or Irish unity, but instead it would act as merely as a facilitator for the wishes of the people of Northern Ireland. In *Realpolitik*, there had been little departure from a bipartisan approach to Northern Ireland between 1981 and 1994, but Labour's stated preferred outcome of that period of a united Ireland was a significant departure from Conservative policy.

According to Labour's Northern Ireland team, the new policy ensured that Labour's approach was 'live not utopian' (Illsley, 1996). The leader of the Ulster Unionist Party asserted that this was a sign that 'in England, unionism is winning the intellectual argument' (Trimble, 1996). The Labour leader, Tony Blair, insisted that he would not 'play politics' with the peace process. The lack of division between the Conservative and Labour parties ensured that the issue of Northern Ireland remained 'uncontested ground' in Westminster politics (Boyce, 1996: 165).

Labour's move away from support for Irish unity was confirmed upon election in 1997, Tony Blair insisting on his first prime ministerial visit:

> My agenda is not a united Ireland and I wonder just how many see it as a realistic possibility for the foreseeable future? Northern Ireland will remain part of the United Kingdom as long as a majority here wish . . . I believe in the United Kingdom. I value the Union . . . Northern Ireland is part of the United Kingdom because that is the wish of the majority of the people who live here. It will remain part of the UK for as long as that remains the case . . . Unionists have nothing to fear from a new Labour Government. A political settlement is not a slippery slope to a united Ireland. The Government will not be persuaders for unity (*Daily Telegraph*, 17 May 1997).

The Labour government was anxious to revive the peace process and move towards multi-party talks. Declaring that the 'settlement train' was leaving, Blair indicated that the peace process was back to the position of early 1996, when the Mitchell Commission reported. Sinn Fein could enter talks in the event of an IRA ceasefire; the IRA would be required to decommission its weapons in parallel with these talks; and Republicans would be obliged to substantially lower their political horizons concerning the outcome of such negotiations.

Although this situation appeared problematical for Republicans, they had several consolations. Firstly, Sinn Fein's electoral successes in 1997 strengthened the mandate of Republicans. Secondly, there was the possibility of a revival of the 'pan-nationalist' coalition following the return to power of Fianna Fail, led by Bertie Ahern, in the Irish Republic in 1997. Thirdly, decommissioning was afforded less priority by a Labour government more anxious than its predecessor to remove barriers to Sinn Fein's entry to talks. Fourthly, the size of the Labour government's parliamentary majority removed the need for short-term political concessions to Unionist parties. Fifthly, negotiations would take place within a closed time frame of less than one year, rather than be allowed to meander indefinitely.

Sinn Fein's final demand, that no outcome to negotiations should be precluded, appeared to be contravened by Blair's specific dismissal of the prospect of a united Ireland. Conflicting interpretations can be provided of why Sinn Fein was prepared to overlook the British Prime Minister's robust denial of the party's political ambition, indeed, arguably, its *raison d'être*. The first is that the peace process was a defeat for Republicans, who would emerge from negotiations with minor cross-border gains, a weakened military wing and internal divisions. Alternatively, Labour's loud public rejection of a united Ireland was a device largely to reassure unionists before negotiations and reduce their hostility to the easing of decommissioning stringencies. Multi-party talks would transform the manner in which Northern Ireland was governed to the point where radical options favoured by many Nationalists emerged, such as joint authority.

As the prospect of multi-party talks in September 1997 was offered to Sinn Fein, Labour's approach confronted Republicans in Northern Ireland with the dilemma of accepting the modest gains offered by new constitutionalism, or pursuing ideological purity and continued violence, with the attendant risk of fruitless political ostracism. Amid considerable scepticism from opponents who feared that Republican options were merely tactical, the IRA indicated a preference for the former approach and renewed its ceasefire in July 1997.

13.9 Conclusion

Peace without political progress offered no permanent remedy to the problems of Northern Ireland. As Edna Longley wrote immediately after the interruption of the IRA ceasefire:

> Peace implies not merely the absence of war, but civilisation, a fully functional civil society. While paramilitaries controlled districts or politicians radically disagreed on institutions, the outward signs of peace such as the demilitarisation of streets, the disappearance of searchers from shop doors and Belfast's consumer and restaurant boon all seemed slightly unreal (*Independent on Sunday*, 11 February 1996).

Despite the difficulties, and the fracturing of the peace process by the IRA in 1996, there was an underlying commitment amongst most parties to a resolution of the conflict. The IRA's return to violence attempted to win a place for Sinn Fein within negotiations, not achieve British withdrawal from Ireland. Political developments resumed with the election of new governments in Britain and Ireland and the announcement of a revived IRA ceasefire in mid-1997.

The inclusion of Sinn Fein offered the prospect of a far-reaching accommodation between the conflicting demands of unionism and nationalism.

The temporary breakdown of the peace process owed much to the acute problems of the Conservative government in the mid-1990s, devoid of a workable parliamentary majority and reliant upon Unionist votes. The return to violence was indicative of a debate within the republican movement over the direction of the peace process, an argument still to be fully played out, but one which moderates and non-militarists would dominate.

Even the constitutional Nationalists of the SDLP complained that the British government 'had not prepared intellectually for the ceasefire' (Attwood, 1996). The cessation of IRA activity had come as a surprise and there had been little thought given to how to proceed after such an event, leading to a succession of stalling devices. Many Unionists argued that suspicion of the motives of the IRA was entirely justified by events in 1996–7. For such critics, the peace process was phoney, as tactical ceasefires could never be equated to a permanent commitment to peaceful methods of conflict resolution. Others were more optimistic, as the demands of Nationalists for change in Northern Ireland had been strengthened by the strongest alliance since partition, from which it would be difficult for the Provisional IRA to re-embark on a permanent campaign. After the Labour government's election victory in 1997, Sinn Fein entered talks and momentum developed towards an agreement embracing unionism and nationalism.

Chapter 14

The Good Friday Agreement

The climax of the peace process arrived in April 1998, as political agreement was reached. The Good Friday (or Belfast) Agreement represented the culmination of exhaustive multi-party, intergovernmental and bilateral talks. Although the talks process was not entirely inclusive, the DUP and UKUP declining to participate, the majority of Northern Irish opinion was represented. The Agreement reflected hard bargaining among historical enemies, allied to compromise. At its heart lay the principle of consent for constitutional change in Northern Ireland. Within this overarching principle lay power-sharing, all-Ireland and confederal dimensions, alongside continued intergovernmentalism. A broad sketch of the constitutional agenda of the Good Friday Agreement had been visible at Sunningdale 25 years earlier. For the new Agreement to form the endgame, a new inclusiveness on non-constitutional issues was needed, embracing an equality agenda and 'end of conflict' measures, such as paramilitary prisoner releases.

14.1 The contents of the Agreement

The Agreement contained several Strands. These were:

- Strand 1: a devolved Northern Ireland Assembly of 108 seats, presided over by a cross-community Executive and headed by a First Minister and a Deputy Minister;
- Strand 2: a North–South Ministerial Council, to establish all-Ireland implementation bodies in at least six policy areas;
- Strand 3: a British–Irish Council, comprising representatives from the British and Irish governments, alongside those from devolved institutions in the United Kingdom. A British–Irish intergovernmental conference, designed to explore the totality of relationships between the two islands, replaced the Anglo-Irish Agreement.

The Irish government also dropped its constitutional claim to Northern Ireland. Henceforth, Articles 2 and 3 of the constitution of the Irish Republic would contain a mere aspiration, rather than assertion, of Irish unity. Aside from constitutional issues, the Agreement also covered human rights, equality, decommissioning, prisoners, security and policing. The main equality-oriented measures were:

- the incorporation of the European Convention on Human Rights into Northern Ireland law; ·
- establishment of a Northern Ireland Human Rights Commission;
- creation of an Equality Commission;
- establishment of a consultative civic forum to allow representation from a wide range of organisations.

On policing, the Agreement established an independent commission to make recommendations for future arrangements (*see* Chapter 7). The Agreement permitted the release of paramilitary prisoners within two years, provided that their organisations maintained a ceasefire. The provisions in respect of decommissioning and security were more ambiguous. All parties were obliged to use 'any influence they may have, to achieve the decommissioning of all paramilitary arms within two years' (HM Government, 1998: 20). The British government promised that it would 'make progress towards the objective of as early a return as possible to normal security arrangements in Northern Ireland, consistent with the level of threat and with a published overall strategy' (HM Government, 1998: 21).

14.2 Negotiating change: party positions

Publication of the document *Propositions on Heads of Agreement*, by the British and Irish governments in January 1998, advanced movement towards serious negotiating positions. *Propositions* laid out the basic format of any agreement. It suggested a Northern Ireland Assembly; North–South bodies; a Council of the Isles and an intergovernmental agreement to replace the Anglo-Irish Agreement. The broad framework of *Propositions* was similar to that in the 1995 Framework Document. However, there were important differences of detail and further movement emerged in the hard bargaining leading to the historic compromise of the Good Friday Agreement.

The Good Friday Agreement attempted to balance Unionist insistence of the retention of Northern Ireland's place in the United Kingdom with the aspiration of Nationalists for internal change and furtherance of Irish political input. Both sides struck bargains in the negotiations leading to the April climax, reflected in significant differences from the 1995 Framework Document and the 1998 *Propositions on Heads of Agreement*. The latter was seen by Nationalists as being too Unionist, whilst the Framework Documents were seen by Unionists as too 'green'. The SDLP was anxious to ensure meaningful power-sharing within a new devolved government. The party opposed the UUP's idea that governance should be based upon a committee system. Instead, the SDLP insisted, with success, upon a powerful, cross-community executive (Hopkins, 1998). Until March 1998, Sinn Fein mobilised its supporters on a 'no return to Stormont' platform. Emphasising its Republican credentials, the party submitted proposals for an independent, united Ireland. No discussions took place around these proposals (Hennessy, 2000). By March 1998, Sinn Fein had softened its position, arguing that the 1995 Framework Document should provide the basis for an agreement, offering the minimum all-Ireland dimension required to satisfy Republicans. The constitutional aspects of the Agreement gave little succour to Sinn Fein. Indeed, for this section of the negotiations, the party appeared to be a captive of its own peace strategy (Hazleton, 1999). Sinn Fein concentrated much of its energies upon the micro-agenda, where gains were possible to partially compensate for the ground lost since the Framework Document. In this area, the party was more successful, with policing and security reforms promised. Sinn Fein's 'hardball' approach to prisoners was also fruitful. Adams indicated to his party's *ard fheis* (annual conference) in 1998 that he made it clear at the outset that there would be 'no deal' without prisoner releases.

In addition to the difficulty of entering a Northern assembly at Stormont, albeit one vastly different from its predecessor, Republicans were also pained by the willingness of the Irish government to relinquish its constitutional claim to Northern Ireland. Some Republicans were scornful of the claim, arguing it had been of little value to defensive Northern Nationalists. As the former IRA member, Martin Meehan, told the 1998 *ard fheis*, the Articles had been 'no use whatsoever in Bombay Street in 1969', referring to how Nationalists were attacked whilst the Irish government did very little. Nonetheless, the Articles had powerful symbolism, emphasising the perception of Republican Ireland of the illegitimacy of the Northern state. The Irish government had always resisted removing the Articles. This time, however, the removal of Articles 2 and 3 appeared to be a non-negotiable item for the UUP. In return, the British government agreed to remove its claim to Northern Ireland under section 75 of the 1920 Government of Northern Ireland Act. Hennessy (2000) argues this was meaningless, as the legal claim to Northern Ireland dated back to the Act of Union of 1800, from which only the 26 counties of the Republic had been removed. Furthermore, the provisions of the 1920 Act were replaced by the 1998 Northern Ireland Act. As such, the removal of the 1920 British claim to Northern Ireland was, in legal terms, 'of no significance' (Hadfield, 1998: 615). Sinn Fein's president, Gerry Adams, nonetheless insisted at the 1998 *ard fheis* that there 'was no longer any great raft of legislation keeping Northern Ireland within the Union'. At that conference, begun in April 1998 and reconvened the following month, Sinn Fein's members voted by 97 per cent to 3 per cent to support entry to Stormont under the terms of the Good Friday Agreement.

The UUP achieved a considerable dilution of the cross-border aspects of the Agreement, compared to what had been tentatively floated in 1995. The Framework Document envisaged an executive North–South Council with a wide range of powers. Fearing any move towards a freestanding, all-Ireland executive body (although this exaggerated the greenness of the Framework Document) Unionists argued that the North–South Council should possess no more than consultative powers. The Unionist parties within the negotiations, the UUP, PUP and UDP, envisaged cross-borderism as a development confined to the sphere of economic logic. The SDLP wished to attach political significance to the North–South Council. Nonetheless, the SDLP conceded from the outset that the all-island dimension 'would have to include accountability by the northern members of the North–South Council to an assembly in Belfast if the council was to be acceptable to unionists' (Farren, 2000: 60).

Bargaining between the two sides meandered, resulting in the chair of the talks, Senator George Mitchell, announcing that a deal needed to be completed by 9 April 1998. During the week leading to this deadline, Mitchell showed the parties the draft agreement produced by the two governments, on the basis of the negotiating stances of the parties. The final deal was much closer to that desired by Unionists. The North–South Council would not be meaningless and six new all-island implementation bodies would be created. Nonetheless, the Council was not invested with executive powers of its own. It was to be a co-ordinating body designed to 'develop consultation, co-operation and action within the island of Ireland – including through implementation on an all-island and cross-border basis' (HM Government, 1998: 11). More importantly, perhaps, the all-Ireland dimension appeared to be ringfenced. There was no built-in dynamic to the North–South Council. The Council was required to identify and agree at least six matters for co-operation and implementation using existing bodies and six with new cross-border bodies. Beyond this, however, further all-island bodies had to be approved by the Northern Ireland Assembly (and Irish parliament). Such consent was unlikely to be forthcoming from even moderate Unionists. Strand 2 appeared to represent the 'necessary nonsense' of an all-Ireland dimension, designed to placate Nationalists and reassure them that their political ambitions were beginning to be recognised (Paul Bew, *The Times*, 29 November 1999). It appeared to do the trick: 69 per cent of SDLP members believed that the Good Friday Agreement brought a united Ireland nearer, and 87 per cent believed that North–South bodies would improve co-operation between the two parts of the island (author's survey, 1999). Sinn Fein persuaded its members that the Agreement was transitional towards Irish unity, although, privately, one senior party figure declared that he 'never believed that the Good Friday Agreement would deliver a united Ireland in 15 to 20 years'. Those outside the negotiations offered similar views to the party (Sinn Fein) they found so objectionable. For the DUP, the Good Friday Agreement represented a clear transition towards Irish unity (as had all previous agreements on Northern Ireland).

14.3 Mixing old and new: central themes of the Agreement

According to the deputy leader of the SDLP, Seamus Mallon, the Good Friday Agreement amounted to 'Sunningdale for slow learners' (quoted by Bew, 1997; Tonge, 2000: 39). In broad constitutional terms, this appeared to be true. Northern Ireland remained in the United Kingdom, whilst the Irish government had some say in the affairs of Northern Ireland. Overall, there were greater similarities than differences between the two agreements, but there was also evidence of policy learning by the two governments and the respective political parties. The old themes of the Good Friday Agreement were consent, cross-borderism, consociationalism and intergovernmentalism.

14.3.1 Consent

The principle of consent underpinned the Agreement. There could be no change in the constitutional status of Northern Ireland without the consent of the majority of its people. The Irish constitution was amended to recognise this principle. In making this change, the Irish government did not abandon its hope of constructing of a thirty-two-county nation state. As such, the new constitution was not post-nationalist. The constitutional imperative of the pursuit of this goal was downgraded, however, to a mere aspiration. There is no demographic 'timebomb' awaiting Unionists. Catholics are much less united on their constitutional preferences than Protestants and the modern difference in Catholic and Protestant birth and emigration rates is negligible. As such, there will be a majority for the retention of Northern Ireland's place in the United Kingdom for the foreseeable future. Given this, the critique of the Agreement offered by the DUP may mystify some observers. The case offered by the Unionist anti-agreement forces is that the influence of the Irish Republic in the affairs of Northern Ireland cannot be reduced. The reiteration of the consent principle is thus undermined by creeping bi-nationalism, followed by eventual Irish unity by stealth, achieved through the creation of all-Ireland executive bodies.

14.3.2 Cross-borderism

One of the difficulties pertaining to the Sunningdale Agreement was the vagueness surrounding the powers that the Council of Ireland would be awarded. The Good Friday Agreement is much more explicit over the remit of the all-island bodies and the North–South Council. Nationalists begin with a higher baseline, in that six new all-island implementation bodies have been created as a result of the Agreement (*see* Chapter 6). However, the greater precision of the 1998 Agreement eliminates much of the potential dynamism of the all-island dimension. A literal reading of the Agreement allows little scope for its expansion, unless Unionists within the Assembly embrace cross-borderism with a hitherto unseen enthusiasm. Without approval from the Northern Ireland Assembly, the powers of the North–South Council cannot expand, nor can the number of cross-border bodies increase. Nonetheless, it is inconceivable that Nationalists will not pressurise Unionists for such increases.

14.3.3 Consociationalism

Enforced power sharing between Unionists and Nationalists was an inevitable element of any deal. Negotiations were based upon the mode of power-sharing rather than the actuality. The Sunningdale Agreement relied upon a grand coalition of the (Faulknerite) UUP, Alliance and SDLP. The Good Friday Agreement moves away from the coalitional model in favour of a more competitive, ethnic bloc approach. Although there is some variance, the model of consociationalism deployed is broadly in line with the principles espoused by Lijphart (1996). It contains cross-community power-sharing, minority protections, community (segmental) autonomy and equality, and weighted majority decision-making on contentious issues (O'Leary, 1999). The First and Deputy Ministers are elected with cross-community consent, whilst the D'Hondt mechanism, based upon party strengths within the Assembly, ensures Unionist and Nationalist representation within the Executive.

The model used is not to everyone's taste, even among supporters of a consociational settlement. The ethnic bloc divisions in Northern Ireland are managed by the Agreement, not removed. There is a fear that the Agreement legitimises the pursuit of vigorous ethnic bloc politics. It assumes (but tries to harness) an essentially competitive rather than co-operative relationship between Nationalists and Unionists, even though the new Assembly will deal with non-reserved (devolved) issues, to which the application of Unionist or Nationalist ideas will often be irrelevant. As an example of this critique, the Alliance Party supports the Agreement, but would prefer a settlement which did not involve the reductionism which leaves the current political centre in Northern Ireland designated as an 'other' party, with Unionist and Nationalist political labels legitimised and supported by the Agreement. The perception of the communities as separate but equal is too segregationist for some. Alliance would prefer a more integrative form of consociationalism, as espoused theoretically by Horowitz (1985). Almost one in three Alliance members believe that the Agreement increases sectarianism by dividing parties into ethnic blocs (Tonge and Evans, 2001b). A majority of Ulster Unionist Council members also offer this criticism, although many are against the Agreement *per se* (Tonge and Evans, 2001b).

Critics of segmental consociational arrangements are accused of 'utopianism, myopia and partisanship' (O'Leary, 1999: 258). Ethnic bloc politics pre-date attempts at consociationalism. Indeed, they are the reason for its deployment as a solution. Ethnic division has been evident under different regime types: devolved, single-party government; direct rule; and now consociational, power-sharing governance. The fuelling of Unionist or Nationalist bloc agendas cannot be directly attributed to the Good Friday Agreement. The strongest charge against the Agreement in this respect is that it formalises existing division, yet the pursuit of vigorous ethnic politics may occur independently from the implementation of consociational political arrangements or the enhancement of intra-ethnic bloc rivalry. As an example, the SDLP became a 'greener', more Nationalist party *after the collapse* of the previous attempt at a consociational settlement in 1974 (Evans, Tonge and Murray, 2000). The party became somewhat disillusioned by the failure of power-sharing and attracted members favouring more stridently Nationalist politics.

14.3.4 Intergovernmentalism

The consociational power-sharing arrangements of the Good Friday Agreement are overarched by a powerful axis of the British and Irish governments. The two governments shaped the Good Friday Agreement and now formally review its progress, with members of the Northern Ireland Assembly 'invited to express views' (HM Government, 1998: 15). Although the Good Friday Agreement replaced the Anglo-Irish Agreement so detested by Unionists, much of the intergovernmental machinery remains in place, subsumed within the standing British-Irish Intergovernmental Conference established under the 1998 Agreement. The difference from the pre-1998 situation is that intergovernmental arrangements no longer pervade 'ordinary' politics in Northern Ireland. A directly elected assembly and indirectly elected executive now assume responsibility for 'low' politics in Northern Ireland. 'High' politics, including those concerning the security of the state, remain a matter for agreement between the two governments, although the role of the Irish Republic is mainly consultative.

Alongside these old themes reside several novel dimensions to the Good Friday Agreement. They include co-determination, confederation, identity politics, co-authority and inclusivity.

14.3.5 Co-determination

One of the most significant aspects of the Good Friday Agreement was that it was endorsed by voters on both sides of the border. For the referendum on the Agreement in May 1998, the electorate throughout the island of Ireland took part in a simultaneous vote for the first time since the last all-Ireland elections of 1918. Such an event was laden with symbolic significance. The referenda were conducted separately north and south of the border. As such, the vote on the Good Friday Agreement amounted to an exercise in co-determination, rather than the 'pure' self-determination demanded by Republicans. Furthermore, the exercise in co-determination did not allow a decision on an outcome which, the text of the Good Friday Agreement acknowledges, is the wish of the majority of Irish people. Page 2 of the Agreement refers to the 'legitimate wish of a majority of the people of the island of Ireland for a united Ireland'. The people of the island were allowed to co-determine whether a specific political compromise, in the form of the Good Friday Agreement, was acceptable. Co-determination emerged, via the Downing Street Declaration of 1993, as a watered-down version of full Irish self-determination proposed under the earlier Hume–Adams dialogue. In effect, Northern Ireland determined its own future, but with the approval of the electorate throughout the island of Ireland. Co-determination thus broadened and reinforced the principle of consent underpinning the Agreement.

14.3.6 Confederation

The British–Irish Council established under Strand 3 links devolved institutions throughout Britain and Ireland. It offers a confederal dimension to the Agreement, bringing all parts of the two islands together under a mutually beneficial arrangement. The establishment of the Council was strongly advocated by Unionists in the negotiations leading to the Good Friday Agreement. It may allow greater cultural interplay of the Agreement and links between devolved institutions in Northern Ireland and Scotland, states with many similarities (Walker, 1997). Whilst the Council may grow in significance, its initial role is not substantial and it has been dismissed as a 'talking shop' (*Guardian*, 14 December 1999). The Council attempts to develop consensus on issues, but, given that it has no powers to force dissenting institutions into programmes of action, bilateral or multilateral agreements between selected devolved institutions are also permissible. The Council's initial role appears to be as a forum for information exchange and consultation.

14.3.7 Identity politics

It is no longer possible to hold a 'disloyal' identity in Northern Ireland. The Agreement allows a range of identities: British, Irish, British-Irish or Northern Irish, and does not discriminate in respect of the validity of any such identity. Furthermore, the Agreement makes no attempt to persuade those regarding themselves as Irish of their Britishness but speaks of their being part of an Irish nation. This emphasis upon identity politics is not entirely new, as such strands have existed since the 1985 Anglo-Irish Agreement. The 1998 version is, however, far more explicit.

14.3.8 Co-authority

Use of the terms joint sovereignty, or co-sovereignty, is too politically sensitive in Northern Ireland. Instead, the British and Irish governments insist that they are each exercising sovereignty within their own jurisdictions to create new political institutions. As such, it is claimed there has been no derogation of sovereignty. This formula is not accepted by Unionist critics of the Agreement. Arguably, the Agreement is a shift towards co-authority (and, ultimately co-sovereignty) over Northern Ireland, through its establishment of all-Ireland executive bodies and the consolidation of British–Irish intergovernmental arrangements. Co-authority does not have to be implemented on a 50–50 basis and the British government clearly remains the dominant partner. Further gains in influence for the Irish Republic may nonetheless move Northern Ireland towards the status of a bi-national state, a minimum objective for many Nationalists.

14.3.9 Inclusivity

Most importantly of all, the Good Friday Agreement was constructed on the basis of inclusivity, designed to bring virtually all shades of opinion into a political process. The process of inclusion had begun by allowing a range of actors some limited input to the 1993 Downing Street Declaration. Inclusion became a primary theme of the Northern Ireland Forum elected in 1996, in which 10 different organisations now had input to the talks process. The Good Friday Agreement was forged by these actors, including three parties linked to paramilitary organisations. Beyond a review of internment, the Sunningdale Agreement, with a mainly constitutional agenda, offered very little to Republicans intent on destabilising Northern Ireland. Although that Agreement was brought down by Loyalists, Sunningdale would, in any case, have failed to secure peace in Northern Ireland, given Republican scorn for its contents. The Good Friday Agreement enticed Republicans, not least because of its radical agenda on the 'three ps' of prisoners, policing and parity of esteem. By summer 2000, all paramilitary prisoners belonging to organisations on ceasefire had been released. Loyalist paramilitaries benefited equally. This, along with the Loyalists' belief that the Union was safe, allowed their political representatives in the PUP and UDP to endorse the Agreement.

14.4 The Good Friday Agreement referenda and Assembly elections

In May 1998, electors in Northern Ireland and the Irish Republic participated in simultaneous, but separate, referenda on the single question of whether to support or reject (via a 'yes' or 'no' vote) the Good Friday Agreement. The results are indicated in Table 14.1.

Across the entire island, 2,119,549 voters registered their support for the Agreement, with only 360,627 voting against. The results in both parts of the island provided the Agreement with a substantial mandate. The institutional arrangements of the Good Friday Agreement could now develop. Notwithstanding the limited nature of the referendum's constitutional choice, the people of the island of Ireland, for the first time in history, had, in effect, voted to accept the partition of their country. There were caveats to the result, for those searching. In the Irish Republic, those not bothering to vote, added to the small number of 'no' voters, almost matched the number of 'yes' voters. This statistic reflected the disinterest in the North felt by many voters in the Irish Republic.

In Northern Ireland, the concern throughout the contest had been whether a majority of Unionists would back the Agreement. With both Nationalist parties endorsing the Agreement, a 99 per cent 'yes' vote was recorded among Catholics, but only 57 per cent of Protestants voted likewise (Hayes and McAllister, 1999). Some 'no' voters opposed what they saw as a constitutional sell-out. The primary concern of others was the moral question of early prisoner releases. Less than half (47 per cent) of Protestants supported the establishment of North–South bodies (Curtice and Dowds, 1999). Even among Protestant

Table 14.1 The Good Friday Agreement referenda 1998

Country	Yes	%	No	%	Turnout (%)
Northern Ireland	676,966	71.1	274,879	28.9	81.0
Republic of Ireland	1,442,583	94.4	85,748	5.6	55.6

Table 14.2 Northern Ireland Assembly elections 1998

Party	Designation	Pro- or anti-Agreement	Vote (%)	Seats
UUP	Unionist	Pro	21.3	28
SDLP	Nationalist	Pro	22.3	24
DUP	Unionist	Anti	18.1	20
SF	Nationalist	Pro	17.6	18
APNI	Other	Pro	6.5	6
UKUP*	Unionist	Anti	4.5	5
Ind. Unionist	Unionist	Anti	2.5	3
PUP	Unionist	Pro	2.5	3
NIWC	Other	Pro	1.6	2

NB: All parties have to designate their Assembly representatives as Unionist, Nationalist, or Other. * The UKUP split in 1999, with four Assembly members forming the Northern Ireland Unionist Party.

'yes' voters, fewer than half supported the establishment of a commission into the future of the Royal Ulster Constabulary and the overwhelming majority opposed early prisoner releases (Hayes and McAllister, 2000). Nonetheless, the Agreement was sold and bought as a compromise package. Opinion was divided over whether the Agreement would bring a lasting peace, although a slight majority believed this would be the result (Evans and O'Leary, 1999).

The referendum campaign yielded some unusual allies, reflecting the inclusivity of the Agreement. Sinn Fein members found themselves urging a 'yes' vote in common with Loyalist former adversaries within the PUP and UDP, whose paramilitary associates had conducted assassination campaigns against Sinn Fein members. Those working-class Loyalists supported many middle-class Unionists within the UUP in urging an end to what they saw as the visionless negativity of 'no' unionism, as espoused most publicly by the DUP. The PUP and UDP argument was that working-class Loyalists had been imprisoned as a consequence of adherence to the fears expressed by the 'siren voices' of unionism. Changes in Republican paramilitarism and the securing of the Union no longer necessitated 'no' unionism. These arguments helped secure a 'yes' vote among many working-class Loyalists, although the sight of Loyalist (and Republican) paramilitaries addressing (separate) rallies in favour of a 'yes' vote may have caused further unease among Unionists unhappy about the apparent moral ambivalence of the deal.

One month after the referendum, the first elections to the new Northern Ireland Assembly were staged (*see* Table 14.2). The results highlighted the divisions within unionism. Of 58 Unionists elected, 30 were from pro-Agreement parties, an uncomfortably slender majority.

Pessimists saw the result as clear indication that 'no' unionism was undefeated. Optimists pointed out that over 70 per cent of voters had supported pro-Agreement parties. Some limited evidence of cross-community electoral politics also emerged, reflected in the willingness of some Unionists to use their lower preference votes to support pro-Agreement candidates, even if such candidates were Nationalists. Unionist transfers to Sinn Fein remained inconceivable, but Sinnott found that in circumstances where lower preference vote transfers to Alliance were not an option, 36 per cent of UUP final transfer votes went to the SDLP (*Irish Times*, 29 June 1998). Similar findings were recorded by Evans and O'Leary (1999). A willingness to vote transfer across the divide is found at a higher level: 15.3 per cent of Ulster Unionist Council members said that they 'definitely' or 'might' consider transferring lower preference votes to the SDLP (Tonge and Evans, 2001a).

14.5 Decommissioning and Executive formation

The issue of the decommissioning of paramilitary weapons dogged the peace process before and after the formation of new political institutions in Northern Ireland. The Good Friday Agreement was ambiguous in respect of whether paramilitary decommissioning was a requirement and over the extent to which such a demand could be linked to particular political parties. The relevant section of the Agreement merely stated that all participants 'reaffirm their commitment to the total disarmament of all paramilitary organisations'(p. 20) and called upon parties to:

> use any influence they may have, to achieve the decommissioning of all paramilitary weapons they may have within two years following endorsement in referendums North and South of the Agreement and in the context of the overall settlement. (HM Government, 1998: 20).

Three years after the clinching of the Good Friday Agreement, the only weapons decommissioned were a handful of guns surrendered by the Loyalist Volunteer Force. The IRA, however, opened two of its weapons dumps to independent inspection. Siren voices within unionism had criticised the Agreement's lack of clarity over whether parties could be linked to the decommissioning of paramilitary associates. Indeed, the Westminster Ulster Unionist MP, Jeffrey Donaldson, walked away from the Agreement at its conclusion, despite his party leader having obtained written assurances on decommissioning from the British Prime Minister. The essential problem for Unionists was that the spirit of the Agreement required decommissioning. A literal reading, however, made it difficult to impose sanctions on parties over the issue. The Agreement did not require IRA decommissioning either in advance of, or simultaneous to, Sinn Fein's entry into government in Northern Ireland.

Sinn Fein and the IRA insisted that the arms issue would be resolved, although IRA weapons had never been surrendered when political parties, such as the main two in the Irish Republic, had emerged from the movement. Gerry Adams did insist that 'the violence we have seen must be for all of us a thing of the past, over, done with and gone', tantamount to saying that the Provisional IRA's violence was over (quoted in Elliott and Flackes, 2000:

130). With Republicans having already crossed a political rubicon in entering Stormont, decommissioning of IRA weaponry would nonetheless be awkward, for several reasons. Firstly, the surrender of weapons, either to the enemy it had been fighting, or on British terms, was the equivalent of an IRA surrender. The leader of the Provisional IRA indicated in 1998 that 'voluntary decommissioning' would be a 'natural part of the peace process' (*Financial Times*, 17 June 1998). The implication was that the dispute lay less over decommissioning than with control of the process. Secondly, the Republican unity evident throughout the peace process would be threatened by such a move. 'Dissident' Republicans labelled even slight co-operation with the International Commission on Disarmament as the 'Provos' final surrender' (*Saoirse*, December 1999). Thirdly, the latent threat of violence, although very distant since 1997 from the Provisional IRA, was thought by some to continue to yield slight political leverage. Finally, Republicans did not draw distinctions between IRA weaponry and the arms held legally by the state. Resolution of the weapons issue could, therefore, occur only within an overall context of 'demilitarisation'. The British government's pledge to return to 'normality' in respect of security still meant the retention of the United Kingdom's only armed police force. The government did, however, remove many security installations from urban areas. The threat from 'dissident' Republicans ensured that the pace of dismantling was slower in border areas.

Republican tactics on the decommissioning issue were apparent from the outset. Firstly, the organisational separation of Sinn Fein and the IRA was emphasised. Secondly, Republicans stated what was apparent from any reading of the Good Friday Agreement. Sinn Fein's electoral mandate, not IRA movement on decommissioning, would entitle the party to seats in government. Thirdly, the sentence in the Good Friday Agreement that spoke of the need to 'achieve the decommissioning of all paramilitary arms within two years', the sole phrase giving Unionists an actual rather than mere moral case, was simply ignored.

Internal Republican difficulties carried little weight within Unionist circles. Unionists attempted to link Sinn Fein's participation in the Northern Ireland Assembly and Executive to progress on IRA decommissioning. Unionist parties reflected their electorate's opinion, with 70 per cent of Protestants believing that Sinn Fein should only be permitted to take seats in the Northern Ireland executive after the IRA has decommissioned weapons or explosives (Evans and O'Leary, 1999). There was broad support for decommissioning: 95 per cent of Protestants and 88 per cent of Catholics believed it should occur (Hayes and McAllister, 2000). The linkage of decommissioning to party representation in new political institutions was, however, much more problematic.

The lack of resolution of the decommissioning issue led to delays in the formation of the Northern Ireland Executive. In May 1999, the British government set a 'final deadline' of 30 June, rapidly revised to another 'final' 15 July deadline. The British and Irish governments produced The Way Forward proposals, allowing an Executive to be formed, to be followed by progress reports on decommissioning. At this stage, only two paramilitary groups, the

UVF and LVF, had contacted the International Commission on Decommissioning. The UUP executive rejected The Way Forward, resulting in farce at Stormont on 15 July. With the UUP absent and the DUP and Alliance parties declining to nominate ministers, an entirely Nationalist executive was formed. Comprising SDLP and Sinn Fein ministers only, this executive lasted 10 minutes before being ruled as in breach of the Good Friday Agreement legislation requiring cross-community executive selection. The Deputy First Minister, Seamus Mallon, resigned (later curiously reinterpreted as a mere offer to resign when the Executive was being reborn) and the entire Good Friday Agreement was placed under a review chaired by Senator George Mitchell.

The essential difficulty of Executive formation lay in choreography, as the Ulster Unionist Party's submission to the Mitchell Review, *Implementing the Agreement*, made clear. Some movement on IRA decommissioning was required. The IRA announced it would appoint a representative to deal with the International Commission on Decommissioning (ICD) after the establishment of the political institutions agreed in the Good Friday Agreement. In November 1999, the Ulster Unionist Council accepted this by 480 votes to 329 (58 per cent to 42 per cent) but built in its own default mechanism. Progress on decommissioning would be reviewed in February 2000 and if no breakthrough had been achieved, the UUP would resign from the Executive. At the end of November, the Executive was formed, headed by the UUP leader, David Trimble. Inaugural meetings of the North–South Council and the British–Irish Council took place during the following month. The UUP had 'jumped first' on the decommissioning issue, but the first Executive lasted a mere 72 days. An IRA statement at the beginning of February 2000, offering 'no threat to the peace process', failed to satisfy Unionists. On 11 February, a gloomy report from General John De Chastelain, Head of the ICD, was made public, indicating little progress on decommissioning. A second, much more optimistic, report was issued later that day, but, given the absence of decommissioning 'product' (i.e. actual weaponry) and the imminence of UUP withdrawal, the Executive was suspended by the Secretary of State.

Having declared that all engagement with the decommissioning body was ended, following the suspension of the Executive, the IRA announced, in May 2000, that it was prepared to 'completely and verifiably put arms beyond use'. The plan involved the regular inspection of arms dumps by the former Finnish president, Martti Ahtisaari, and the former Secretary General of the African National Congress, Cyril Ramaphosa. The Ulster Unionist Council was urged to accept this offer by David Trimble, who had survived a leadership challenge in March from the Rev. Martin Smyth by the uncomfortably narrow margin of 57 per cent to 43 per cent (*see* Chapter 4). That UUC meeting also made the restoration of the Executive conditional upon the retention of the Royal Ulster Constabulary. This time, Trimble's margin was even narrower, at 53 per cent to 47 per cent. Considerable cynicism had developed over the tortuous sequencing on decommissioning and Executive formation. *The Times* columnist, Simon Jenkins, wrote before the May UUC decision: 'Don't laugh;

this is another crucial week in the peace process' (22 May). If the weariness was understandable, the May 2000 UUC vote was crucial and led to the restoration of the Executive. An IRA proposal on decommissioning had been accepted by the ruling body of unionism's largest party, without any conditions attached to the reformation of the Executive. Accordingly, the collapse of the Executive was much less likely than hitherto. The Executive was duly reformed, containing representatives from the UUP, SDLP, DUP and Sinn Fein.

The decommissioning issue had not been resolved and Trimble resigned as First Minister in summer 2001 in the absence of substantial movement. Unionists rejected the argument of Sinn Fein's TD in the Irish Republic, Caoimhghin O Caolain, that the guns should be left to 'rust in peace'. Republicans and Unionists had been obliged to shift their positions. Unionists were obliged to drop their insistence upon IRA decommissioning as a pre-condition for Sinn Fein's presence in government in Northern Ireland. The UUP entered government with Sinn Fein, despite the absence of any handover of weapons. The IRA, for the first time in its history, allowed its armoury to be inspected by externals.

14.6 Republican 'dissidents'

The Good Friday Agreement was portrayed by the British and Irish governments as a balanced constitutional settlement. All the people of Northern Ireland were deemed winners if the Agreement could endure and a lasting peace be created in Northern Ireland. This did not prevent parties from selling the Agreement to supporters as a vindication of their own political outlook. Pro-Agreement Unionists argued that it secured the Union. Anti-Agreement Unionists contended that the Agreement created structures which would lead to a united Ireland. Nationalists and Republicans said the same things as anti-Agreement Unionists, the main difference being that they regarded such a development as favourable. The Good Friday Agreement secured the Union for the foreseeable future, enshrining the consent principle. It acknowledged the need for recognition of the Irishness of Nationalists. This was effected through cultural means, notably in Irish language provision and in political terms by all-Ireland executive bodies and British–Irish intergovernmentalism. In this respect, the Agreement reflected most closely the political thinking of the SDLP (Murray, 1998).

Republicans declined to formally endorse the consent principle, as its acceptance legitimised the state of Northern Ireland. Nonetheless, the presence of Republicans in a government of Northern Ireland at Stormont signalled tacit acceptance. Sinn Fein's leadership pre-empted criticism of the Agreement from their own constituency by acknowledging that the Good Friday Agreement was not a Republican document. For Republican 'dissidents', compromise was unacceptable. The extent of Republican unity, given the acceptance by the Sinn Fein leadership of a settlement substantially short of Republican objectives, might be seen as a major achievement. Republican Sinn Fein and the tiny Continuity IRA still clung to a purist view of republicanism rejecting 'partitionist parliaments' north and south of the border. A more serious split in the IRA occurred in 1997, with the formation of the 'Real IRA' and its political outlet, the 32 County Sovereignty Committee. Ironically, these Republican 'dissidents' emerged because they believed the words of a British Prime Minister. Tony Blair's first major speech on Northern Ireland after his 1997 election victory made clear that a united Ireland would not emerge, either now or through the eventual outcome of a negotiated settlement. Given this, hardline militarists within the Republican movement argued, why renew an IRA ceasefire? The decision of the IRA to renew its cessation of violence led to the creation of the breakaway Real IRA in the autumn of 1997, linked to the 32 County Sovereignty Committee. The criticism of the Provisionals for 'selling out' was more wounding than that emanating from Republican Sinn Fein, given that Bernadette Sands-McKevitt, the sister of the hunger-striker and dead Republican hero, Bobby Sands, was a prominent member of the 32 County Sovereignty Committee. Sands-McKevitt insisted that 'Bobby did not die for cross-border bodies with executive powers. He did not die for nationalists to be equal British citizens within the Northern Ireland state' (*Irish Times*, 8 January 1998; Hennessy, 2000: 112). Any hopes that the Real IRA may have entertained of attracting large numbers of disaffected Provisional IRA members diminished with its disastrous bombing of Omagh in August 1998, killing 29 civilians (*see also* Chapter 5).

14.7 Conclusion

The Good Friday Agreement was a subtle agreement that displayed a considerable amount of policy learning from Sunningdale. Its broad constitutional terms were not dissimilar from those on offer 24 years earlier. Acceptance of the Good Friday Agreement owed far more, therefore, to changes within republicanism than fundamental changes in British policy towards Northern Ireland. Republicanism, as expressed through the political and military actions of Sinn Fein and the IRA, was not defeated, yet it could not alter the constitutional status quo. As Hennessy (2000: 20) puts it, the British 'only need a draw to win' in this respect. The main constitutional change instead came from the Irish government, with its abandonment of a claim to Northern Ireland under Articles 2 and 3 of the constitution. This allowed the development of an unthreatening external (cross-border) dimension to the Good Friday Agreement, one which did not impinge upon an internal consociational settlement (O'Leary, 2001). The basic contest within the constitutional clauses of the Agreement, wrapped in the language of self-determination, was that of consent versus transition (to Irish unity). Although the latter came off second best, this was not apparent to many Unionists, who remained sceptical of the deal.

Aside from reworn assertions of the consent principle, the Good Friday Agreement offered much that was novel. Belatedly, the British government realised the futility of the strategy of exclusion of groups it disliked. Support for republicanism was acknowledged and Sinn Fein was incorporated within the political process. The new strategy of inclusivity was equally effective on the Loyalist side. This forced an important divorce between sections of working-class loyalism, willing to act positively in favour of the deal, and the siren voices of Paisleyites and others, still hostile to radical change.

The mere fact that the Agreement had, by 2001, survived three years of periodic Unionist revolts, increased support for 'no' campaigners, prisoner releases and an absence of decommissioning, led to limited optimism concerning its durability, although even a sympathetic analyst feared that at times it was in 'mortal danger' (O'Leary, 2001: 484). Its vulnerability was highlighted by the temporary suspension of institutions in 2000 and 2001. Nonetheless, 'no' Unionists were pitted against a considerable range of forces. The Secretary of State for Northern Ireland, John Reid, insisted that the Agreement 'remains the only show in town' (*Independent*, 3 May 2001). Gerry Adams argued that 'if it (the Good Friday Agreement) collapses on Monday, on Tuesday we have to put it together again' (*Guardian*, 30 April 2001). Often precarious, unloved by many and criticised by others, the greater inclusivity of the Good Friday Agreement at least allowed it to enjoy a healthier balance of political support than its ill-fated 1974 predecessor.

Chapter 15

Political stability in Northern Ireland?

15.1 The problem in context

During the Troubles, there were commentators who, perhaps unsurprisingly, declared that 'there is no solution' (Rose, 1976: 139). The plethora of failed initiatives in the 1970s and 1980s, added to the long history of Britain's 'Irish problem' and Ireland's 'British problem', gave that view credence. The conflict appeared enduring and intractable. The violence in Northern Ireland was protracted, but it was also seen as 'manageable'. Tomlinson makes the point that the 3,400 deaths between 1969 and 1994, although extraordinary by European standards, were 'relatively minor' on a global scale of conflict (Tomlinson, 1995: 1). The inhabitants of Northern Ireland were more likely to be killed in a car accident than die as a result of the conflict (O'Leary and McGarry, 1996). Against this, the scale of the conflict amongst a small population reveals some startling comparative statistics. Extrapolating the figures for Northern Ireland during the period 1969–98, half a million people in Britain would have been charged with a terrorist offence and 111,000 would have been killed (Hayes and McAllister, 2000).

The 'no solution' approach was not merely based upon sheer pessimism, but reflected the multi-faceted nature of the problem. It appeared impossible to find a single answer which dealt with all these facets. Darby (1991) made the point that conflict is found in all societies. He argued that management of the conflict in Northern Ireland should focus upon the eradication of violence, which gave the problem in Northern Ireland its distinctiveness, rather than attempting a holistic solution. The Good Friday Agreement attempted to end violence permanently and manage existing political and cultural differences in the hope of ultimate reconciliation. The Agreement amounted to a large package of measures. Conflicting identities, beliefs, religions, ambitions, cultures, histories and economies are not easy to 'treat' in isolation.

There has been an absence of consensus surrounding the main causes of conflict. There are still those who see the Northern Ireland problem as essentially one of British colonialism (Miller, 1998b). Miller argues that a *colonial* explanation, often overlooked in academia, offers the clearest historical and contemporary account of why the British government claims sovereignty over Northern Ireland. He argues that Northern Ireland is a 'possession which the

British state has tried to present as an integral part of the state' (Miller, 1998b: 4). Miller criticises exponents of the view that the Northern Ireland problem is an ethnic one, asking when it ceased to be colonial, given that all of Ireland was once a colony of Britain.

The *ethno-religious* dimension to the problem, although perhaps an unfashionable modern explanation, is still aired (Bruce, 1986; 1994). This argument stresses the centrality of the Protestant religion within Unionist identity. Although the Northern Ireland problem is not centred upon theological differences, the sense of Protestant-Britishness felt by Unionists gives them a special sense of identity.

McGarry and O'Leary (1995) argue that the problem is *ethno-national*, with the two peoples of Northern Ireland, British and Irish, wishing their state (of Northern Ireland) to be part of their nation (Britain or Ireland). To some extent, the Good Friday Agreement acknowledges this argument and ethno-national explanations now represent orthodoxy. Believing such an Agreement was possible, even during a period when pessimists outnumbered optimists, McGarry and O'Leary (1990: ix) wrote:

> [We want] to counter one facile, thought-stopping, and pessimistic article of faith which has come to dominate academic, administrative and intelligent journalistic commentary on Northern Ireland . . . the notion that there is *no* solution to the conflict.

In rejecting more cynical assertions over prospects for Northern Ireland, the assumption of the above argument was that the seemingly irreconcilable goals of nationalism and unionism could be reconciled, or at least accommodated in a manner broadly acceptable to supporters of either. The Good Friday Agreement was based upon accommodation of the constitutional status quo and acknowledgement of the aspiration for change. Northern Ireland remains part of the United Kingdom, but the Irish government is allowed a special relationship with Northern Nationalists. The Good Friday Agreement is not a permanent settlement. It manages and harnesses divisions and places them within institutional frameworks. It may, however, lead to ultimate reconciliation. The difficulty for the Agreement's critics is in devising an alternative with sufficiency of consensus.

15.2 Alternatives to the Good Friday Agreement?

A number of remedies to the Northern Ireland problem were proposed prior to the Good Friday Agreement. Many may now look dated, as the population has become increasingly accustomed to political compromise and relative peace, but alternative macro-solutions still have their supporters. Some of these alternatives also represent compromises, although others, notably the full integration of Northern Ireland into Britain or a united Ireland, are 'winner takes all' suggestions. Arthur and Jeffery (1996: 124) claim that 'such simple solutions are . . . only for the simple-minded'.

15.2.1 The restoration of direct rule

15.2.1.1 Definition
A return to direct rule of Northern Ireland from Westminster is the most likely scenario should the Good Friday Agreement prove unsustainable. Such a reversion occurred briefly from February until May 2000. Under direct rule, power is exercised by the Secretary of State for Northern Ireland and the Northern Ireland Office. Legislative powers and the scrutiny of legislation by MPs in Northern Ireland are very limited.

15.2.1.2 Advantages
Although rarely seen as a solution to the problem, it might be argued that direct rule is the least of all evils. It provided Northern Ireland with a temporary solution to the problem of governance. The period of direct rule from 1972 to 1998 saw the abolition of much of the overt discrimination against the Nationalist population. Direct rule avoided the need for political thinking. Experiments with solutions sometimes led to increases in violence, as occurred, for example, after the Anglo-Irish Agreement of 1985. Direct rule emerged as a 'solution' by default.

15.2.1.3 Disadvantages
No political group wished to see indefinite direct rule. As such, its continuation was not a permanent solution. Apart from brief ceasefires, there was never a period devoid of violence under direct rule. Direct rule merely filled a vacuum created by the lack of internal agreement. Direct rule was initially intended as a temporary, emergency measure. Accordingly, it could not be described as a means of conflict resolution.

15.2.2 Full integration into the United Kingdom

15.2.2.1 Definition
Northern Ireland would be governed in a manner identical to any other part of the United Kingdom. Legislation for Northern Ireland would be passed using the methods employed elsewhere in the United Kingdom.

15.2.2.2 Advantages
Favoured by a substantial section of the Unionist population and by a sizeable number within the Ulster Unionist Party, full integration is supported on the ground that it would end uncertainty over the future of Northern Ireland. Advocates believe that violence is fostered by encouraging violent Nationalists that political logic is in their favour. Full integration would reverse this process and impose a final defeat. The citizens of Northern Ireland would be treated as equals within the United Kingdom. Their place within that Kingdom would no longer be conditional.

15.2.2.3 Disadvantages

There is no such thing as identical treatment. Scotland and Wales are treated separately and differently within the United Kingdom. Many supporters of integration do not desire political integration, in which mainland British political parties would contest elections in Northern Ireland. Perhaps due to self-interest, they want to preserve their own political parties, by favouring only administrative integration. Tactically, therefore, such limited integrationists wish Northern Ireland to be treated as a place apart.

Political integration remains the 'untried solution' (Cunningham and Kelly, 1995: 20). Whether political or administrative, full integration takes no account of the Irish identity of the minority population in Northern Ireland. The suggestion may further polarise British versus Irish identities and increase violence.

15.2.3 United Ireland

15.2.3.1 Definition

Ireland would be governed on an independent, thirty-two-county basis, by a parliament based in Dublin. The British government would renounce sovereignty over Northern Ireland, which would be absorbed into a unitary Irish state.

15.2.3.2 Advantages

This solution might please the majority of people on the island of Ireland and in Britain. Although few are prepared to undertake sacrifices for its establishment and many would fear the consequences, the creation of a united Ireland remains a long-term aspiration for most citizens in both countries. If one takes a utilitarian view that the business of government is to create the greatest happiness for the greatest number, the British and Irish governments ought to facilitate British withdrawal and create an independent Ireland. The case for a united Ireland relies upon a wider geographical application of the consent principle, currently confined to Northern Ireland. Nationalists note that national consent was not granted for the division of Ireland.

15.2.3.3 Disadvantages

Consent within Northern Ireland for absorption within a united Ireland will not be forthcoming for the foreseeable future. It is inconceivable that Unionists in Northern Ireland would accept a united Ireland. Nationalists in Northern Ireland and the majority of citizens in the Irish Republic supported the Good Friday Agreement, which kept Northern Ireland within the United Kingdom. An agreed Ireland does not exist, but the majority of Irish voters, North and South, accepted the Good Friday Agreement, in effect maintaining partition but with North–South links.

A section of the Unionist population might offer armed resistance to enforced entry into a united Ireland. The dual minority thesis applies. A united

Ireland would merely replace the present Nationalist minority in Northern Ireland, desirous of Irish unity, with a larger Unionist minority, unwilling to accept a united Ireland. Even if their British 'prop' were withdrawn, many Unionists would not recognise a unitary Irish state. Simplistic assertions concerning an overall majority for Irish unity are inadequate, failing to take account of qualitative differentials. The strength of Unionist opposition to a united Ireland remains stronger than Nationalist support for its establishment.

15.2.4 Joint authority

15.2.4.1 Definition
Britain and Ireland would jointly assume responsibility for the management of Northern Ireland. The two countries would together control the legal, political and executive governance of the region, as co-equals. Sovereignty would be shared.

15.2.4.2 Advantages
Joint authority moves away from the 'winner-takes-all' models of British rule or a united Ireland. No recent political agreements have suggested a purely internal solution is possible in Northern Ireland. The Good Friday Agreement offers a slight nudge towards joint authority through its cross-border and intergovernmental dimensions. Arguably, therefore, a momentum is gathering for such an approach. Joint authority would provide clear institutional recognition of parity of esteem between the Nationalist and Unionist communities.

15.2.4.3 Disadvantages
Joint authority would be vigorously opposed by Unionists who see no democratic basis in the proposal. It would also be seen as an inevitable forerunner of a united Ireland. Militant Republicans would be unlikely to accept a continued British presence in Northern Ireland. The mechanics would also be difficult. The idea runs the risk of creating segregated authority, in which the sovereign power is forced to act separately according to the area being governed. Legislation would be difficult to pass, requiring the approval of both parliaments or an executive council of representatives from both governments.

15.2.5 European authority

15.2.5.1 Definition
Northern Ireland would be neither exclusively British nor Irish. Its citizens would adopt a common European identity, with Northern Ireland governed as a region within a federal Europe.

15.2.5.2 Advantages
For all member states within the European Union, the provisions of the Maastricht Treaty create a further pooling of sovereignty (Boyle and Hadden, 1994). The notion of exclusive sovereignty over territory appears dated. By

placing Northern Ireland under European law, there may be a transfer of the loyalties of citizens towards neutral Europe. National loyalty may be transferred. Supporters of the European argument point to the subtle shifts of identity that have occurred in the last 30 years in Northern Ireland. A primary Ulster identity has been displaced by a British identity amongst Unionists. Identity is, therefore, impermanent.

There may be a withering of the importance of partition as a range of crossborder institutions develop, promoted by European Union initiatives. The European Union is already active in providing assistance in this field. Nationalists adopt a neofunctionalist approach to cross-border co-operation. This foresees rolling integration of the North and South of Ireland developing as a logical and technocratic consequence of the need for greater economic cooperation. This co-operation extends beyond economic activity.

15.2.5.3 Disadvantages

The European Union may be able to promote a certain range of cross-border initiatives based on mutual co-operation, but the project may be limited. Transfers of identity towards Europe assume the existence of a spillover effect, in which economic cross-border initiatives prove to be the catalyst for new institutions and new loyalties. People in Northern Ireland and the Republic may support the promotion of economic co-operation within the European Union, but equally may desire that this is 'ringfenced' co-operation, restricted to that sphere. The political transfer of loyalties is another matter. As Porter (1996: 39) puts it: '. . . sovereignty is not so easily disposed of, borders are not so magically spirited away and political identities are not so effortlessly relocated'.

Unionists would have more to lose by the pooling of sovereignty over Northern Ireland. British sovereignty is actual; the Republic's is no longer even claimed. Furthermore, as with joint British–Irish authority, the mechanics would be difficult. A British police force would probably remain, as might nominal British sovereignty, even if real legislative power lay with Europe. Northern Ireland would probably remain a region under nominal British jurisdiction within a Europe of the Regions.

15.2.6 Devolved power-sharing without cross-border bodies

15.2.6.1 Definition

Devolution to a Northern Ireland Assembly would take place as now, but without the all-Ireland dimension of the Good Friday Agreement. Devolution without cross-border bodies continues to receive overwhelming support within the Democratic Unionist Party. It is also the favoured solution of nearly half of the Ulster Unionist Council (Tonge and Evans, 2001a).

15.2.6.2 Advantages

Consociational arrangements, basically involving the sharing of power amongst élites, have worked elsewhere in divided societies, particularly bi-communal ones such as Northern Ireland. Unionist critics of the Good Friday Agreement argue that it is impossible to develop Nationalist loyalty to Northern Ireland when the role of the Irish government is enhanced through cross-border bodies. Such critics believe that the most appropriate means of developing loyalty to the state of Northern Ireland is to discourage this external reference point for Northern Nationalists. From the 1960s onwards, Nationalists realised that simple anti-partitionist politics are inadequate. Sharing power strictly within Northern Ireland provides them with a stake in the state, but cross-borderism concurrently undermines that state.

15.2.6.3 Disadvantages

Power-sharing within Northern Ireland has to have external dimensions because most of the citizens of Northern Ireland have external loyalties. The absence of cross-border bodies would mean that there would be no settlement, as Nationalists would be disinterested. Few in Northern Ireland look exclusively inwards for the means of political settlement. Nationalists see themselves as part of an Irish nation and look towards the institutional vehicle of that nation, the Irish government. Unionists look east to 'mainland' Britain. It is inconceivable that power-sharing arrangements will lack all-Ireland and inter-governmental arrangements. The broad shape of a political agreement in Northern Ireland has been evident since the 1973 Sunningdale Agreement. The 1998 Good Friday Agreement repeated many of the constitutional aspects of that Agreement, being described by the deputy leader of the SDLP, Seamus Mallon, as 'Sunningdale for slow learners' (Tonge, 2000).

15.2.7 Repartition

15.2.7.1 Definition

The border between Northern Ireland and the Republic would be shifted. The size of Northern Ireland would be reduced, with parts transferred to the Republic.

15.2.7.2 Advantages

Repartition has been employed successfully on several occasions in Europe in, for example, Belgium, Switzerland, Greece and Turkey (Whyte, 1990; Boyle and Hadden, 1994). Under one formula, the size of Northern Ireland might be reduced to four counties as Nationalist majorities exist in two. Alternatively, the border could be redrawn on the basis of local administrative units. Half of Northern Ireland's 26 local-government districts contain a Catholic majority. With the exception of Moyle in the North, the border could easily be moved north-eastwards to absorb these areas. The obvious advantage of such a proposal is that it 'releases' many Nationalists into the Irish Republic, whilst securing the remaining state of Northern Ireland against the problem of a rising Nationalist population. The location of the border was designed as temporary.

Arguably repartition would provide recognition of the trend towards communal separation in Northern Ireland. Segregation has increased as populations have shifted to their 'own territory'. In the first three years of the Troubles, the population movement in Northern Ireland was the largest in western Europe since the Second World War (Murphy, 1978).

15.2.7.3 Disadvantages
Beset by practical difficulties, repartition has rarely been regarded as a credible solution. Unless the new border were based upon unprecedented contortions, Belfast would remain in Northern Ireland. Yet Belfast now has a Nationalist majority and contains 100,000 Catholics, many of whom might wish to join the Irish Republic. They would not wish to remain in a redrawn, British, Northern Ireland. Protestants in the counties handed over to the Republic would be equally unhappy. It is, therefore, impossible to redraw the border on the basis of an agreed local consensus. Alternatively, the proposal is based upon the fallacy that *all* Catholics would support a redrawing. Even if repartition were desirable, it would need to take account of the strength of nationalism in an area, not merely the religious affiliation of the local population.

15.2.8 Independent Northern Ireland

15.2.8.1 Definition
Northern Ireland would be ruled by neither London nor Dublin governments. Instead it would exist as a country in its own right, governed by the people contained within its borders.

15.2.8.2 Advantages
Supporters argue that an independent state is also the only way to guarantee genuine parity of esteem between the two communities in Northern Ireland. Without independence, there are only two alternatives: firstly, second-class status for Nationalists within a British state or similar subordinate status for Unionists within an all-Ireland republic; secondly, an insecure Northern Ireland, in which sectarian division is perpetuated through the fostering of external allegiances. Nationalists are encouraged to look to the Irish Republic; Unionists look to the British state. The Good Friday Agreement does not offer a sufficient basis for loyalty to Northern Ireland, but generates instability in reassuring Unionists of their Britishness and Nationalists that their dreamed-of republic might come about. Only by generating loyalty to Northern Ireland can this instability be overcome. A significant number of Catholics are prepared to describe themselves as 'Northern Irish'. Similarly, for Protestants, the self-identification of 'Northern Irish' is preferred to the label of 'Irish'. An independent Northern Ireland, although small, would not be the tiniest state in Europe. Other viable states of smaller size exist. Supporters could offer the prospect of 'independence in Europe', an option favoured by advocates of Scottish independence.

15.2.8.3 Disadvantages
Few advocate an independent Northern Ireland nowadays. Indeed, the earlier attempts of the Ulster Defence Association to sell the idea to Loyalists have

been described as an 'abject failure' (McCullagh and O'Dowd, 1986: 5). Militant Nationalists would oppose an independent Northern Ireland as a denial of the goal of Irish unity. Moderate Catholics might be fearful of being dominated in a state in which there was a greater number of Protestants without, ironically, British intervention to guarantee rights. Opponents might be sceptical of any guarantees offered regarding their rights within such a state, despite the categorical assurances of Loyalists. An independent Northern Ireland would struggle to be economically viable, despite the fast growth rate of recent years. The weakness of local industry has been disguised by the amount of assistance to the Province provided by the European Union, America, and, above all, Britain. The survival of Northern Ireland might rely upon continued support from these quarters, as Britain might be less than willing.

15.3 Public attitudes

The 71 per cent 'yes' vote in Northern Ireland in the referendum on the Good Friday Agreement indicated the willingness of its population to accept a constitutional compromise. Ironically, Unionists were divided to a far greater extent than Nationalists, even though the Agreement confirmed Northern Ireland's place in the United Kingdom for the foreseeable future. Nationalists overwhelmingly endorsed an Agreement which, whilst keeping a united Ireland as a possibility, rejected its creation prior to the existence of a majority in favour of change within Northern Ireland. The desire among Catholics for an overturn of the constitutional status quo is far from overwhelming, although a united Ireland remains comfortably the largest preferred option among this group (Table 15.1). Unionist constitutional preferences among Protestants are greater than aggregate Nationalist sentiments found among Catholics.

The results indicate the division in attitudes over the constitutional future of Northern Ireland, although Unionists and Nationalists can find support for their respective cases. Most Protestants want to remain part of the UK; fewer than one-fifth of Catholics share this view as a long-term aim. Although Catholics are less supportive of a united Ireland than Protestants are of maintaining the Union, there is little difference in the percentage of Protestants or Catholics prepared to identify themselves as Unionists and Nationalists respectively (Table 15.2).

Table 15.1   Constitutional preferences for Northern Ireland

Q. Do you think the long-term policy for Northern Ireland should be for it . . .

	Protestant	Catholic	Total (%)
To remain part of the UK	87	16	56
To reunify with the rest of the island	3	48	21
To become independent	4	18	11
Other/Don't know	6	18	12

Source: adapted from Northern Ireland Life and Times Survey, 1999.

Table 15.2   The extensiveness of unionism and nationalism in Northern Ireland

Q. Generally speaking, do you think of yourself as a unionist, nationalist or neither?

	Protestant	**Catholic**	**Other/no religion**	**Total (%)**
Unionist	71	1	36	39
Nationalist	70	1	7	29
Neither	27	26	54	30
Other/Don't know	2	3	3	2

Source: adapted from Northern Ireland Life and Times Survey, 1999.

Table 15.3   British attitudes to the constitutional future of Northern Ireland

Option	**Percentage in favour**
Irish reunification	52
Remain part of the UK	30
Other	5
Don't know	13

Source: adapted from Northern Ireland Social Attitudes Survey, 1991; British Election Survey, 1992; Hayes and McAllister (1996: 72).

Nearly one-third of the population does not see itself as either Unionist or Nationalist. This is not transferred into support for those parties in the political centre in Northern Ireland, Alliance and Women's Coalition, sympathising with such an approach. Their combined vote is less than 10 per cent of Northern Ireland's voters. Electorally, the population supports parties freely labelling themselves as Unionist or Nationalist and which designate themselves as such within the Northern Ireland Assembly established under the Good Friday Agreement.

The attitude of the British public towards Northern Ireland has been a source of disappointment for Unionists. There has been persistent support for British withdrawal from Northern Ireland, although the majority for this option has declined (Hayes and McAllister, 1996). Ironically, support in Britain for Irish unity may be as great as is found amongst Northern Ireland's Catholics. Support for Irish reunification is lowest in Scotland, possibly a reflection of the salience of Northern Ireland politics in parts of the west of Scotland. Table 15.3 indicates majority British support for Irish reunification.

Support for withdrawal can partly be attributed to the fact that the British public might not have to live with the consequences of such an action. Other likely factors include genuine support for Irish unity, weariness towards the Northern Ireland problem, disenchantment over the financial cost and resentment over British casualties sustained during the conflict. Whatever the reason, the stances of the British public have persistently been at odds with the bipartisan decisions taken by their elected representatives.

Interest in Northern Ireland is not great within the Irish Republic, compared to other issues, although the level does fluctuate. One survey found that 41 per cent of people in the Republic thought that Northern Ireland was 'very important' (Market Research Bureau of Ireland Poll, April 1991, cited in Hussey, 1995: 187). There was majority support in the Irish Republic for changes in respect of Ireland's constitutional claim to Northern Ireland. Over half the population favoured either the replacement of Articles 2 and 3 or its amendment to an aspiration for unity (King and Wilford, 1997: 187). A united Ireland is the long-term solution most favoured in the Irish Republic, but the overwhelming endorsement of the Good Friday Agreement by voters in the Republic on the 1998 Good Friday Agreement emphasised the largely aspirational nature of this desire. Three-fifths of the Republic's population support a united Ireland (Marsh and Wilford, 1994: 210). The citizens of the Irish Republic have not abandoned Northern Nationalists. However, recognition of the need for Unionist consent for change and awareness of the sensitivities of Northern Protestants to the nature of the Republic required 'jettisoning some nationalist shibboleths' (Chubb, 1992: 28). Another contributory factor was the economic burden that Northern Ireland would create for the Irish Republic if absorbed, although the rapid growth of the Northern Ireland economy in recent years has eroded this factor. The new awareness of the unionist position and lack of support for an imposed united Ireland means that a distinction can be drawn between the 'post-nationalist' population in the South and the 'highly nationalist' section of the population in the North (Boyce, 1995: 429).

15.4 The micro-agenda

Aside from constitutional issues, the Good Friday Agreement was concerned with an equality agenda. This tended to be linked with the promotion of human rights. Discrimination against Catholics during the period of 1920–72 left many feeling second-class citizens. It has been much more difficult since this period to maintain that there has been systematic economic discrimination against Catholics, but inequalities persist. Some Nationalists continue to claim the existence of economic and cultural inequality.

15.4.1 Economic equality

On average, Catholics remain poorer than Protestants and endure a significantly higher rate of unemployment, despite a plethora of fair employment initiatives and legislation. Equality is not easily achievable. A succession of anti-discrimination measures have reduced inequality. Structural factors and some continuing discrimination have combined to prevent full parity. Arguments for economic equality are unconvincing when offered in isolation as a remedy to the Northern Ireland problem. The growth of a Nationalist middle-class has nonetheless been important in stabilising Northern Ireland. Mainly supportive of the SDLP and prepared to compromise on historical constitutional ambitions, this section of the Catholic population was an infertile recruiting ground for Republicans, whose core support remained among disadvantaged Nationalists.

Economic parity does not necessarily have an impact upon ethnic identity. Middle-class Nationalists see themselves as Irish; middle-class Unionists regard themselves as British. Furthermore, economic change in the Irish Republic made no impact upon Unionist political aspirations. Unionists remain as opposed as ever to absorption within an all-Ireland state, despite the huge economic progress made by the South in recent years. Assisted by its position as the largest beneficiary of EU assistance, economic growth in the 'emerald tiger' of the Republic outstripped that of the United Kingdom during the 1990s.

15.4.2 Human rights

Established under the Good Friday Agreement, the Northern Ireland Human Rights Commission placed statutory obligations upon public authorities to promote equal opportunities. These obligations were accompanied by the incorporation of the European Convention of Human Rights into Northern Ireland law, direct access to the courts for aggrieved citizens and the granting of powers to the courts to overturn Assembly legislation. The Agreement mooted the possibility of the establishment of a dedicated Department of Equality, but this did not materialise. A Human Rights Commission was also established south of the border, with the two bodies to be linked by a joint Human Rights Committee. The Agreement does not acknowledge economic disparities between Unionists and Nationalists. Much of its focus in the 'rights, safeguards and equality of opportunity' section is upon cultural aspects, notably the promotion of 'linguistic diversity', through encouragement of the Irish language and the new-found interest among some Unionists of 'Ulster-Scots'.

Critics of the rights-based approach to conflict transformation are unhappy over the lack of democratic legitimacy of bodies designed to maintain rights. Transfers of powers to such bodies involve a forfeiture of rights. The Parades Commission, for example, is an unelected and unaccountable organisation, responsible for determining when organisations have the right to march and through which areas. Its main role has been to prevent the right of the Orange Order to march through areas inhabited mainly by Nationalists. The freedom of assembly has been ranged against the freedom to live without offence, with the Parades Commission deciding which is the 'superior' freedom.

15.5 Conclusion

Alternatives to the Good Friday Agreement do not possess cross-community consensus. Each provides too many losers. The approach of the British government has been to support power-sharing with internal and external dimensions. The Good Friday Agreement appeared to survive at times by default, not greatly cherished, but perhaps better than the alternatives. Referenda on the Agreement confirmed that long-term aspirations for Irish unity among Northern Nationalists and the Republic's voters could easily be channelled into short- and medium-term compromises. There remain a small number of rejectionists who are not prepared to accept compromises falling considerably short of an independent, united Ireland. Unionist hostility to the Agreement has concentrated partly on its constitutional aspects, but has been directed mainly at other aspects of the package, notably decommissioning and policing. Unionist constitutional preferences are marked by their unanimity, although a majority of Unionists appear prepared to compromise on the modern form of that Unionism, accepting a new working relationship with the Irish Republic.

Conclusion

Northern Ireland moved slowly into a post-conflict era. The 1998 Good Friday Agreement frequently looked vulnerable, but, even in the event of collapse, a return to earlier levels of conflict appeared most unlikely. Conflict receded, whilst change accelerated, albeit not at the pace expected by optimists. The Good Friday Agreement was not a final political settlement, but instead the creator of a set of institutions in which ongoing differences were to be managed peacefully. Former revolutionary Republicans and militant Loyalists were drawn together within the Northern Ireland Assembly and its committees. Members of Sinn Fein who had wished to destroy the state found themselves administering its health and educational services.

This book has argued that the peace process was facilitated by changes within republicanism. Republicans were forced to concede that their historical objectives needed to be negotiated. Without abandoning ultimate goals, the Republican movement was obliged to ditch parts of its historical baggage. This included a belief in military victory for the IRA and the perception of republicans as the sole 'liberators' of Ireland. Sinn Fein and the IRA appeared to tacitly accept the view espoused in the 1990s by a former Taoiseach, Albert Reynolds, that the physical-force tradition within republicanism had run its course because 'it could go no further' (Mansergh, 1995). Sinn Fein's move towards constitutionalism arose from the limitations of the 'armalite and ballot box' strategy of the 1980s, in which a party coming into ever closer contact with the state was simultaneously attempting its destruction. Sinn Fein was also obliged to abandon its hopes of the early 1990s that the British government would act as a clear persuader to Unionists for a united Ireland. Instead, Republicans have been obliged to settle for limited gains falling considerably short of an all-Ireland Republic. The moribund abstentionism which characterised Nationalist politics for four decades after partition was displaced by a ruthless paramilitary campaign and a concurrent vibrant electoralism, each yielding some results, but not victory. Unionist hegemony was quickly ended, discrimination largely eradicated and an all-Ireland dimension conceded. Provisional IRA prisoners were eventually released. The two parts of Ireland have been drawn together via the North–South Ministerial Council. Aside from prisoner releases, some of these items were on offer as early as 1974, 20 years before the Provisional IRA began its decisive move away from armed struggle.

The constitutional basis of the Good Friday Agreement was based upon consent, and in this respect satisfied most Unionists, even though other aspects of the Agreement were less palatable. In other constitutional aspects, the Agreement reflected much of the political thinking of the SDLP, conceding an Irish dimension. The British government has long acknowledged that there is no purely internal settlement to be found in Northern Ireland. For fear of further offending Unionists, it cannot use the term 'shared sovereignty' in respect of its proposals for the province, but the logic of the Good Friday Agreement arguably runs in that direction and certainly not towards integration of Northern Ireland within the United Kingdom. Shared sovereignty can only be built slowly. The Republic has some say in the affairs of Northern Ireland. The debate has moved on to the extent of influence. A literal reading of the Good Friday Agreement ought to provide much solace for Unionists. The cross-border dimension of the Agreement is weak and ringfenced.

The sceptical view

Many doubted the durability of the Good Friday Agreement. Its institutions were temporarily suspended in 2000 and 2001 and, in the absence of decommissioning by paramilitary groups, often appeared fragile and impermanent. For critics, the peace process merely produced the brightest of a number of false dawns. Bruce argued that the process was 'wonderfully inappropriately named' (Bruce, 1996). Often it floundered amid stalemate, apparently rescued only by the promise that paramilitary organisations could keep their weapons as their political associates sit in government and decline to support the state's police service. Sixty-five people were killed by paramilitaries in the three years following the Agreement. In 2000 alone, there were 262 punishment shootings and beatings. Republican ultras in the Real IRA and Continuity IRA indicated that violence would continue whilst Ireland remained partitioned.

Nonetheless, the popular support for the Agreement demonstrated in the 'yes' referendum vote (albeit unconvincingly on the Unionist side) highlighted the huge groundswell of public support for peace and for devolved, inclusive government in Northern Ireland. What the peace process achieved, in the words of one Loyalist participant, was 'conflict-transformation' by ending 'bellicose rantings' in favour of negotiation (David Ervine, quoted in the *Irish World*, 5 April 1996). The same practitioner highlighted how identity politics have shaped the process when he declared: 'I have the right to be British; Gerry Adams has the right to describe himself as Irish' (Ervine, 1996).

The pursuit of conflicting goals

The goals of Irish nationalism and British unionism are seemingly irreconcilable. The Good Friday Agreement seeks merely their management without conflict, in settled political institutions which enjoy a popular legitimacy always denied to Northern Ireland's previous political arrangements. Participation by all in these internal and bi-national institutions will form the major element of what the UUP leader, David Trimble, described as the:

> historic and honourable task of this generation, to raise up a new Northern Ireland in which pluralist unionism and constitutional nationalism can speak to each other with the civility that is the foundation of freedom (*Belfast Telegraph*, 22 June 1998; Bew and Gillespie, 1999: 368).

Nonetheless, the strength of competing nationalisms and identities, British and Irish, ensures a lack of consensus politics and an inability to forge a common British-Irish identity, based upon Northern Irishness. The Good Friday Agreement does not attempt to overcome these nationalisms, but instead strives to reduce their competitiveness, whilst recognising their equal validity. Parity of esteem is the vogue. The pursuit of the goals of Irish nationalism and British unionism is now mainly constitutional. Violence has always been a minority taste on either side, abhorred by substantial Nationalist and Unionist majorities. Despite this, there was sufficient tacit support amongst the Nationalist and Unionist communities to sustain violence. The policy of the British government for most of the Troubles was to reduce violence by reassuring both communities that the stated goals used to justify violence can be accomplished by peaceful means. The Good Friday Agreement climaxed this strategy. For Nationalists, this means that Britain would not stand in the way of a united Ireland if there is majority consent in Northern Ireland. For Unionists, the Union is safe until such a point is reached.

In this respect there is little new in British government policy. The position of Northern Ireland within the United Kingdom has technically been conditional since 1949, when the Ireland Act declared that its status could change with the consent of the parliament of Northern Ireland. Obviously this condition overwhelmingly favoured Unionists. Nowadays, British policy provides a more overt recognition of the aspirations of Nationalists. This recognition has arrived through concerted pressure from Irish Nationalists. The policy learning of the British government was demonstrated not in constitutional terms, but through the inclusiveness of the Good Friday Agreement. The British and Irish governments treated paramilitary prisoners as prisoners of war, to be released at the end of the conflict. Their political representatives were entitled to take their seats in government or within the Northern Ireland Assembly. This made the deal 'sellable' to Republican and Loyalist constituencies.

Divided unionism

Under pressure from a widening tactical coalition of Nationalist forces since the 1980s, Unionists have been obliged to rethink their politics. The unanimity of Unionist constitutional preferences has been matched by disunity over the best means of attainment. This disunity was highlighted by the near 50–50 split over whether to support the Good Friday Agreement, a fault-line which has not disappeared. Previously, the basic choice for unionists lay between the promotion of cultural unionism, emphasising an exaggerated sense of Protestant-Britishness, or a liberal unionism centred upon equal citizenship for all within the United Kingdom (Porter, 1996). Now, Unionists have been obliged to decide whether to support a civic model, embracing new economic and political relationships with an Irish Republic no longer claiming need of the 'reintegration of the national territory'. It remains difficult for civic Unionists to move decisively towards a new pluralist politics, which would weaken the link between Unionist politics and its cultural and religious heritage.

Ethnic bloc politics

Northern Ireland remains a non-consensual state, divided by ethnicity. The links between Catholic denomination and support for Irish Nationalist parties and between Protestant affiliation and support for British Unionist parties remain very strong. Measured this way, the old centre ground, as represented by the Alliance Party, has become even narrower. Inter-ethnic rivalry remains strong, with little sense of collective responsibility among the rival Unionist and Nationalist representatives within the Northern Ireland Executive. Intra-ethnic bloc rivalries may accentuate this problem. Parties may play to the 'ethnic gallery' (their electoral bloc) and defend the interests of this bloc rather than seek the common good. The Good Friday Agreement is based upon the consociational idea that party leaders are relatively insulated from such demands from below and will share power in a co-operative spirit with élites from the 'other' bloc (see Deane, 2001).

Thus far, the evidence is that ethnic bloc, zero-sum politics remain the dominant form and that cross-community bridging of the electoral divide is still exceptional. The Good Friday Agreement may be culpable in the promotion of Unionist–Nationalist rivalries, but it hardly invented them. Furthermore, there are examples of cross-community co-operation, within the Assembly and in wider society. At Executive level, however, the performance of a rainbow non-coalition has not always impressed, preferring on occasion to maintain party or ethnic bloc rivalries over a sense of collective responsibility (Wilford, 2001). The long-term eradication of ethnic bloc politics remains unlikely among the electorate or political parties. As such, although Northern Ireland's conflict has subsided and substantial change has arrived, consensus politics remain a distant prospect.

Chronology

1886 First Home Rule Bill fails in parliament.

1893 Second Home Rule Bill fails in parliament.

1912 Third Home Rule Bill passed but shelved due to World War I. 471,000 declare Solemn Covenant of Opposition in Ulster. Ulster Volunteer Force is formed to provide armed resistance.

1916 Easter Rising in Dublin. Execution of its leaders by the British stirs Nationalist sentiment.

1918 Sinn Fein wins last all-Ireland elections, gaining 73 of the 105 seats.

1920 Government of Ireland Act 1920 creates two parliaments, both under British control. One in Belfast would govern certain affairs in six Northern counties; the other in Dublin would have limited control over the remaining 26 counties in Ireland. The Act is accepted in the North, but rejected in the South.

1921 Anglo-Irish War produces the Anglo-Irish Treaty, giving greater autonomy for the Southern 26 counties, which receive dominion status and become the Irish Free State. The partition of Ireland is confirmed as Northern Ireland declines participation in the affairs of the Southern state.

1922–3 Irish Civil War fought between pro- and anti-treaty forces ends in victory for supporters of the treaty.

1937 New Southern Irish constitution claims jurisdiction over the entire island of Ireland.

1939–45 The Free State remains neutral during World War II.

1949 The Free State leaves the Commonwealth and becomes the Republic of Ireland. The British government passes the Ireland Act, insisting that the status of Northern Ireland can only change with the consent of its parliament.

1956–62 IRA Border Campaign ends in failure.

1967 Northern Ireland Civil Rights Association founded.

1968–9 Civil rights demonstrations meet Unionist resistance. Widespread disruption follows. British troops sent to Northern Ireland to restore order.

1970 Provisional IRA formed.

1971 The British government introduces internment. Official and Provisional IRA attacks increase.

1972 The worst year of the Troubles begins with 'Bloody Sunday' in which the British Army shoots dead 13 civilians in Derry. The Official IRA blows up the Aldershot barracks of the regiment responsible but kills cleaners and clergy. The Officials declare a ceasefire which is not rescinded. The Provisional IRA carries out hundreds of bombings and shootings. The most notorious was 'Bloody Friday' in which 22 bombs were detonated in one hour in Belfast, killing nine civilians.

1973   Sunningdale Conference agrees the establishment of a power-sharing executive in Northern Ireland, a Council of Ireland and affirmation that the constitutional status of Northern Ireland can only be changed with the consent of a majority in the province.

1974   Eleven of Northern Ireland's 12 MPs elected in the February election oppose the power-sharing executive, which collapses after five months following an Ulster Workers' Council Strike.

1975   Northern Ireland Constitutional Convention fails.

1976–7   Peace People Initiative mobilises citizens against violence but ends in failure. Labour government pursues Ulsterisation and criminalisation policies, treating paramilitaries as common criminals and using the RUC where possible to deal with security.

1979   INLA murders Shadow Northern Ireland Secretary, Airey Neave, with a car bomb at the House of Commons. The IRA kills Lord Mountbatten and 18 British soldiers in a single day.

1981   IRA and INLA prisoners renew their hunger strike in support of special-category status, resulting in the death of 10 Republicans. One of the prisoners, Bobby Sands, is elected as an MP. After his death his election agent is elected. Sinn Fein begins its 'armalite and ballot box' strategy.

1982   Secretary of State, James Prior, begins the rolling devolution initiative, designed to return powers to Northern Ireland. A Nationalist boycott leads to its failure.

1985   Anglo-Irish Agreement confirms that there can be no change in the status of Northern Ireland without the consent of the majority. However, its creation of an Anglo-Irish secretariat and a consultative role for the Dublin government in the affairs of Northern Ireland provokes Unionist outrage.

1986   Sinn Fein ends abstentionism in elections to the Republic's parliament, the Dail.

1987   The SAS kills eight Provisional IRA members at Loughall. The IRA bombs a Remembrance Day parade in Enniskillen, killing 11.

1988   Hume–Adams talks begin.

1990   Northern Ireland Secretary of State, Peter Brooke, declares that Britain has 'no selfish strategic or economic interest in Northern Ireland'.

1993   A series of atrocities, including IRA bombs in Warrington killing two children and in the Loyalist Shankill killing nine, with Loyalist paramilitary responses, do not prevent political movement. The Downing Street Declaration is issued by John Major and the Irish Taioseach, Albert Reynolds, on 15 December. It confirms that there is to be no change in the constitutional status of Northern Ireland without the consent of the majority. The future of Ireland should be self-determined by the Irish people on a North and South basis.

1994   IRA calls a 'complete cessation of operations'. Loyalist paramilitaries reciprocate six weeks later.

1995   Framework Documents issued, calling for a devolved Northern Ireland Assembly and cross-border political and economic bodies.

1996   Mitchell Commission proposes decommissioning of paramilitary weapons in parallel with all-party talks. The British government calls elections to a 'Peace Forum'. The IRA resumes violence, as a bomb at Canary Wharf kills two. Sinn Fein are excluded from multi-party peace talks.

1997   New Labour government insists that the 'settlement train is leaving' at round-table talks in September. IRA renews its ceasefire in July to facilitate Sinn Fein's entry to those talks.

1998 Multi-party talks lead to the Good Friday Agreement in April. A Northern Ireland Assembly, North–South Ministerial Council, British–Irish Council and British–Irish Intergovernmental Conference are all established. Prisoner releases begin, completed by summer 2000.

Sinn Fein votes overwhelmingly (331–19) at its annual conference in May to enter Stormont as part of the Good Friday Agreement.

'Yes' votes for the Agreement in Northern Ireland (71 per cent) and the Irish Republic (95 per cent) are recorded in simultaneous referenda, held separately in each country in May.

Elections are held to the Northern Ireland Assembly in June and it sits for the first time in July.

A Real IRA bomb kills 29 at Omagh, the worst atrocity committed in Northern Ireland during the conflict.

1999 Power is devolved to a Northern Ireland Assembly for the first time for 25 years. Inaugural meetings of the North–South Council and British–Irish Council are held.

The Patten Report recommends changes to the name, size, culture and ethos of the RUC.

2000 Devolved government is suspended temporarily, in February. It is restored in May 2000 following Provisional IRA hints of movement on decommissioning.

2001 David Trimble resigns as First Minister, due to the absence of weapons decommissioning.

Further reading

There is a wealth of books and articles dealing with political conflict in Northern Ireland. It is important to stress that the following are merely a small number of recommendations from a vast choice. Most items cited here are books. Students of Northern Ireland's politics should also read journals or periodicals, such as *Irish Political Studies*, *Fortnight* and *Irish Studies Review*.

1. The roots of modern problems

Michael Laffan (1983) *The Partition of Ireland 1911–1925* provides an excellent account of the conflicting pressures which led to the division of the country. He also provides an authoritative account of the rise of republicanism in his 1999 work, *The Resurrection of Ireland: The Sinn Fein Party 1916–1923*. A.T.Q. Stewart (1967) *The Ulster Crisis* offers a detailed account of the threat of armed Unionist resistance to Home Rule. For a discussion of alternative views of the period, read Chapters 6 to 9 inclusive of D. George Boyce and A. O'Day (eds) (1996) *Modern Irish History. Revisionism and the Revisionist Controversy*. O'Leary and McGarry (1993) *The Politics of Antagonism* provide informative coverage of the 1918 all-Ireland elections.

2. An 'Orange state': Northern Ireland 1921–68

Michael Farrell's (1980) *Northern Ireland: The Orange State* remains perhaps the most important sustained and detailed critique of the Unionist regime. Its successor *Arming the Protestants* (1983) is read less, but is of at least equal value. Bryan Follis provides a thorough, objective account in *A State under Siege* (1995). Tom Wilson rejects many of the claims of discrimination in *Ulster: Conflict and Consent* (1989). The revisionist work of Bew, Gibbon and Patterson (1996) *Northern Ireland 1921–1996: Political Forces and Social Classes* is particularly valuable. It uses the archives of the Northern Ireland state to highlight conflict between London and Belfast and to suggest an internal dynamic to Unionist politics. McGarry and O'Leary's *Explaining Northern Ireland* (1995) provides a cogent critique of denials of discrimination.

3. From civil rights to armed insurrection

The chapter by Christopher Hewitt, 'The Roots of Violence; Catholic Griev-ances and Irish Nationalism during the Civil Rights Period' in P.J. Roche and B. Barton (1991) *The Northern Ireland Question: Myth and Reality* provides a sound account. Bob Purdie's article 'Was the Civil Rights Movement a Republican/Communist Conspiracy?' (1998, *Irish Political Studies*, vol. 3) ought to be read, as should his *Politics in the Streets: The Origins of the Civil Rights Movement in Northern Ireland* (1990). One of the most interesting accounts of the split in the IRA is found in either version of Henry Patterson's *The Politics of Illusion* (1989; 1997).

4. Unionist and Loyalist politics

Surprisingly, there remains a dearth of literature dedicated to the party system in Northern Ireland. Mitchell and Wilford's edited collection, *Politics in North-ern Ireland* (1999), offers perhaps the best recent chapters. John Whyte provides a seminal interpretation of Nationalist and Unionist positions in *Interpreting Northern Ireland*, which, although published in 1990, still has value. McGarry and O'Leary's exposition in *Explaining Northern Ireland* (1995) must also be read. Norman Porter's *Rethinking Unionism* (1996) is cogent. Eloquent guides can also be found in Chapters 4–5 and 8–9 of Aughey and Morrow (eds) *Northern Ireland Politics* (1996) and Arthur and Jeffery's *Northern Ireland since 1968* (1996). A useful account of the politics of the main Unionist party during the Troubles is offered by David Hume's 1996 work, *The Ulster Unionist Party 1972–92*. The same applies to Feargal Cochrane's *Unionist Politics* (1997). Bruce (1986; 1994) offers insights into the DUP, via *God Save Ulster!* and *At the Edge of the Union*.

5. Nationalist and Republican politics

In order to understand the historical analyses of various Nationalist parties, see the policy papers submitted to the Forum for Peace and Reconciliation in 1995, published as *Paths to a Political Settlement in Ireland* (1995). McGarry and O'Leary's *Explaining Northern Ireland* (1995) is again useful in outlining political thinking. Gerry Murray's 1998 book, *John Hume's SDLP*, provides the most detailed account of the development of the party. In a sympathetic examination of the organisation, Murray argues that the Good Friday Agree-ment was a triumph for the SDLP. McGovern's chapter in Gilligan and Tonge's *Peace or War: Understanding the Peace Process in Northern Ireland* (1997) should be read.

There is a much larger literature on republicanism. Books on republicanism that ought to be read are Henry Patterson's *The Politics of Illusion: Republican-ism and Socialism in Modern Ireland* (1989), later revised and retitled *The Politics of Illusion: A Political History of the IRA* (1997); Pat Walsh's *Irish*

Republicanism and Socialism: The Politics of the Republican Movement 1905 to 1994 (1994); and Brendan O'Brien's *The Long War: the IRA and Sinn Fein* (1999). Well sourced and highly readable accounts are also offered by Bishop and Mallie (1988) *The Provisional IRA*; Peter Taylor (1997) *Provos*; Bowyer-Bell (1989) *The Secret Army: The IRA 1916–1979*; and Tim Pat Coogan (1987) *The IRA*. M.L.R. Smith's *Fighting for Ireland? The Military Strategy of the Irish Republican Movement* (1995) is also worth reading, whilst Gerry Adams' own book, *Free Ireland: Towards a Lasting Peace* (1995) is a clear exposition of Republican thinking.

6. Governing Northern Ireland

Much of the literature requires updating. O'Leary's chapter on 'The Belfast Agreement and the Labour Government', in Seldon (2001) *The Blair Effect*, is useful. Otherwise, works tend to be dated. Connolly's concentration upon modes of governance in *Politics and Policy-making in Northern Ireland* (1990) is helpful for pre-Good Friday Agreement analysis. Bew and Patterson provide an older critique of aspects of state policy in *The British State and the Ulster Crisis* (1985). Readers interested in the European influence on the Northern Ireland polity should begin with Chapter 5 in Boyle and Hadden (1994) *Northern Ireland: The Choice*.

7. Policing Northern Ireland

'A New Beginning: Policing in Northern Ireland', the Independent Commission on Policing for Northern Ireland's 1999 report (the *Patten Report*), must be read. O'Leary's chapter in Seldon (*see* Chapter 6) indicates how legislation varied from Patten.

McGarry and O'Leary offer their own critique and remedies in *Policing Northern Ireland: Proposals for a New Start* (1999). Criticisms of aspects of policing in Northern Ireland are found in the writings of Paddy Hillyard.

8. The roles of religion

Steve Bruce's *God Save Ulster!* (1986) is regarded as the most important account of the religious dimension to Paisleyism. Even if one rejects the assertions in the final chapter, it remains a vital read. Scholars should examine McGarry and O'Leary's *Explaining Northern Ireland* (1995) for the refutation. Other useful works include Fulton (1991) *The Tragedy of Belief*; Chapter 2 of Whyte (1990) *Interpreting Northern Ireland*; and Chapter 21 of Aughey and Morrow (eds) (1996) *Northern Ireland Politics*. A very sympathetic account of the Orange Order is presented by Ruth Dudley Edwards in *The Faithful Tribe* (1999). Haddick-Flynn provides a very detailed account of the Loyal Orders, with isolated factual errors. He offers 'neither tar nor whitewash', in *Orangeism: The Making of a Tradition* (1999).

9. Political failures 1972–84 _____

Bew and Patterson (1985) *The British State and the Ulster Crisis* and Chapter 6 of *Northern Ireland 1921–1996: Political Forces and Social Classes* (1996) are useful. Wichert offers a measured basic account in both editions of *Northern Ireland since 1945* (1991; 1999), a comment equally applicable to D. George Boyce (1996) *The Irish Question and British Politics 1868–1996* (Chapter 4). Chapter 17 of Wilson (1989) *Ulster: Conflict and Consent* should be read. Personal accounts by practitioners are sometimes useful. Read Brian Faulkner (1978) *Memoirs of a Statesman* concerning the failure of power-sharing.

10. The Anglo-Irish Agreement _____

As suggested by the title, Aughey offers a strident critique in *Under Siege* (1989). Kenny's *The Road to Hillsborough* (1986) is good on the background to the Agreement. Also worth reading is Michael Cunningham's *British Government Policy in Northern Ireland, 1969–1989* (1991; second edition 2001). Dermot Quinn provides a useful beginner's guide in *Understanding Northern Ireland* (1993).

11. The logic of the peace process: changes in republicanism ___

One of the most provocative accounts is provided in Mark Ryan's work *War and Peace in Ireland: Britain and the IRA in the New World Order* (1994). Ryan suggests that the peace process was a product of a lowering of Republican horizons. Good coverage of changes in Republican thinking is provided in Kevin Bean's article, 'The New Departure? Recent Developments in Republican Strategy and Ideology' (1995) in *Irish Studies Review*, no. 10. McIntyre also offers an intellectual critique in *Irish Political Studies*, 1995, arguing that British state strategies have always undermined republicanism. Gerry Adams' own book, *Free Ireland: Towards a Lasting Peace* (1995) is a thoughtful analysis of the development of republicanism. Brendan O'Brien's *The Long War: the IRA and Sinn Fein* (1999) provides lots of detail of the discussions with the Republican movement.

12. The development of the peace process _____

Several chapters in Cox, Guelke and Stephen's edited collection, *A Farewell to Arms? From 'Long War' to Long Peace in Northern Ireland* (2000), are useful. The book is particularly strong on the international and comparative dimensions to the peace process.

Events are recorded in Bew and Gillespie (1999) *Northern Ireland: A Chronology of the Troubles*. Tim Pat Coogan (1995) *The Troubles: Ireland's Ordeal 1966–1995 and the Search for Peace* and Mallie and McKittrick (1996) *The Fight for Peace* are highly readable and informative accounts of the careful construction of the process. Discussion of the Downing Street Declaration is provided in the afterword of McGarry and O'Leary (1995) *Explaining Northern Ireland*. Gilligan and Tonge (eds) (1997) *Peace or War? Understanding the Peace Process in Northern Ireland* offer a number of mainly critical perspectives.

13. War and peace: the long road to negotiations 1995–7 _____

Most of the reading for Chapter 12 is relevant. Read also pp. 312–69 of O'Leary and McGarry (1996) *The Politics of Antagonism*. Volume 21 of the *Irish Reporter*, What Peace Process?, contains a number of interesting arguments. A special edition of *Race and Class*, vol. 37, 1995 also needs perusal. *The Northern Ireland Peace Process* by Thomas Hennessey (2000) is also essential reading.

14. The Good Friday Agreement _____

O'Leary offers a detailed examination of the consociational basis of the Agreement in 'The Nature of the British–Irish Agreement', *New Left Review*, 233 (1999). Again, the same author's chapter in Seldon (2001) *The Blair Effect* should be visited. Hennessey (2000, *see* Chapter 13) draws very sensible conclusions concerning winners and losers from the Agreement. Tonge explores similarities and dissimilarities between the Good Friday Agreement and the Sunningdale Agreement in *Contemporary British History*, vol. 14, no. 3 (2000). Cox *et al.* (2000, *see* Chapter 12) should be used for coverage of a large range of actors and organisations during the peace process.

15. Political stability in Northern Ireland _____

Although now dated, John Whyte's *Interpreting Northern Ireland* (1990) explores older options in dispassionate fashion. *Ireland: A Positive Proposal* by Kevin Boyle and Tom Hadden (1985) offers a brisk rebuttal of simplistic solutions. The same authors return to these themes in *Northern Ireland: the Choice* (1994). McGarry and O'Leary (1995) *Explaining Northern Ireland* and (1993) *The Politics of Antagonism* argue the case for joint authority and a maximisation of community authority. They are engaged in acrimonious debate with Paul Dixon in *Irish Political Studies*, vol. 11 (1996). The opening chapter of Miller (1998) *Rethinking Northern Ireland* offers a blistering attack from the editor on the unwillingness of the academic community to consider Northern Ireland as a British colony.

Finally, three books of a rather different type are recommended as important additions to the sum of human knowledge. Elliott and Flackes (1999) *Northern Ireland: A Political Directory 1968–1999* is a mine of useful information. The same can be said of Bew and Gillespie (1999) *Northern Ireland: A Chronology of the Troubles*. McKittrick *et al.* (1999) *Lost Lives* is a grimly compulsive account of each of the deaths during the Troubles.

References

Adams, G. (1985) in Collins, M. (ed.) *Ireland after Britain*, London: Pluto.

Adams, G. (1995) *Free Ireland: Towards a Lasting Peace*, Dingle: Brandon.

Alliance Party (1995) submission to the Forum for Peace and Reconciliation in *Paths to a Political Settlement in Ireland: Policy Papers submitted to he Forum for Peace and Reconciliation*, Belfast: Blackstaff.

Arthur, P. (1992) 'The Brooke Initiative', *Irish Political Studies*, vol. 7, pp. 111–15.

Arthur, P. (1996) 'Anglo-Irish Relations' in Aughey, A. and Morrow, D. (eds) *Northern Ireland Politics*, Harlow: Longman.

Arthur, P. and Jeffery, K. (1996) *Northern Ireland since 1968*, 2nd edn, Oxford: Blackwell.

Attwood, A. (1996) 'The SDLP and the Peace Process'. Lecture to University of Salford students, Queen's University Belfast, 22 March.

Aughey, A. (1989) *Under Siege: Ulster Unionism and the Anglo-Irish Agreement*, London: Hurst.

Aughey, A. (1994) 'Contemporary Unionist Politics' in Barton, B. and Roche, P.J. (eds) *The Northern Ireland Question: Perspectives and Policies*, Aldershot: Avebury.

Aughey, A. (1996) 'Direct Rule' in Aughey, A. and Morrow, D. (eds) *Northern Ireland Politics*, Harlow: Longman.

Aughey, A. and Morrow, D. (eds) (1996) *Northern Ireland Politics*, London: Longman.

Aunger, E. (1983) 'Religion and Class: An Analysis of 1971 Census Data' in Cormack, R.D. and Osborne, R.J. (eds) *Religion, Education and Employment: Aspects of Equal Opportunity in Northern Ireland*, Belfast: Appletree.

Bambery, C. (1990) *Ireland's Permanent Revolution*, London: Bookmarks.

Bardon, J. (1992) *A History of Ulster*, Belfast: Blackstaff.

Barritt, D. and Carter, C. (1962) *The Northern Ireland Problem*, Oxford: Oxford University Press.

Barton, B. and Roche, P.J. (eds) (1994) *The Northern Ireland Question: Perspectives and Policies*, Aldershot: Avebury.

Bean, K. (1995) 'The New Departure? Recent Developments in Republican Strategy and Ideology', *Irish Studies Review*, no. 10, pp. 2–6.

Bean, K. (2001) 'An Agenda for Discussion', *Fourthwrite*, no. 5, spring, pp. 6–7.

Beerman, J. and Mahony, R. (1993) 'The Institutional Churches and the Process of Reconciliation in Northern Ireland: Recent Progress in Presbyterian–Roman Catholic Relations' in Keogh, D. and Haltzel, M. (eds) *Northern Ireland and the Politics of Reconciliation*, Cambridge: Cambridge University Press.

Bennett Report (1979) *Report of the Committee of Enquiry into Police Interrogation Procedures in Northern Ireland*, Cmnd 7497, London: HMSO.

Bennett, R. (1996) 'New Labour and Northern Ireland', *New Left Review*, no. 220, pp. 153–9.

Bew, P. (1995) 'Seizing the Interval – The Northern Ireland Peace Process', *British Association of Irish Studies Newsletter*, no. 8, pp. 3–5.

Bew, P. (1997) *Sunday Times*, 20 April.

Bew, P. (1998) 'Unionist Potholes on the Roadway to Realism', *Sunday Times*, 12 April.

Bew, P. and Dixon, P. (1994) 'Labour Party Policy and Northern Ireland' in Barton, B. and Roche, P.J. (eds) *The Northern Ireland Question: Perspectives and Policies*, Aldershot: Avebury.

Bew, P., Gibbon, P. and Patterson, H. (1996) *Northern Ireland 1921–1996: Political Forces and Social Classes*, 2nd edn, London: Serif.

Bew, P. and Gillespie, G. (1996) *The Northern Ireland Peace Process 1993–1996: A Chronology*, London: Serif.

Bew, P. and Gillespie, G. (1999) *Northern Ireland: A Chronology of the Troubles*, Dublin: Gill and Macmillan.

Bew, P. and Meehan, E. (1994) 'Regions and Borders: Controversies in Northern Ireland about the European Union', *Journal of European Public Policy*, vol. 1, no. 1, pp. 47–63.

Bew, P. and Patterson, H. (1985) *The British State and the Ulster Crisis*, London: Verso.

Bew, P. and Patterson, H. (1987) 'Unionism: Jim Leads On', *Fortnight*, no. 256.

Bishop, P. and Mallie, E. (1988) *The Provisional IRA*, London: Corgi.

Boal, F.W., Campbell, J. and Livingstone, D. (1991) 'The Protestant Mosaic: A Majority of Minorities' in Roche, P.J. and Barton, B. (eds) *The Northern Ireland Question: Myth and Reality*, Aldershot: Avebury.

Bowyer-Bell, J. (1989) *The Secret Army. The IRA 1916–1979*, 3rd edn, Dublin: Poolbeg.

Boyce, D.G. (1995) *Nationalism in Ireland*, 3rd edn, London: Routledge.

Boyce, D.G. (1996) *The Irish Question and British Politics, 1868–1996*, London: Macmillan.

Boyle, K., Hadden, T. and Hillyard, P. (1980) *Ten Years On in Northern Ireland: The Legal Control of Political Violence*, London: Cobden Trust.

Boyle, K. and Hadden, T. (1984) 'How to Read the New Ireland Forum Report', *Political Quarterly*, vol. 55, no. 4, pp. 402–17.

Boyle, K. and Hadden, T. (1985) *Ireland: A Positive Proposal*, London: Penguin.

Boyle, K. and Hadden, T. (1989) *The Anglo-Irish Agreement: Commentary, Text and Official Review*, London: Sweet and Maxwell.

Boyle, K. and Hadden, T. (1994) *Northern Ireland: The Choice*, London: Penguin.

Breen, S. (2000a) 'On the One Road', *Fortnight*, no. 388.

Breen, S. (2000b) 'Backfire!', *Fortnight*, no. 390, December.

Broughton, D. (1996) 'The Perceptions of Peace: Public Opinion and the Peace Process in Northern Ireland'. Paper presented at the Annual Meeting of the American Political Science Association, San Francisco, August–September.

Bruce, S. (1986) *God Save Ulster! The Religion and Politics of Paisleyism*, Oxford: Oxford University Press.

Bruce, S. (1987) 'Ulster Loyalism and Religiosity', *Political Studies*, vol. 35, no. 4, pp. 643–8.

Bruce, S. (1992) *The Red Hand: Protestant Paramilitaries in Northern Ireland*, Oxford: Oxford University Press.

Bruce, S. (1994) *At the Edge of the Union: The Ulster Loyalist Political Vision*, Oxford: Oxford University Press.

Bruce, S. (1996) 'The Future of Loyalism'. Paper presented to the Understanding the Peace Process in Ireland seminar series, European Studies Research Institute, University of Salford, 27 March.

Buckland, P. (1981) *A History of Northern Ireland*, Dublin: Gill and Macmillan.

Calvert, J. (1972) 'Housing Problems in Northern Ireland; A Critique', *Community Forum*, vol. 2, no. 2, pp. 18–20.

Cameron Report (1969) *Disturbances in Northern Ireland: Report of the Commission Appointed by the Governor of Northern Ireland*, Cmnd 532, Belfast: HMSO.

Campbell, G. (1987) *Discrimination: the Truth*, Belfast: Democratic Unionist Party.

Campbell, G. (1995) *Discrimination, Where Now?* Belfast: Democratic Unionist Party.

Campbell, G. (1996) 'The Democratic Unionist Party and the Peace Process'. Presentation to the Understanding the Peace Process in Ireland seminar series, European Studies Research Institute, University of Salford, 28 February.

Carmichael, P. (2001) 'The Northern Ireland Civil Service: Characteristics and Trends since 1970'. Paper presented to the PSA British Territorial Politics Conference, University of Wales Cardiff, January.

Chubb, B. (1992) *The Government and Politics of Ireland*, 3rd edn, Harlow: Longman.

Cochrane, F. (1993) 'Progressive or Regressive? The Anglo-Irish Agreement as a Dynamic in the Northern Ireland Polity', *Irish Political Studies*, vol. 8, pp. 1–20.

Comerford, R. (1981) 'Patriotism as Pastime: The Appeal of Fenianism in the Mid-1860s', *Irish Historical Studies*, vol. 22, pp. 239–50.

Compton Report (1971) *Report of the Enquiry into Allegations against the Security Forces of Physical Brutality in Northern Ireland Arising out of the Events on 9th August 1971*, Cmnd 4823, London: HMSO.

Connolly, M. (1990) *Politics and Policy-making in Northern Ireland*, Hemel Hempstead: Philip Allan.

Connolly, M. and Loughlin, J. (1986) 'Reflections on the Anglo-Irish Agreement', *Government and Opposition*, vol. 21, no. 2, pp.146–60.

Coogan, T.P. (1987a) *The IRA*, London: Fontana.

Coogan, T.P. (1987b) *Disillusioned Decades: Ireland 1966–87*, Dublin: Gill and Macmillan.

Coogan, T.P. (1995) *The Troubles: Ireland's Ordeal 1966–1995 and the Search for Peace*, London: Hutchinson.

Coulter, C. (1994) 'The Character of Unionism', *Irish Political Studies*, vol. 9, pp. 1–24.

Coulter, C. (1999) *Contemporary Northern Irish Society: An Introduction*, London: Pluto.

Cox, M. (2000) 'Northern Ireland after the Cold War', in Cox, M., Guelke, A. and Stephen, F. (eds) *A Farewell to Arms? From 'Long War' to Long Peace in Northern Ireland*, Manchester: Manchester University Press.

Cox, M., Guelke, A. and Stephen, F. (eds) (2000) *A Farewell to Arms? From 'Long War' to Long Peace in Northern Ireland*, Manchester: Manchester University Press.

Cox, W. H. (1987) 'Public Opinion and the Anglo-Irish Agreement', *Government and Opposition*, vol. 22, no. 3, pp. 336–51.

Crawford, C. (2001) 'A Reluctant Ceasefire', *Fortnight*, no. 392, February.

Crawford, R. (1987) *Loyal to King Billy. A Portrait of the Ulster Protestants*, London: Hurst.

Cronin, M. (1994) 'Sport and a Sense of Irishness', *Irish Studies Review*, no. 9, pp. 13–17.

Cunningham, M. and Kelly, R. (1995) 'Standing for Ulster', *Politics Review*, pp. 20–23.

Curtice, J. and Dowds, L. (1999) 'Has Northern Ireland Really Changed?'. Paper presented to the CREST/QUB Conference, '"Agreeing to Disagree?" The Voters of Northern Ireland', Queen's University Belfast, June.

Darby, J. (1976) *Conflict in Northern Ireland: The Development of a Polarised Community*, Dublin: Gill and Macmillan.

Darby, J. (ed.) (1983) 'The Historical Background' in *Northern Ireland: The Background to the Conflict*, Belfast: Appletree.

Darby, J. (1991) *What's Wrong with Conflict?* University of Ulster: Centre for the Study of Conflict Occasional Paper, no. 2.

Deane, S. (2001) 'Factions in Northern Ireland: Factional Power in the Pursuit of Peace'. Paper presented to the Political Studies Association of the United Kingdom Annual Conference, University of Manchester, April.

Democratic Unionist Party (1995) *The Framework of Shame and Sham*, Belfast: Democratic Unionist Party.

Dickson, B. (1991) 'The Legal Response to the Troubles in Northern Ireland' in Roche, P.J. and Barton, B. (eds) *The Northern Ireland Question: Myth and Reality*, Aldershot, Avebury.

Dickson, B. (2000) 'Policing and Human Rights after the Conflict' in Cox, M., Guelke, A. and Stephen, F. (eds) *A Farewell to Arms? From 'Long War' to Long Peace in Northern Ireland*, Manchester: Manchester University Press.

Dillon, M. (1990) *The Dirty War*, London: Arrow.

Diplock Report (1972) *Report of the Commission to Consider Legal Procedures to Deal with Terrorist Activities in Northern Ireland*, Cmnd 5185, London: HMSO.

Dixon, P. (1994) '"The Usual English Doubletalk": The British Political Parties and the Ulster Unionists 1974–1994', *Irish Political Studies*, vol. 9, pp. 25–40.

Douds, S. (1995) 'God and the LOL', *Fortnight*, vol. 343.

Doyle, M. (1995) 'Just Say Yes' *Fortnight*, vol. 343.

Dudley Edwards, R. (1999) *The Faithful Tribe: An Intimate Portrait of the Loyal Institutions*, London: HarperCollins.

Dumbrell, J. (1995) 'The United States and the Northern Irish Conflict 1969–94: From Indifference to Intervention', *Irish Studies in International Affairs*, vol. 6, pp. 107–25.

Elliot, R. and Hickie, J. (1971) *Ulster: A Case Study in Conflict*, London: Longman.

Elliott, S. and Flackes, W. (1999) *Northern Ireland: A Political Directory*, Belfast: Blackstaff.

Ellison, G. and Smyth, J. (1999) *The Crowned Harp: Policing Northern Ireland*, London: Pluto.

Ervine, D. (1996) 'The Progressive Unionist Party and the Peace Process'. Lecture in the Understanding the Peace Process in Ireland seminar series, European Studies Research Institute, University of Salford, 20 March.

Evans, G. and O'Leary, B. (1999) 'Northern Irish Voters and the British–Irish Agreement: Foundations of a Stable Consociational Settlement?'. Paper presented to the PSA Elections, Parties and Opinion Polls Annual Conference, University College Northampton, September.

Evans, J., Tonge, J. and Murray, G. (2000) 'Constitutional Nationalism and Socialism in Northern Ireland' in Cowley, P., Denver, D., Russell, A. and Harrison, L. (eds) *British Elections and Parties Review*, vol. 10, London: Frank Cass.

Eveleigh, R. (1975) *Peace Keeping in a Democratic Society*, London: Hurst.

Fanning, R. (1983) *Independent Ireland*, Dublin: Helicon.

Farrell, M. (1980) *Northern Ireland: the Orange State*, London: Pluto.

Farren, S. (1996) 'The View from the SDLP. A Nationalist Approach to an Agreed Peace', *Oxford International Review*, vol. 7, no. 2, pp. 41–6.

Farren, S. (2000) 'The SDLP and the Roots of the Good Friday Agreement' in Cox, M., Guelke, A. and Stephen, F. (eds) *A Farewell to Arms? From 'Long War' to Long Peace in Northern Ireland*, Manchester: Manchester University Press.

Fisk, R. (1983) *In Time of War: Ireland, Ulster and the Price of Neutrality 1939–45*, London: Andre Deutsch.

Fitzgerald, G. (1991) *All in a Life. Garret Fitzgerald: An Autobiography*, London: Macmillan.

Fitzgerald, G. (1996) 'Ireland in the next millennium', *Irish Studies Review*, no. 17, pp. 2–7.

Flackes, W.D. (1983) *Northern Ireland: A Political Directory 1968–83*, London: Ariel.

Flanagan, R. (1998) 'Maintaining Law and Order in Northern Ireland', *RUSI Journal*, August, pp. 12–17.

Follis, B.A. (1995) *A State under Siege. The Establishment of Northern Ireland 1920–1925*, Oxford: Oxford University Press.

Ford, D. (1996) 'The Alliance Party and the Peace Process'. Lecture to visiting University of Salford students, Queen's University Belfast, 22 March.

Frazer, H. and Fitzduff, M. (1990) *Improving Community Relations*, Belfast: Community Relations Council.

Fulton, J. (1991) *The Tragedy of Belief*, Oxford: Clarendon.

Gafikin, F. and Morrisey, M. (1990) *Northern Ireland: The Thatcher Years*, London: Zed.

Gardiner Report (1975) *Report of a Committee to Consider, in the Context of Civil Liberties and Human Rights, Measures to Deal with Terrorism*, Cmnd 5847, London: HMSO.

Geddes, A. and Tonge, J. (eds) (1997) *Labour's Landslide*, Manchester: Manchester University Press.

Gibney, J. (1996) 'From the Collapse of the Peace Process to Real Negotiations', *Irish Reporter*, no. 22, pp. 13–17.

Greer, A. (1996) *Rural Politics in Northern Ireland: Policy Networks and Agricultural Development since Partition*, Avebury: Aldershot.

Greer, S.C. (1987) 'The Supergrass System in Northern Ireland' in Wilkinson, P. and Stewart, A.M. (eds) *Contemporary Research on Terrorism*, Aberdeen: Aberdeen University Press.

Guelke, A. (1988) *Northern Ireland: the International Perspective*, Dublin: Gill and Macmillan.

Guelke, A. (1994) 'The Peace Process in South Africa, Israel and Northern Ireland; A Farewell to Arms?' *Irish Studies in International Affairs*, vol. 5, pp. 93–106.

Guelke, A. (2000) ' "Comparatively Peaceful": South Africa, the Middle East and Northern Ireland' in Cox, M., Guelke, A. and Stephen, F. (eds) *A Farewell to Arms? From 'Long War' to Long Peace in Northern Ireland*, Manchester: Manchester University Press.

Gurr, T. (1970) *Why Men Rebel*, Princeton: Princeton University Press.

HM Government (1972) *The Future of Northern Ireland*, London: HMSO.

HM Government (1973) *Northern Ireland Constitutional Proposals*, Cmnd 5259, London: HMSO.

HM Government (1974) *The Northern Ireland Constitution*, Cmnd 5675, London: HMSO.

HM Government (1982) *Northern Ireland: A Framework for Devolution*, Cmnd 8541, London: HMSO.

HM Government (1995) *Frameworks for the Future*, Belfast: HMSO.

HM Government (1996) *Northern Ireland (Entry to Negotiations, etc.) Act 1996*, London: HMSO.

HM Government (1998) *The Agreement* (Good Friday/Belfast Agreement), Belfast: HMSO.

Haagerup, N. (1984) *Report Drawn up on Behalf of the Political Affairs Committee on the Situation in Northern Ireland*, European Parliament working documents, 1–1526/83.

Hachey, T. (1984) *Britain and Irish Separatism*, Chicago: Rand McNally.

Hadden, T., Irwin, C. and Boal, F. (1996) 'Separation or Sharing?', *Fortnight*, vol. 356.

Haddick-Flynn, K. (1999) *Orangeism: The Making of a Tradition*, Dublin: Wolfhound.

Hadfield, B. (1998) 'The Belfast Agreement, Sovereignty and the State of the Union', *Public Law*, winter, pp. 599–616.

Hadfield, B. (1999) 'The Nature of Devolution in Scotland and Northern Ireland: Key Issues of Responsibility and Control', *Edinburgh Law Review*, vol. 3, issue 1, pp. 3–31.

Hamill, D. (1986) *Pig in the Middle: The Army in Northern Ireland 1969–85*, London: Methuen.

Harkness, D. (1996) *Ireland in the Twentieth Century: Divided Island*, London: Macmillan.

Harris, R. (1986) *Prejudice and Tolerance in Ulster*, Manchester: Manchester University Press.

Hartley, T. (1994) 'Charter for Justice and Peace in Ireland', *Starry Plough*, autumn, pp. 2–7.

Hayes, B. and McAllister, I. (1996) 'British and Irish Public Opinion towards the Northern Ireland Problem', *Irish Political Studies*, vol. 11, pp. 61–82.

Hayes, B. and McAllister, I. (1999) Who Voted for Peace? Public Support for the 1998 Northern Ireland Agreement'. Paper presented to the CREST/QUB Conference, '"Agreeing to Disagree?" The Voters of Northern Ireland', Queen's University Belfast, June.

Hayes, B. and McAllister, I. (2000) 'Sowing Dragon's Teeth: Public Support for Political Violence and Paramilitarism in Northern Ireland'. Paper presented to the Political Studies Association of the United Kingdom Annual Conference, London School of Economics and Political Science, April.

Hazleton, W. (1994) 'A Breed Apart. Northern Ireland's MPs at Westminster', *Journal of Legislative Studies*, vol. 1, no. 4, pp. 30–53.

Hazleton, W. (1999) 'Devolution in Northern Ireland: Diffusion of Power as a Flexible Approach to Conflict Management'. Paper presented to the Political Studies Association of Ireland Annual Conference, Wexford, October.

Hazleton, W. (2001) 'The Good Friday Agreement and Practical Politics: Conflict Resolution through Institution Building'. Paper presented to the Political Studies Association Annual Conference, University of Manchester, April.

Hennessey, T. (2000) *The Northern Ireland Peace Process: Ending the Troubles?*, Dublin: Gill and Macmillan.

Hickey, J. (1984) *Religion and the Northern Ireland Problem*, Dublin: Gill and Macmillan.

Hillyard, P. (1983) 'Law and Order' in McAllister, I. *Northern Ireland: The Roots of the Conflict*, Belfast: Appletree.

Holland, J. (1996) 'Keeping Peace at Arm's Length', *Irish Post*, 2 March.

Holland, J. and McDonald, H. (1994) *INLA: Deadly Divisions*, Dublin: Torc.

Hopkins, S. (1998) 'The Good Friday Agreement in Northern Ireland', *ECPR News*, vol. 10, no. 1, pp. 15–16.

Hoppen, K.T. (1980) *Ireland since 1800: Conflict and Conformity*, Harlow: Longman.

Horowitz, D. (1985) *Ethnic Groups in Conflict*, Berkeley: University of California.

Hughes, J. (1994) 'Prejudice and Identity in a Mixed Environment' in Guelke, A. (ed.) *New Perspectives on the Northern Ireland Conflict*, Aldershot: Avebury.

Hume, D. (1996) *The Ulster Unionist Party 1972–92*, Armagh: Ulster Society.

Hume, J. (1993) 'A New Ireland in a New Europe' in Keogh, D. and Haltzel, M. (eds) *Northern Ireland and the Politics of Reconciliation*, Cambridge: Cambridge University Press.

Hunt Report (1969) *Report of the Advisory Committee on Police in Northern Ireland*, Cmnd 535, Belfast: HMSO.

Hussey, G. (1995) *Ireland Today*, London: Penguin.

Illsley, E. (1996) 'The Labour Party and the Peace Process'. Paper presented to the Understanding the Peace Process in Ireland seminar series, European Studies Research Institute, University of Salford, 14 February.

Irish Episcopal Conference (1984) *Submission to the New Ireland Forum*, Dublin: Verita.

Irvine, M. (1991) *Northern Ireland: Faith and Faction*, London: Routledge.

Jackson, A. (1994) 'Irish Unionism 1905–21' in Collins, P. (ed.) *Nationalism and Unionism: Conflict in Ireland 1885–21*, Queen's University, Belfast: Institute of Irish Studies.

Johnson, D. (1985) 'The Northern Ireland Economy 1914–39' in Kennedy, L. and Ollerenshaw, P. (eds) *An Economic History of Ulster 1820–1939*, Manchester: Manchester University Press.

Joint Unionist Manifesto (1987) *To Put Right a Great Wrong*, Belfast: Ulster Unionist Party and Democratic Unionist Party.

Joint Unionist Task Force (1987) *An End to Drift*, Belfast: Joint Unionist Task Force.

Kee, R. (1976) *The Bold Fenian Men. The Green Flag Volume Two*, London: Quartet.

Kennedy, D. (1988) *The Widening Gulf*, Belfast: Blackstaff.

Kennedy, D. (ed.) (1995) *Steadfast for Faith and Freedom: 200 Years of Orangeism*, Belfast: Grand Lodge of Ireland.

Kenny, A. (1986) *The Road to Hillsborough: The Shaping of the Anglo-Irish Agreement*, Oxford: Permagon.

Keogh, D. (1994) *Twentieth Century Ireland: Nation and State*, Dublin: Gill and Macmillan.

Keogh, D. and Haltzel, M. (eds) (1995) *Northern Ireland and the Politics of Reconciliation*, Cambridge: Cambridge University Press.

Kilbrandon, Lord (1984) *Northern Ireland: Report of an Independent Inquiry*, London: The Independent Inquiry.

Kilby, S. (1996) 'The Voyage of Cruiser', *Fortnight*, no. 354.

King, S. and Wilford, R. (1997) 'Irish Political Data 1996', *Irish Political Studies*, vol. 12, pp. 148–210.

Labour Party (1988) *Towards a United Ireland. Reform and Harmonisation: A Dual Strategy for Irish Unification*, London: Labour Party.

Laffan, B. (1994) 'Managing Europe' in Collins, N. (ed.) *Political Issues in Ireland Today*, Manchester: Manchester University Press.

Laffan, M. (1983) *The Partition of Ireland 1911–1925*, Dublin: Dublin Historical Association.

Laffan, M. (1999) *The Resurrection of Ireland. The Sinn Fein Party 1916–1923*, Cambridge: Cambridge University Press.

Lambkin, B.K. (1996) *Opposite Religions Still?*, Aldershot, Avebury.

Lawlor, S. (1983) *Britain and Ireland 1914–23*, Dublin: Gill and Macmillan.

Leonard, A. (1999) 'The Alliance Party and the Third Tradition in Northern Ireland'. Unpublished MSc thesis, University College Dublin.

Lijphart, A. (1996) 'The Framework Document in Northern Ireland', *Government and Opposition*, vol. 31, no. 3, pp. 267–74.

Lyons, F.S.L. (1973) *Ireland since the Famine*, London: Fontana.

Lyons, P. (1999) 'Data Section', *Irish Political Studies*, vol. 14, pp. 191–256.

MacIver, M.A. (1987) 'Ian Paisley and the Reformed Tradition', *Political Studies*, vol. 35, no. 3, pp. 359–78.

MacStiofain, S. (1975) *Memoirs of a Revolutionary*, London: Gordon Cremonesi.

McAllister, I. (1977) *The Northern Ireland Social Democratic and Labour Party*, London: Macmillan.

McAllister, I. and Wilson, B. (1978) 'Bi-Confessionalism in a Confessional Party System: The Northern Ireland Alliance Party', *Economic and Social Review*, vol. 9, no. 3, pp. 207–25.

McAuley, J. (1991) 'Cuchullain and an RPG-7: The Ideology and Politics of the Ulster Defence Association' in Hughes, E. (ed.) *Culture and Politics in Northern Ireland 1960–1990*, Milton Keynes: Open University Press.

McAuley, J. (1997) 'Flying the One-Winged Bird: Ulster Unionism and the Peace Process' in Shirlow, P. and McGovern, M. (eds) *Who are the People? Unionism, Protestantism and Loyalism in Northern Ireland*, London: Pluto.

McAuley, J. (2001) 'What is New about New Loyalism?'. Paper presented to the Political Studies Association of the United Kingdom Annual Conference, University of Manchester, April.

McCann, E. (1980) *War and an Irish Town*, 2nd edn, Harmondsworth: Penguin.

McCann, E. (1992) *Bloody Sunday in Derry*, Brandon: Dingle.

McCullagh, M. and O'Dowd, L. (1986) 'Northern Ireland; The Search for a Solution', *Social Studies Review*, vol. 1, no. 4, pp. 1–10.

McDowell, D. (1995) 'Lessons from Labour', *Ulster Review*, Winter, pp. 7–9.

McGarry, J. (2000) 'Police reform in Northern Ireland', *Irish Political Studies*, vol. 15, pp. 173–82.

McGarry, J. and O'Leary, B. (1990) Preface, in McGarry, J. and O'Leary, B. (eds) *The Future of Northern Ireland*, Oxford: Clarendon.

McGarry, J. and O'Leary, B. (1995) *Explaining Northern Ireland*, Oxford: Blackwell.

McGarry, J. and O'Leary, B. (1999) *Policing Northern Ireland: Proposals for a New Start*, Belfast: Blackstaff.

McGinty, R. (1999) 'Biting the Bullet: Decommissioning in the Transition from War to Peace in Northern Ireland', *Irish Studies in International Affairs*, vol. 10, pp. 237–47.

McIntyre, A. (1995) 'Modern Irish Republicanism: the Product of British State Strategies', *Irish Political Studies*, vol. 10.

McKittrick, D. (1995) *The Nervous Peace*, Belfast: Blackstaff.

McKittrick, D., Kelters, S., Feeney, B. and Thornton, C. (1999) *Lost Lives. The Stories of the Men, Women and Children Who Lost their Lives as a Result of the Northern Ireland Troubles*, Edinburgh: Mainstream.

Mallie, E. and McKittrick, D. (1996) *The Fight for Peace: The Secret Story of the Irish Peace Process*, London: Heinemann.

Mansergh, M. (1995) 'The Background to the Peace Process', *Irish Studies in International Affairs*, vol. 6, pp. 145–58.

Marsh, M. and Wilford, R. (1994) 'Irish Political Data 1993', *Irish Political Studies*, vol. 9, pp. 189–245.

Marsh, M., Wilford, R., King, S. and McElroy, G. (1996) 'Irish Political Data 1995', *Irish Political Studies*, vol. 11, pp. 213–308.

Miller, D. (1978) *Queen's Rebels. Ulster Loyalism in Historical Perspective*, Dublin: Gill and Macmillan.

Miller, D. (ed.) (1998a) *Rethinking Northern Ireland*, London: Longman.

Miller, D. (1998b) 'Colonialism and Academic Representations of the Troubles' in Miller, D. (ed.) *Rethinking Northern Ireland*, London: Longman.

Minogue, D. (1996) 'The Divorce Referendum in the Republic of Ireland' in Hampsher-Monk, I. and Stanyer, J. (eds) *Contemporary Political Studies*, Exeter: Political Studies Association.

Mitchell, G. (2000) *Making Peace: The Inside Story of the Making of the Good Friday Agreement*, London: Heinemann.

Mitchell, P. (1999) 'The Party System and Party Competition' in Mitchell, P. and Wilford, R. (eds) *Politics in Northern Ireland*, Oxford: Westview.

Mitchell, P. and Gillespie, G. (1999) 'The Electoral Systems' in Mitchell, P. and Wilford, R. (eds) *Politics in Northern Ireland*, Oxford: Westview.

Mitchell, P. and Wilford, R. (eds) (1999) *Politics in Northern Ireland*, Oxford: Westview.

Mitchell Report (1996) *Report of the International Body on Arms Decommissioning*, Belfast: HMSO.

Moloney, E. and Pollok, A. (1986) *Paisley*, Dublin: Poolbeg.

Montgomery, G. and Whitten, J. (1995) *The Order on Parade*, Belfast: Grand Orange Lodge of Ireland.

Morrison, D. (1985) in Collins, M. (ed.) *Ireland after Britain*, London: Pluto.

Moxon-Browne, E. (1983) *Nation, Class and Creed in Northern Ireland*, Aldershot: Gower.

Moxon-Browne, E. (1991) 'National Identity in Northern Ireland' in Singer, P. and Robinson, G. (eds) *Social Attitudes Survey*, Belfast: Blackstaff.

Murphy, D. (1978) *A Place Apart*, London: Penguin.

Murphy, J. (1995) *Ireland in the Twentieth Century*, Dublin: Gill and Macmillan.

Murphy, R. and Totten, K. (2000) 'Data Section', *Irish Political Studies*, vol. 15, pp. 249–335.

Murray, G. (1998) *John Hume's SDLP*, Dublin: Irish Academic Press.

Murray, R. (1990) *The SAS in Ireland*, Dublin: Mercier.

Needham, R. (1999) *Battling for Peace. Northern Ireland's Longest Serving Minister*, Belfast: Blackstaff.

Nelson, S. (1976) 'Andy Tyrie', *Fortnight*, no. 123.

Nelson, S. (1984) *Ulster's Uncertain Defenders: Loyalists and the Northern Ireland Conflict*, Belfast: Appletree.

New Ireland Forum (1984) *Report of the New Ireland Forum*, Dublin: Stationery Office.

Newsinger, J. (1995) 'British Security Policy in Northern Ireland', *Race and Class*, vol. 37, no. 1, pp. 83–94.

New Ulster Political Research Group (1979) *Beyond the Religious Divide*, Belfast: New Ulster Political Research Group.

North Report (1997) *Independent Review of Parades and Marches*, Belfast: HMSO.

Northern Ireland Office (2000) *Report of the Independent Commission on Policing for Northern Ireland Implementation Plan*, Belfast: HMSO.

O'Bradaigh, R. (1996) 'The Evil Fruit Has Ripened Once More', *The Irish Reporter*, no. 21, pp. 19–22.

O'Brien, B. (1999) *The Long War: the IRA and Sinn Fein*, Dublin: O'Brien.

O'Brien, C. (1972) *States of Ireland*, London: Hutchinson.

O'Dochartaigh, F. (1994) *Ulster's White Negroes*, Edinburgh: AK Press.

O'Farrell, P. (1975) *England and Ireland since 1800*, Oxford: Oxford University Press.

O'Halloran, C. (1987) *Partition and the Limits of Irish Nationalism: An Ideology under Stress*, Dublin: Gill and Macmillan.

O'Kane, E. 'Anglo-Irish Relations and the Peace Process: From Exclusion to Inclusion'. Paper presented to the Political Studies Association of the United Kingdom Annual Conference, University of Manchester, April.

O'Kelly, M. and Doyle, J. (2000) 'The Good Friday Agreement and Electoral Behaviour – An Analysis of Transfers under PRSTV in the Northern Ireland Assembly Elections of 1982 and 1998'. Paper presented to the Political Studies Association of Ireland Annual Conference, University of Cork, October.

O'Leary, B. (1985) 'Explaining Northern Ireland: A Brief Study Guide', *Politics*, vol. 5, no. 1, pp. 35–41.

O'Leary, B. (1999) 'The Nature of the British–Irish Agreement', *New Left Review*, 233, pp. 66–96.

O'Leary, B. (2001) 'The Belfast Agreement and the Labour Government' in Seldon, A. (ed.) *The Blair Effect*, London: Little, Brown and Company.

O'Leary, B. and McGarry, J. (1996) *The Politics of Antagonism: Understanding Northern Ireland*, 2nd edn, London: Athlone.

O'Muilleoir, M. (1999) *Belfast's Dome of Delight: City Hall Politics 1981–2000*, Belfast: Beyond the Pale.

O'Neill, T. (1972) *The Autobiography of Terence O'Neill, Prime Minister of Northern Ireland 1963–69*, London: Hart-Davis.

Paisley, I. (1997) 'Measured and Consistent Action', *The House Magazine*, vol. 22, no. 755, p. 16.

Patten Report (1999) The Independent Commission on Policing for Northern Ireland, '*A New Beginning: Policing in Northern Ireland*', London: HMSO.

Patterson, H. (1989) *The Politics of Illusion. Republicanism and Socialism in Modern Ireland*, London: Hutchinson.

Patterson, H. (1997) *The Politics of Illusion. A Political History of the IRA*, London: Serif.

Patterson, H. and Moore, L. (1995) 'Ulster Protestants: A Community in Retreat?', *Renewal*, vol. 3, pp. 43–54.

Peace People (1976) *Strategy for Peace*, Belfast: Peace People.

Phoenix, E. (1994) 'Northern Nationalists, Ulster Unionists and the Development of Partition 1900–21' in Collins, P. (ed.) *Nationalism and Unionism: Conflict in Ireland 1885–1921*, Queen's University Belfast: Institute of Irish Studies.

Pimlott, B. (1992) *Harold Wilson*, London: HarperCollins.

Police Authority for Northern Ireland (1997) *Listening to the Community: Working with the RUC: The Work of the Police Authority, 1 July 1995 to 31 March 1997*, Belfast, PANI.

Pollak, A. (ed.) (1993) *A Citizens Inquiry: the Opsahl Report on Northern Ireland*, Dublin: Lilliput.

Porter, N. (1996) *Rethinking Unionism. An Alternative Vision for Northern Ireland*, Belfast: Blackstaff.

Price, J. (1995) 'Political Change and the Protestant Working Class', *Race and Class*, vol. 37, no. 1, pp. 57–69.

Probert, B. (1978) *Beyond Orange and Green: The Political Economy of the Northern Ireland Crisis*, London: Zed.

Purdie, B. (1988) 'Was the Civil Rights Movement a Republican/Communist Conspiracy?', *Irish Political Studies*, vol. 3, pp. 33–41.

Purdie, B. (1990) *Politics in the Streets: The Origins of the Civil Rights Movement in Northern Ireland*, Belfast: Blackstaff.

Quinn, D. (1993) *Understanding Northern Ireland*, Manchester: Baseline.

Randall, N. (1998) 'New Labour and Northern Ireland: From Moribund Peace Process to Shadow Assembly', Manchester Papers in Politics 6/98.

Republican Education Department (1969) *Ireland Today and Some Questions on the Way Forward*, Dublin: RED.

Roche, P.J. and Barton, B. (eds) (1991) *The Northern Ireland Question: Myth and Reality*, Aldershot: Avebury.

Rose, R. (1971) *Governing Without Consensus: An Irish Perspective*, London: Faber.

Rose, R. (1976) *Northern Ireland: A Time of Choice*, London: Macmillan.

Rowan, B. (1995) *Behind the Lines: The Story of the IRA and Loyalist Ceasefires*, Belfast: Blackstaff.

Royal Ulster Constabulary (1996) *Chief Constable's Annual Report 1996*, Belfast: RUC.

Ruane, J. and Todd, J. (1996) *The Dynamics of Conflict in Northern Ireland: Power, Conflict and Emancipation*, Cambridge: Cambridge University Press.

Ryan, M. (1994) *War and Peace in Ireland. Britain and the IRA in the New World Order*, London: Pluto.

Ryan, M. (1995) 'The Deconstruction of Ireland', *ECPR News*, vol. 6, no. 3, pp. 26–8.

Scarman Report (1972) *Violence and Civil Disturbances in Northern Ireland in 1969: Report of the Tribunal of Enquiry*, Cmnd 566, Belfast: HMSO.

Shirlow, P. and McGovern, M. (eds) (1997) *Who are the People? Unionism, Protestantism and Loyalism in Northern Ireland*, London: Pluto.

Sinn Fein (1987) *Scenario for Peace*, Belfast: Sinn Fein.

Sinn Fein (1992) *Towards a Lasting Peace*, Belfast: Sinn Fein.

Sinn Fein (1994) *Setting the Record Straight: An Account of Sinn Fein–British Government Dialogue*, Belfast: Sinn Fein.

Sinn Fein (1995a) 'Initial discussion of A New Framework for Agreement'. Submission to the Forum for Peace and Reconciliation, Dublin Castle, 5 May.

Sinn Fein (1995b) 'Self-determination, Consent, Accommodation of Minorities and Democracy in Ireland: Second Response to Dr Asbjorne Eide's First Draft'. Submission to the Forum for Peace and Reconciliation, Dublin Castle, 13 September.

Sinn Fein (1995c) 'The Nature of the Problem and the Principles Underlying its Resolution'. Submission to the Forum for Peace and Reconciliation, Dublin Castle, 25 November.

Sinnott, R. 'Interpreting Electoral Mandates in Northern Ireland: The 1998 Referendum'. Paper presented to the CREST/QUB Conference, '"Agreeing to disagree?" The Voters of Northern Ireland', Queen's University Belfast, June.

Smith, D. and Chambers, G. (1991) *Inequality in Northern Ireland*, Oxford: Clarendon.

Smith, M.L.R. (1995) *Fighting for Ireland? The Military Strategy of the Irish Republican Movement*, London: Routledge.

Smyth, C. (1987) *Ian Paisley: Voice of Protestant Ulster*, Edinburgh: Scottish Academic Press.

Smyth, J. (1996) 'Ceasefire in Northern Ireland – The Phoney Peace', *Capital and Class*, vol. 58, pp. 7–18.

Social Democratic and Labour Party (1972) *Towards a New Ireland*, Belfast: SDLP.

Social Democratic and Labour Party (1973) *A New North, A New Ireland*, Belfast: SDLP.

Stalker, J. (1988) *Stalker*, London: Harrap.

Stevenson, J. (1996) *'We Wrecked the Place': Contemplating an End to the Northern Irish Troubles*, New York: Free Press.

Stewart, A.T.Q. (1967) *The Ulster Crisis*, London: Faber.

Stewart, A.T.Q. (1977) *The Narrow Ground; Aspects of Ulster, 1609–1969*, London: Faber.

Teague, P. (1996) 'The European Union and the Irish Peace Process', *Journal of Common Market Studies*, vol. 34, no. 4, pp. 549–70.

Thatcher, M. (1993) *The Downing Street Years*, London: HarperCollins.

Tomlinson, M. (1995) 'Can Britain Leave Ireland? The Political Economy of War and Peace', *Race and Class*, vol. 37, no. 1, pp. 1–22.

Tonge, J. (1997) 'Northern Ireland: Last Chance for Peace?' in Geddes, A. and Tonge, J. (eds) *Labour's Landslide*, Manchester: Manchester University Press.

Tonge, J. (2000) 'From Sunningdale to the Good Friday Agreement: Creating Devolved Government in Northern Ireland', *Contemporary British History*, vol. 14, no. 3, pp. 39–60.

Tonge, J. and Evans, J. (2001a) 'Do the Members Like It? Party Attitudes to Devolved Government in Northern Ireland'. Paper presented to the Political Studies Association of the United Kingdom Annual Conference, University of Manchester, April.

Tonge, J. and Evans, J. (2001b) 'Northern Ireland's Third Tradition(s): The Alliance Party Surveyed', in Tonge, J., Bennie, L., Denver, D. and Harrison, L., *British Elections and Parties Review 11*, London: Frank Cass.

Toolis, K. (1995) *Rebel Hearts*, London: Picador.

Townshend, C. (1983) *Political Violence in Ireland: Government and Resistance since 1848*, Oxford: Clarendon.

Trimble, D. (1996) Address to Ulster Unionist Party Annual Conference, Galgorm Manor Hotel, 19 October 1996.

Trimble, D. (1997) 'Bridging the Democratic Deficit', *The House Magazine*, vol. 22, no. 755, p. 15.

Ulster Defence Association (1987) *Common Sense*, Belfast: Ulster Defence Association.

Ulster Unionist Information Institute (1995) *Unionism Restated: Statement of Aims*, no. 16.

Ulster Unionist Party (1996) *The Democratic Imperative*, Belfast: Ulster Unionist Party.

Urban, M. (1992) *Big Boy's Rules: The SAS and the Secret Struggle against the IRA*, London: Faber and Faber.

Walker, G. 'The Northern Ireland Factor in the Scottish Constitutional Debate'. Paper presented to the Political Studies Association of the United Kingdom Annual Conference, University of Ulster, 1997.

Wall, M. (1966) 'Partition: The Ulster Question' in Williams, D. (ed.) *The Irish Struggle 1916–26*, London: Routledge.

Walsh, P. (1994) *Irish Republicanism and Socialism: The Politics of the Republican Movement 1905 to 1994*, London: Athol.

Ward, A. (1993) 'A Constitutional Background to the Northern Ireland Crisis' in Keogh, D. and Haltzel, M. (eds) *Northern Ireland and the Politics of Reconciliation*, Cambridge: Cambridge University Press.

Ward, R. (1997) 'The Northern Ireland Peace Process: A Gender Issue?' in Gilligan, C. and Tonge, J. (eds) *Peace or War? Understanding the Peace Process in Northern Ireland*, Aldershot: Avebury.

White, B. (1984) *John Hume: Statesman of the Troubles*, Belfast: Blackstaff.

Whyte, J. (1980) *Church and State in Modern Ireland 1923–79, 2nd edn*, Dublin: Gill and Macmillan.

Whyte, J. (1983) 'How Much Discrimination Was There under the Unionist Regime 1921–68?' in Gallagher, T. and O'Connell, J. (eds) *Contemporary Irish Studies*, Manchester: Manchester University Press.

Whyte, J. (1990) *Interpreting Northern Ireland*, Oxford: Clarendon.

Whyte, J. (1991) 'Dynamics of Social and Political Change in Northern Ireland' in Keogh, D. and Haltzel, M. (eds) *Northern Ireland and the Politics of Reconciliation*, Cambridge: Cambridge University Press.

Wichert, S. (1991; 2nd edn 1999) *Northern Ireland since 1945*, London: Longman.

Widgery Report (1972) *Report of the Tribunal Appointed to Inquire into the Events of Sunday 30 January 1972 which Led to the Loss of Life in Connection with the Procession in Londonderry on that Day*, Cmnd 220, Belfast: HMSO.

Wilford, R. (2001) 'Northern Ireland One Year On: A Discursive Narrative'. Paper presented to the PSA British Territorial Politics Group Conference, University of Wales Cardiff, January.

Wilson, A. (1995) *Irish America and the Ulster Conflict 1968–1995*, Belfast: Blackstaff.

Wilson Report (1965) *Economic Development in Northern Ireland*, Cmnd 479, Belfast: HMSO.

Wilson, T. (ed.) (1955) *Ulster under Home Rule*, Oxford: Oxford University Press.

Wilson, T. (1989) *Ulster: Conflict and Consent*, Oxford: Blackwell.

Wright, F. (1987) *Northern Ireland: A Comparative Analysis*, Dublin: Gill and Macmillan.

Index